To Hannah Sherbersky and Reenee Singh

Good Relations

Cracking the code of how to get on better

JANET REIBSTEIN

GREEN TREE
LONDON · OXFORD · NEW YORK · NEW DELHI · SYDNEY

GREEN TREE
Bloomsbury Publishing Plc
50 Bedford Square, London, WC1B 3DP, UK
29 Earlsfort Terrace, Dublin 2, Ireland

BLOOMSBURY, GREEN TREE and the Diana logo are trademarks of
Bloomsbury Publishing Plc

First published in Great Britain 2023

A catalogue record for this book is available from the British Library

Library of Congress Cataloguing-in-Publication data has been applied for add
where a UK originated single-ISBN edition for which we own US rights

ISBN: HB: 978-14729-9238-3; eBook: 978-14729-9237-6; ePdf: 9781472992369

2 4 6 8 10 9 7 5 3 1

Typeset in Fournier MT Std by Deanta Global Publishing Services, Chennai, India
Printed and bound in Great Britain by CPI Group (UK) Ltd, Croydon, CR0 4YY

To find out more about our authors and books visit www.bloomsbury.com and
sign up for our newsletters

CONTENTS

Introduction: Better relating

Maybe you picked up this book because you're having a tricky time with someone – a partner, a relative, a friend, a child. After all, there are just so many ways to get it wrong, aren't there? But maybe part of you also knows that when things go well in a relationship it feels amazing. If you're willing to think differently about yourself as you interact, moment to moment, with others, particularly when things get tricky, and if you're willing to practise the skills this book describes, I promise you'll get better and better at relating to other people. If you can do that, your life will be immeasurably enhanced.

Perhaps you're sceptical that relationships are a code that can be cracked, but I assure you they can, because this book is based on science, on evidence from my research, from my clinical work and from the work of other researchers too, as well as programmes devised to teach all of us about how to be better at relating to each other. I am Professor Emerita in the School of Psychology at the University of Exeter, in the UK. For over forty years I've been a psychologist training professionals, treating people clinically, researching what makes for good relating and how to achieve that, as well as how to manage when relationships break up – including helping to create programmes for separated and divorced parents. From all that came a method of psychotherapy based on evidence for what works best that's in use in the UK both in the NHS and in private practice. I have advised and consulted to businesses, organisations and governmental agencies on a plethora of aspects of relationships and I teach them how to work on their relationship skills, but this knowledge hasn't been freely available and explained – until now.

Sibling scenario

A woman is walking home from the station. Her phone rings. It's her brother. He lives in a different city, not too far away, and has three small children. They have always been close, although finding time to meet up is often hard, but the relationship between the sister and the brother's wife is more difficult. As a consequence, he feels trapped in the middle and his sister feels pushed to the side. After a few weeks of not getting together, the brother and his family are due to visit for the day that coming weekend.

She is tired – it's been a long day at work and she went shopping at lunchtime to buy presents for her nephews – and seeing her brother's number she immediately feels angry, because she thinks he's calling to say they're not coming.

'Yes,' she says, her tone tight, aggressive, imagining her brother at the other end about to cancel. 'What?'

He is also at the end of his day and as he pictures her grimacing face, he's grimacing, too. 'Oh,' he says. 'That's the way you say hello? You never change.'

On hearing this she imagines she knows what's coming. 'Right,' she says. 'So, she's managed to persuade you not to come. You've got better things to do . . .'

This makes her brother see red. 'Listen to yourself,' he yells. 'Forget it. Just forget it. All I was going to tell you is that we're completely overbooked this weekend. The kids have a whole lot of stuff I didn't expect or know about, so we were going to come after lunch now and leave before supper, so they can still do at least some of their activities, but you're so hostile, we aren't coming at all now.'

This is too much for his sister. 'Yeah, well, right,' she yells back, furious that everyone else's needs come before hers and that she's misjudged the situation. 'Don't bother. You're far too busy. I wouldn't want you to have to squeeze me in. You've a far more important life to be getting on with. Forget it is right. Just forget it.'

And they both hang up.

What a sad and angry interaction. Both brother and sister want their relationship, they want to see each other, but it's not straightforward. However, instead of falling into the usual pattern that's built up between them, what if one of them had done something different? What if the sister had talked herself down from anger, been calm, and managed to think about her brother, the demands of having a family, and the split loyalty he feels to her and to his wife? What if she'd accepted both her sadness and their mutual love, and been able to greet him warmly with, 'Hi, what's up?' Because if she had, she would probably have got a friendly, welcoming response in return, something like, 'Hi, not much. Just checking in to fine-tune arrangements for this weekend and looking forward to seeing you'! If this had been you, with your sibling, wouldn't this have made you feel you'd achieved a better outcome?

You might recognise this as a pattern between you and, say, your best friend. Maybe they continually cancel on you, break promises, and maybe when that happens you don't say anything and accept their excuses, which always sound sort of reasonable, but quietly you stew. Or maybe you squabble with a sibling over the most trivial things, which leaves a sour taste and, even though you make up, the taste somehow remains. Or maybe your mother texts you that she's waiting to hear about your next visit to her. Implied in the text is that you've been ignoring her, and you feel guilty and deliberately don't text back, thinking you'll wait till you figure out a decent reply. You wait too long, forgetting about it, because you have so much else going on, so the next day you get an angrier text from her and now you're not just guilty but cross.

If you'd been able to text your mother in the right way . . . If you'd been able to foresee what might set off your sibling and said something different . . . If you'd understood your friend better and had managed to say something constructive . . . If only . . . If you had, in each of these scenarios, you'd have ended up in a better place. You'd have been happier. You'd have felt better.

Happy people

Our lives are a lot easier when we get on well with our families, friends, colleagues and those we come into contact with on a daily basis. In general, most of us want to get along with others. There is robust scientific evidence to show that the three top things you need for wellbeing and happiness are: a healthy diet, not to smoke and thriving relationships.

There is now ample research that says people who get on with people are the happiest people in the world. They are the most successful and the healthiest. Science has even singled them out and given them a special name: the 'relationally capable'. This roughly translates as the ones who know how to 'do' relationships, relationships being the stuff that goes on, moment to moment, between people. Relationally capable people are skilful. They're the kind of people who can identify what they want and need, but who can also identify what others want and need. Because they're so skilful and secure the best outcomes, they generally end up being the happiest and healthiest people in the world.

We all know how good we feel when we're enjoying and experiencing friendship, when we're in love, when we've had

4

a positive interaction with someone at work or in our extended family. If you're a parent, hearing from teachers that your child seems to make friends or does well socially will no doubt fill you with a greater sense of relief and happiness than if you're told they're good at maths (although that's great, too). And your pleasure at hearing this is correct, because studies have shown that the ability to do well socially is more important for health, wellbeing, financial security, success and happiness than academic excellence or high IQ.

We all also know how the nightmare – imagined or real – of loneliness feeds into our fear of old age, but loneliness can hit us at any time and the consequences can be catastrophic. We *need* to be in relationships. Life is risky without them and research shows that when men's romantic relationships break down they are more likely to die, more likely to get seriously ill and more likely to be admitted to psychiatric units than women. They're more vulnerable than women, because women tend to prioritise time and energy for their families and friendships, and have wider, more robust and more intimate networks to call upon, although they are not without the risk of loneliness.

People do need people, but they need to be in *good* relationships with them. Bad relationships are hurtful and can even be dangerous. They create risk factors for mental and physical illness, for one. Sexual and physical abuse, even murders, all occur more within families and intimate partnerships than they do with strangers. Relating to people *well* is the key to staving off illness, loneliness and depression. Being able to relate *well* to others is what will keep you safe, secure and thriving. We also need to be good at relationships, because it's within them that we learn most about ourselves and feel most connected to life itself. When severely depressed people are asked what draws them back from the cliff top, stops them from taking that final step, they often answer that they couldn't do that to their family or their best friend.

5

In the moment

So, while the case for good relationships is clear, how we create them is not so obvious. Do you know how to turn tricky conversations into productive ones? Do you want to learn the tools to reverse the decline of a once-treasured friendship? Or even to end it with grace? I bet most people are quite adept at figuring out how they feel and why in those situations, but equally I bet that much of the anguish generated by tricky relationships comes from not being sure whether you're managing things in the best way possible.

Self-help books on relationships tend to spend an inordinate amount of time on advising us to focus on how we feel and why, and that has its place, but few ask us to turn our attention to what happens in those moments when people interact with each other. Relationships are simply the product of those moments: they exist as 'good 'or 'bad' because of how those moments build and are then felt between two people. That's where you're going to get the most pay-off in doing relationships better – focusing on those interactions. Why am I so sure? Because I'm a psychologist who's spent my professional life observing relationships. It's been an interesting ride for me and slowly, over time, it's revealed some truths, but it's time to share those truths.

The good news is that you can learn to form good, healthy and lasting relationships. But how does it work? What do we need to understand about ourselves, about the other person in the relationship, about the way we come together in those interactions? How do we learn to be better at communicating what we need from others and also at understanding what they need from us? What do we need to do to behave better with others – and be better, happier people for it?

This book will show you how and teach you the skills for interacting well. This is a game-changer and if you follow my steps you'll quite simply have better relationships. I've seen the most unlikely cases – people with legacies of horrendous childhoods – turn a relationship around, so instead of replicating the pain they create a relationship that can sustain them. I've seen, too, how for people with chronic or acute disorders, like OCD or depression or bipolar diagnoses, strengthening a relationship can mean the difference between thriving and becoming emotionally disabled.

I have seen how, when relationships break down, when we are not able to relate well to each other, there can be dire consequences. Sometimes these are short-term, but sometimes not, leading us to harm ourselves and others. I've worked with many, many people undergoing separation and divorce, so I've seen how a mother's or father's totally understandable depressive symptoms have had knock-on effects for their children, because depression has short-circuited their ability to parent at a time when it is most critical. And I've seen how, if you teach these warring parents to alter how they relate to each other as they divorce, they can cope with parenting their children, and limit the damage and pain. I have seen how the fall-out from people's failure to manage competition – something which is crucial in the workplace – makes people rashly leave jobs, because their relationships have imploded through unmanaged, aggressive competition. Yet had they changed their focus they might have stayed and been able to turn those soul-destroying competitions into creative collaborations in which they could have flourished.

What about in your life? Are you short-changing yourself, stifling anger or expressing it too often when you feel undervalued or frustrated at work? Is your relationship with your partner going around in circles? Are you stuck in a friendship that feels draining or unequal, but you can't think how to shift things? Or are you too often caught between wanting to say what you feel, but not wanting to offend or hurt? In order to change how you interact, you don't need to go to a therapist. All you need

7

is a willingness to examine why you act and think in a certain way; why someone else thinks and acts differently to you; and how to open yourself to change and do things better for you and the other person. Trust makes relating thrive; lack of it stops it short. Through this book you'll learn the skills to create trust, because creating trust means you've got a platform of shared understanding and these four basic skills will get you there:

+ **Emotional management:** This is the ability to calm yourself when you begin to become emotional; when you're tense, ruffled, upset or angry.
+ **Mentalising:** This is placing yourself in the other person's position and feeling for them, but also understanding them as different from you.
+ **Collaborative communication:** This is making sure your communication is clear and concise, and phrasing things in order to invite people to think along with you.
+ **Making repairs:** This is putting things back on track, including apologies when there's been hurt or upset, and also rewinding communications, when there's been a break in understanding, to ensure you understand each other again.

In the next chapter you'll find out all about them, what they look like and how they can be used, and we'll go back to the warring brother and sister we met at the outset. If they had put these simple skills into practice they would have had a much happier outcome, an outcome that they both actually wanted.

2

Skills: Learning to interact

I magine that you are the brother whose sister snaps when you ring her to fine-tune your weekend plans. You're also rushing back from work and you use those precious ten minutes on the walk home to ring your sister before the onslaught of children, dinner, homework, baths and bedtime hits you. You intend to make the call quick, but then her anger derails you. You can't believe she thinks *she's* got it hard – what is wrong with her? – and you immediately fight back: anger meets anger.

The interchange leaves you feeling triumphant and justified, but as you walk on your anger fades to irritation and is joined by a sense of being put upon, because you've now got this bad feeling between you to deal with as well. Perhaps by the time you put the key in the door you're feeling sad that your relationship has come to this once again when you'd thought you'd got to a better place recently. Whichever way you think about it, it was a negative interaction and you feel bad.

The higher the proportion of positive interactions in your life, the better for your wellbeing. You can learn skills to keep that proportion as high as possible and, as you'll see, you're largely in control of whether things go well or badly. The manner in which an interaction starts gives it a positive or negative direction, but the response and then the response to that can take it in the same direction or change the direction. Interactions are feedback loops and each person's behaviour shapes the other person's.

You, when it's your turn, and the other person, when it's theirs, have the power to make it go well – or not. If your interactions with someone are going well you're in sync, you're allies, you're on the same side, and that's good relating. It makes you feel good and is associated with wellbeing. Too much conflict and a lack of understanding is not. When there's conflict the skills you'll start to develop in this chapter will help interactions that have already gone sour, or hang in the balance, go well.

Of course, even if you use your skills deftly most of the time, you will still have those negative loops, but when you do, knowing you can make things better helps you to note where they went wrong, so you can use your skills to make them go right next time and work towards making a life of mostly positive interactions.

Changing the negative direction of loops, especially in ongoing relationships, is also important because small instances of negative loops can build to bigger ones. A series of bad interactions can lead to resentment, cruelty and then disengagement. If you get more and more of what you feel is poor treatment, you feel like you just want to hurt back. Why should you be nice to someone who isn't nice to you? If that happens the relationship remains gridlocked in negativity. It doesn't feel good or safe to be around someone likely to bite your head off and they don't feel good around you either. The proportion of negative interchanges rises and your wellbeing suffers.

In our scenario the brother – or the sister – could have turned things around gently, without making a big deal of it. Or, if that wasn't possible, next time he could greet her warmly, smoothing over the recent small disruption, or apologise for his tone. But let's imagine for a moment he had just enough bandwidth to catch his breath, realise he was about to lose it and calm down, and think for just a moment about his sister and appreciate that she is beleaguered, unhappy, probably envious.

If he had done those things, and felt a glimmer of affection and then compassion for her, he would be employing the first two of the skills – emotional management and mentalising. And if he did, in a split second he could use the next skill – collaborative communication – and reverse the negative direction by saying kindly, sympathetically, 'So how are you, Sis? It's nice to hear your voice.'

Or perhaps he didn't have the energy or time at that point. In that case, his skills could kick in later. Imagine you're the brother and it's the next morning. In fact, the night before the kids were on really good form, and after they were in bed you and your wife kicked back with a nice glass of wine, and listened to music and read together. You felt replenished, which, by the way, is what good relating can do. You had a good night's sleep, but before you dropped off you thought about sending your sister a short email, trying to make things better, except you couldn't really think of the right words or weren't sure how she'd take them. So, you slept on it, a bit uneasily, but because you felt so much more optimistic and energised by having a good time with your family, you felt hopeful and were able to park it and go to sleep.

It's morning now. You've just had a nice breakfast with your wife and kids, and there are no lost socks or unexpected texts from work. On your walk to the train you're feeling so much lighter than yesterday, but, even so, there's this vestige of discord in your gut from your unresolved spat with your sister. So, you think about the skills you didn't use – nor did she, of course – and you wonder if you could do something differently. In fact, you could try phoning her now, while you've got the chance, but – disappointingly – when she answers it's with a sullen, 'Yeah?' This time, though, you *do* have the bandwidth and you use the skills, the skills which I'll take you through, and this time you turn things around. Afterwards the heaviness in your gut is gone. You feel good about the day ahead and more optimistic about your relationship with your sister. You were out of sync with her before. Now the two of you are in sync again.

Different skillset

Of course, we'd all like a life free of confrontations, but they do happen and that's where your skills can help you minimise the chances of a disagreement becoming worse or turn a relationship that threatens to go into decline into a thriving one. The big shift this book asks you to make is to learn skills that focus your attention on what happens between you and the other person, moment to moment. You saw that the brother and sister created bad feelings. The same can happen for good feelings and, because it's a two-way street, either person has the power to make it better.

Now calm, the next morning the brother is able to do skilful things, so he doesn't snap back when his sister is sullen answering the phone. He now can think interactively. First, he plays back what happened, 'watching' what his sister said and did, including her non-verbal communication – in this case her tone of voice. Next, he notices his own reaction to her and is taken aback. He then thinks about the 'why' and realises it would be more helpful to their relationship, and kinder to his probably unhappy sister, if he is now friendly and even placatory. Unlike the evening before, this time the brother notices the interaction, not just his own feelings. By focusing on their interactions he takes a 'relational' approach that focuses on his own perspective and his sister's perspective.

The positive interaction between him and his sister becomes about what he wants to happen, which is to make things okay, rather than his need to feel justified, which he realises was motivating him the evening before: *she* shouldn't be angry, because *he* had the right to be! We've imagined ourselves to be the brother in this scenario, but it could easily have been the sister who turned things around and followed the same steps. She, too, could have healed things between them and felt better herself.

Having the skills I teach doesn't negate the need to be right, or make you right in every scenario, but they can help you be heard, and becoming skilled at getting the other party to hear your point is key. For example, the sister might really need to establish with her brother that she feels dismissed by his wife. However, she certainly wasn't going to get him to hear it during the angry phone call, because they were in conflict with each other. To be able to listen, people have to feel unthreatened, because if they're busy defending their own position they won't be listening at all. Trying to establish that you are in the right is a waste of breath until you're both sufficiently in sympathy with each other to listen.

A note of caution here: of course, there are situations that are resistant to change. When there have been years of obstruction and non-cooperation changing characteristic ways of interacting with someone takes conscious effort and persistence, sometimes over a very long time, and you might, on balance, think the effort isn't worth it. In addition, some people are resistant to any changes, perhaps stemming from a pathological condition or deep damage which affects their ability to trust anyone. And sometimes to try, especially in the face of potential real damage – for instance in sexually, physically, financially or deeply psychologically abusive situations – prolongs your risk. Should you continue to try for change? That's a judgement call.

Relationships might be complicated, but you can boil what you need to master down to four main skills: **emotional management**, **mentalising**, **collaborative communication** and **repairs**.

Emotional management

I recently watched a four-year-old boy stepping away from a table of noisy four-year-olds and whispering to his father, 'Shy!' I know that father had worked on his painfully shy son to help him label what he felt when he felt uncomfortable around other people. He'd given him the word 'shy'. It was useful for him. The little boy accepted what he felt when he felt it, because his parents had explained it, labelled it for him and accepted it in him. They'd given him some ways to manage it, so if someone he trusted was around he could go to that person, who could comfort and support him, and perhaps help him negotiate his way towards a solution. And that's exactly what happened: his father led him back to the table, sat down next to his son and gently helped him settle in with the initially scary crowd.

There are three emotional management steps to know about here: labelling, body awareness and relaxation. It helps to know what an emotional state is; to give it a label. The four-year-old labelled his feeling. Taking a step away from the feeling towards thinking calms down whatever surge of adrenaline might be accompanying it. Adrenaline gets in the way of thinking. It means you're operating from the primitive part of the brain, the instinctual one that makes you fight or flee, rather than from the part that gives you the capacity to think more clearly about what's going on and to make choices about how to behave.

Can you think of a time when you realised you were in a 'state'? That you were rattled, annoyed, upset, anxious, worried, hurt? You'd been 'triggered'. You might also have realised that just by noticing and labelling what was happening – 'I've been triggered' or 'I'm not calm' – you were calming down. That's because you were being self-reflective, not automatic or impulsive.

14

The brother in our scenario labelled his emotions, from anger and feeling justified all the way through to feeling put upon and sad, but labelling emotions doesn't mean it's necessarily okay to act on them. By the next morning the brother wasn't endorsing them, even though he accepted why he'd felt them. He wanted to act on something kinder and more conciliatory. Being calm and reflective meant he could choose to do that. If you're managing your emotions, you're able to think about them and consider whether you want to act on them or not.

The little four-year-old boy has learned about himself and warned his father, 'I'm in an uncomfortable state. What can I do to calm myself down?' The angry sister could have stopped – it only takes a millisecond – and that self-reflection would have given her the chance not to jump down her brother's throat. She could have, as her brother did the following day, calmed down, reflected and approached her brother differently in their next encounter.

Suppose they, like the little boy, could have labelled in the moment. The angry sister might have noticed her tense body, her tight voice tone, her sharp greeting. She might have noted 'I'm tense' or 'I'm angry.' When you're triggered, in a negative emotional state, your primitive brain dominates. You don't want to be in that state, because it shrinks the possible choices to only two: 'I either fight back and do something aggressive or I flee and do something passive aggressive.' Labelling is a move towards reflecting and calming.

The sister could then have taken the next steps and, after noting her state and becoming aware of how her body felt, told herself, 'I need to relax.' Relaxation puts you in what we've come to know as a 'mindful' position, which simply means you notice your 'here and now'. Your focus is on right now, not the moment that got you there and not the moment you're pulled to next. You hold emotions in your body, so if you change your body, you change your emotional state. To relax your body is a shortcut to changing the emotional climate.

So, right now, how's your body awareness? Where are your shoulders? Are they hunched? What about your jaw? Clenched? Your hands? Fisted? Is your breathing shallow? Is it coming from your chest, rather than your diaphragm? All of these are signs of tension – and primitive brain control. Shift your posture, soften your shoulders, slacken your jaw, unclench your fists, spread your toes, sink yourself comfortingly back into your chair, and breathe more deeply as you place your hands on your diaphragm to check that it's expanding with air, then deflating as you breathe slowly out. You're on the pathway to calming and giving your relating a better chance.

As your body softens and opens, so your mind opens. Rationality comes back. In fact, taking three deep breaths from the diaphragm and counting to six as you exhale almost magically transforms a tense moment into a calm one. It has been proven that doing just this small and simple breathing exercise and practising it, randomly but regularly, through the day can change the quality of your emotional state radically. Taking these steps to relaxation takes seconds and is imperceptible. You can even do it in the midst of an interaction.

Now imagine you're the sister and you've just done this labelling, body awareness and relaxing. You now think about what you want. Your brother is phoning you, you very much want him to come to your house this weekend and you want it to be a nice time, but you also want to tell him that you expected him to hurt you again, because his wife is unkind to you and he needs to know that upsets you. What should you do next? First you need to think about him, because that will help you manage your eventual communication to him. You need mentalisation.

Mentalisation

You're already conscious of how you feel, so now you're going to engage with how the other person might feel and why. You will be trying to do this so that together you can reach a position of shared understandings. Emotional management is the necessary first step and the sister is now neutral, so she's able to think about how she sounded to her brother, about how he felt – angry, because he showed it – but also to imagine why he might have been impatient, not just angry, with her. She reflects: 'He has so much on. He does feel the loyalty battles between me and his wife. He's trying to please everyone and he also has kids who have lives that pull him in different directions. He's trying to please me too. My sharpness was probably just one more thing, one more reminder of how he can't get it right for everyone.'

She's mentalising when she thinks this way. She's imagining how the other person felt, but guessing from what she knows about her brother. Mentalisation is a shift from yourself to the other; in this case from the sister's anger and imagined rejection to her brother. It's the ability to interpret and understand the emotions and behaviours of the other person, by imagining what the other person might be thinking or feeling. It's compassionate imagining.

Mentalising includes feeling empathy, but goes beyond it. Empathy's great – it certainly defuses the situation and makes the atmosphere kinder. The sister and brother each came to feel empathy, they felt bad for the other person, but they then went on and thought about how they are different. Relating skilfully is about people feeling understood – you and the other person. By understanding that his sister is *different* to him he was mentalising: the brother was not expecting her to behave just the way he would have. The danger with empathy alone is that it can make you tend to think the reasons someone feels the way they do are the same as your reasons. Mentalising means you keep in mind the differences between you. It means that you hypothesise.

In some situations, when you have the energy and time, mentalising can be done within a problematic interaction, on the spot. If you think about times in your own life when you've been triggered, but 'bit your tongue,' you might recognise that you've done this. Then you might have done or said something that was compassionate to the other person to smooth things over, even while realising they'd been thoughtless. Perhaps you realised without articulating it to yourself consciously that the other person had other troubling things happening, making them short-tempered. Or that they'd had too much to drink. If so, you did some compassionate imagining, some mentalising, without labelling it as that and probably without realising you'd done it.

Obviously, if you don't know the other person your ability to mentalise is limited, but even so you can keep an open mind, and don't assume that because you felt and behaved a certain way, that's the only way to feel and behave. Clearly, the more intimate the relationship, the more you've got to go on, so the easier it is to fine-tune your mentalising. In intimate relationships you'll know a lot about what makes someone tick – for instance, whether your sister often feels rejected by you – and be able to make good guesses as to why. With strangers, you have to make best guesses with paltry information. Even so, you can never know the inside of someone completely. Your best guesses about why someone's feeling and behaving the way they are, are just that: best guesses. There could be other explanations – they're called 'hypotheses' – and mentalising rests on them, because they're all we've got to go on.

Maybe the sister had just had a fight with her boyfriend and she's just taking her anger out on her brother; maybe she hadn't had a single thought about the weekend and how he'd possibly reject her. If you are too sure you're right – that there simply can't be any other way to think about it – you could be in trouble. The sister demonstrates this – she jumped to conclusions and was so sure that her brother was calling to cancel because he was choosing his family over her – that she shouted at him straightaway. The interaction went south.

When you mentalise, rather than 'knowing', you're open to increasing your understanding of the other person, to having shared meanings. You 'get' them. When I did a study of long, happy love relationships I interviewed a couple in their late fifties who'd been together since their teens. They described their relationship as volatile, but loving. I asked him, in a separate interview, how he now managed his anger when arguments erupted. 'I take the dog for a walk,' he told me. 'At first, I am only thinking about how *I* feel hurt, but by the time I've walked round the park once I'm not thinking that way. I've thought about the dog, looked at the houses, cleared my mind. I'm not hurting. By the time I am ready to do another circuit I find I'm thinking about *her*, and how and why *she's* hurting – how I used to hurt her with my words and even more, and then, that, of course, my words will carry hurt for her. I'm thinking about her, how it feels and why. Then I want to go back and say sorry.'

Once he's back, he told me, they talk gently and things are calm. His wife wants their alliance, not their estrangement, as much as he does and they find their way back to it. By removing himself, getting some fresh air, time with his dog, he's found his method. He knows that by first labelling, then removing himself – walking the dog around the block – he can rely on staying calm, which then means he can think compassionately – mentalise – about his wife. He returns to her with the intention to repair their fracture. He is in a state to offer himself back to her, safe and trustworthy, and trusting her again.

So, you've mentalised and now you're ready for what happens: what you each do in response to each other and how things are communicated.

Collaborative communication

She snapped and he bit back – what you do moment to moment is what creates trust and safety or distrust and threat. In this case, there was no safety for either party. She attacked and he attacked back. This was not collaborative communication. If you want to make things right with the other person you need to build alliances and shared understanding, and that rests on how you phrase things – what you say and how you say it – but you also need to use non-verbals that communicate safety, making your tone of voice and posture inviting.

Make it safe

People will listen if they know it's safe to listen; if they know you're not going to hit them with something horrible. Once a teacher began a parents' evening about my young son with, 'Is he deaf?' I was so shocked that I stopped listening for most of what she next said. If she'd begun, as the previous year's teacher had done, with, 'I wish I had a whole class like your son,' I would have listened and then found out that he was a bit too dreamy and sometimes appeared not to listen. We would have been allies, collaborating in thinking about my son's behaviour and ways in which he could progress.

The teacher might have said to me, 'Your son seems really imaginative and it seems to me that he gets lost in his thoughts. Do you think that's a fair description?' She didn't know for sure if that was right – he may have been deaf and we didn't know about it – but that would have shown me she was supportive and wanted to have a genuine discussion.

Be brief

It turns out people can only take in a little bit of information at a time when they're in conversation. Once I was in a restaurant with an Italian friend whose English was rudimentary. The waiter rattled off a load of menu choices, describing things in complicated language, hopelessly losing my friend, whose bemused expression seemed to annoy the waiter, perhaps offended that his glorious descriptions had landed badly. Use language in bite-sized chunks that matches the other person's capacities (that's why you use simple language with children).

Be clear and focused

People's attention can wander, so you need to focus on a single point. There's a reason short, snappy catchphrases catch on: they're quickly heard, interpreted and digested. There are, of course, different rules during lectures or plays, communications that aren't interactive, because you can take in a lot more if you're not preparing your own response, but in interactions you need to stick to the single point you want to make and make it concisely.

Clarity also comes from your 'optics' aligning with your content. What you say and how you say it should look and sound the same. Otherwise, the other person won't know what you really mean. If you say, 'I'm sorry,' but say it aggressively, they will be confused and unlikely to be convinced that you are contrite.

You might yearn to bring up other points about them, perhaps that they're too sensitive or quickly become self-righteous, but this is not the time for that. Stay with your main point, because if you go on to other points that one will get lost. When you share understanding you are in an alliance, on the same side. In ongoing relationships there will be occasions to bring up other points, one by one, in a way and at times when they can be heard.

Speak from your own experience

Refrain from telling the other person who they are and what they're thinking. When you're convinced you 'know' how someone is feeling and behaving, and you tell them, the other person will rebel. That's particularly true when you tell someone that you 'know' their mind. Minds are private spaces. You would stop listening and jump to protect yours from outside invasion, too.

Anyway, even though you 'know' you know, you could well be wrong. We make wrong inferences all the time, especially about people we know well. That's partly because we have so many pieces of 'evidence' to back us up. But maybe we've read at least some of the evidence wrongly. What if at least some of the times you've thought the other person was acting self-righteously, they weren't? What if you'd caught them talking passionately about a principle in which they believe instead? If you've closed your mind and jumped to conclusions, you've likely made some wrong ones.

Use your own phrasing

Reassurance that you're not telling someone what and how they think comes in another form, too: stating things from your own experience, rather than insisting that because you see it one way that's how it must be. When you're making an observation, you can only communicate what you, yourself, have felt or what you, yourself, have perceived. It's fundamentally the case that perceptions can be wrong.

Phrasing things so it shows you know that it's coming from an entirely subjective position by making it about your own experience means saying things like, 'I could be mistaken, but it seems to me . . .' or 'I might be wrong, but I can imagine that you might have felt . . .' or 'It's been my experience . . .' or 'I was left *feeling* that I was disrespected . . .'

22

The perception is yours, the feeling is yours, even if you could have been wrong about the incident. In fact, maybe you were wrong, but you've left it open, through your phrasing, for the other person to confirm or deny the accuracy of your perception.

Indeed, speaking from your experience, but not imposing, can yield really productive conversations. Maybe you've misread intentions. The other person is in listening, receptive mode, hearing that you're open to hearing you've misread the situation, which may give them pause for thought about how they came across to you

Invitational, collaborative phrasing

You're trying to convey that you want the other person to think about what you're saying. You're offering it to them for consideration. You've got a common interest. In the case of the brother and sister, it's looking forward to a good weekend together. However, let's assume the siblings are already back on track, it's a different time and place, and you as the brother think now is a good time to bring up the fact that that incident on the phone was, to you, an example of your sister becoming 'self-righteous'. How would you do that?

Safety first, of course, so you need to assure her you are speaking not just from your heart and experience, but in the interests of something you can both collaborate over: in this case, smoothing your relationship further. That means you are caring for her as much as for yourself and you want to establish collaboration, to invite her to be collaborative with you, so you phrase your comments with that intention.

You might say something like, 'I can imagine you might very easily feel I'm always about to leave you out – I look like I've got a million other things on – and I want you to know I don't want you to feel that, if that's true. I want to know how you think about it. Is there something we could both do differently?'

You've made it safe, collaborative, and you've invited her to think jointly with you.

You use language that's open and inviting, and you convey that you're interested in understanding. You phrase things in a calm – or if appropriate, warm or sympathetic – and engaging way that shows you want the person to help you understand, clarify, explain, and you invite them to contribute from their perspective. Invitational, collaborative phrasing is tentative: phrases such as 'I might be wrong . . .' 'It seems to me . . .' or 'I can imagine that . . .' Going back to their angry phone exchange the brother might offer, 'I can imagine that you would be hurt by my sharpness in reply to you . . .' or 'I might be wrong, but it might be that, from things in the past, you could have been frightened I was going to cancel . . .'

Then, taking things further, you might invite your sister to reflect further with you, together, ensuring a smoother future together, with phrases such as, 'Can we think or try to understand, perhaps imagine how to do it differently, so we don't keep ending up in the same place?' The operative words here are the question 'Can . . .?' and 'we'. They are both invitational and collaborative.

Using courteous language helps, too: 'Please could you help me so we can both understand . . .?' might really help invite your sister to think with you. And when she does respond with information from her experience – 'Yes, you're right. I still don't feel I know your wife very well and you do juggle us, which makes me very uncomfortable' – saying to her, 'Thank you for helping us get some clarity' also joins you collaboratively.

All these skills can come at any time – then and there, or later – to get you both on the same page. You've calmed and thought about yourself as part of the interaction. You've thought about the other person, as another person reacting to or reaching out to you. You've then thoughtfully shaped how you want to come across to them so they'll hear you and understand. That's being skilful, but it's a learning process and you'll make errors. You can certainly become skilled in managing emotions, mentalising and communicating collaboratively, but you'll never be perfect, so you also need to learn how to make repairs.

Repairing breakages

Your close friend who lives abroad has promised to come for a big birthday celebration, one of those that ends with zero. Ten years ago they disappointed you at the last minute by cancelling their attendance at a similar celebration – their dog was being put down. At the time you tried to empathise and, not being a dog lover yourself but knowing they were, you felt proud of yourself that you didn't lose your cool, but rode out that disappointment with grace and understanding. This time another big party's been planned. You want them there. You think you've been clear. And a week before the party you get another cancellation from them: they are unwell and their son has a major exam. You are sceptical of the excuse. You guess there is something else. You don't trust them. They say you are so important to them, but their actions suggest otherwise and, anyway, you are clearly not a priority.

You are hurt and incandescent. You fire off an angry email, citing the time ten years ago when you 'forgave' them and saying you don't know if you can do that again. An angry one comes in reply, accusing you of insensitivity. This could be the end of a friendship, especially with so much distance between you. Is that what you want?

And then you reflect: your friend used to have a flying phobia. You thought they'd overcome it, because they have flown to visit you and you had assumed it was gone. But maybe – and another of your other friends has helped you think about it from

25

the point of view of your friend – just maybe your friend is not being honest either with you or themself about it. Having phobias is humiliating; thinking maybe you've cracked it and then realising you haven't is demoralising. Could that be what's happening? That seems not just plausible but the likeliest explanation, knowing what you do about your friend. You feel upset with yourself for having been what the friend has labelled 'insensitive'. What do you do?

When an interaction breaks down, it needs repairing. Repairs are gestures and/or words of empathy and remorse for causing hurt. You want to get things on track. You take responsibility for re-establishing trust. Repairs turn things around; make growls into smiles. They also take bravery. You might be rebuked if your timing is wrong – if you've hurt someone, they need to calm down to receive your attempt to repair. Maybe your friend is still smarting and still embarrassed that they can't manage to get on a plane. They might need some time, as you did, to reflect, to realise the friendship is at risk from the angry emails and to want to put it right.

As the songs correctly say, 'Sorry' – the key repair word – is the hardest word. Apologies are difficult, in part because no one wants to feel they might have caused hurt, to be the 'bad guy'. Your instinct is to defend hurtful behaviour by saying it was retaliatory. And it might have been. But trust is destroyed when there's breakage and, if you want to be allies again, you need to rebuild it. Apologies are mainly for the effect on the other person. They'll trust you again if you apologise for that, at least.

Apologies are magical, but do need patience around timing. When there's been a big rupture like the one between you and your flying-phobic friend – and in this case, both sides caused hurt so each needs to apologise – apologies look like something this: 'I'm really sorry for the hurt I caused . . . You must have really been upset by what I said/did/didn't say/didn't do . . . I shouldn't have said what I said in the way I said it . . . I recognise its effect was just all wrong/must have been misunderstood/ must or could have been hurtful/made you angry . . . I should have done things differently, because I recognise how wrong/ hurtful/upsetting it must have been.'

So, you could say to the friend, 'I am really sorry for firing off that email without thinking. I imagine it really upset you; it would certainly have upset me.' And, further, it helps to contextualise your error: 'I was so disappointed, of course, that you wouldn't be here with me to celebrate and I just lashed out, lashed out at someone I care so much about – the irony is that that's why I was so upset in the first place!'

Or there can be small interactional breakages. They, too, need repairs. For instance, suppose you say something you don't mean as awkward, but which clearly, from the reception it gets, is. The other person may go momentarily silent or they may reply oddly, but either way, even though you may not know why, you know something's gone askew. There's been a breach, but how do you get it back on track?

You go back to that point where, for example, the other person went silent, and you ask about that so you can understand. You rewind to the moment when you were not in sync. Then – and here comes the importance of phrasing, again – you *invite* them back so you can understand and you're on the same page again: 'Wait a minute – can we go back so we're sure we're not talking at cross-purposes? . . . I think somewhere there's been a misunderstanding – could have been me.' Or if you think it might be because you used an off-putting phrase, you say something like, 'I'm sorry – maybe it was badly put . . . I just want to clarify we understand each other – can I check?' You've repaired the small breakage in mutual understanding. Again, in ongoing relationships you can reflect on it and do this later.

There are apologies for content and apologies for the manner in which something's been said or done. The effect of your manner − thoughtlessness, flippancy, harshness − can destroy trust as much as the content of what you say. Then there's the content, the point you're trying to make, and that, too, might cause pain and mistrust.

In the earlier scenario, the sister was angry, because she thought her brother was calling to cancel, and her angry manner hurt her brother. 'I'm sorry for shouting', apologises for her manner and paves the way for her point to be heard. But, as it happened, she was wrong. Her content was incorrect and he wasn't cancelling and about to make her feel devalued, so she owes an apology for the content too: 'I jumped the gun and got it wrong.' If she apologises on both counts he's likely to be more sensitive to her in the future, because she's shown sensitivity to him. They will be on each other's side again.

Putting it all together

Here's a scenario played out from the top, turning a vicious loop into a virtuous one, in the moment and using all the skills mentioned. Let's start with the sister. If she had calmed and soothed herself, so she didn't jump to an angry conclusion (emotional management), was open to hearing him and thinking more broadly about his life, not just hers (mentalising), she might have opened with something like (emotional management, using collaborative communication in an inviting tone), 'Hi, there. What's up?' That would have been more likely to get her a warm response, something like, as we saw earlier, 'Hi, not much. Just checking in to fine-tune about this weekend. Looking forward to seeing you'!

Or her brother could have turned things around. At the first sign of his sister's anger, he might have calmed and soothed himself (emotional management), thought about her life and not just his (mentalising), and then responded to her hostility with kindness, his tone warm, with something like (collaborative communication), 'Hey, I'm glad to hear you, hope it's an okay time to talk. Really looking forward to seeing you, so if you aren't busy right now can we talk about this weekend?'

The sister or the brother might also have turned things around at the time by thinking about what they'd done to antagonise the other (mentalising) and saying (repairing), 'Hey, I'm sorry. I really shouldn't have said what I just did. It wasn't fair. Let's start again.' And the vicious cycle would have turned virtuous.

You've now got the toolkit for navigating well when there are ruptures, conflicts or misunderstandings. In the following chapters you're going to learn how to put managing emotions, mentalising, collaborative communication and repairing into action in your own life across a range of different relationships, but first let's think about our instincts and the learning process itself.

3

Foundations: Building blocks of success

Have you ever watched a newborn with their mother? The wordless choreography that melds the two – the baby crying, the mother feeding, the baby settling, the mother at ease? Or watched parents smile when their babies smile at them and grimace when their babies grimace? Scientists have watched, too, and established that it's how you behave together that matters. It's true from the very beginning, we need security and positive interactions to thrive.

Scientific observations in natural and experimental settings of parents with infants and toddlers have shown the clear effect on babies of sensitive and caring parental responsiveness. Babies smile, are soothed and their heart rates settle when this happens. It's true physiologically: pleasurable interactions show increased levels of oxytocin, the 'love hormone'. Good interactions lead to good feelings. Babies 'know' when they are 'understood'. Their caregivers respond with what they need when they cry and their caregivers know they're right because the babies stop crying. The behaviours exchanged are the crux of the matter.

This mutual smiling and grimacing is called mirroring. Mirror neurons are neurons in all of us that make you feel as if you are actually having the same experience as someone else, in your own different, separate bodies. Mirror neurons are almost magical, bonding us physically as we interact in deep understanding with each other.

If good interactions make us feel good, it follows that if we feel bad then some good interactions might make us feel better. Let's look at therapy. People who go into therapy usually want to 'feel better.' If you go into therapy it's useful to look at what it is in therapy that enables you to change or feel better. I always think of therapy as being like a laboratory of change – the principles that hold for change in therapy can also hold for real life. We practise in the therapy room with our therapist, and then go out to try and make these changes in our day-to-day lives.

We now know that one of the keys to effecting change in therapy is a focus on behaviour. Learning how to behave and communicate better is crucial, and working on how you each relate to each other is an especially powerful way to achieve change.

You do need to understand yourself, too, it's true – why you think the way you do, why you find some things difficult to do, what might prevent you making changes and why. In fact, if there's insight behind any changes you make, studies show that the changes will last longer, although insight on its own isn't anywhere near enough.

At the beginning of my career, a lot of what happened in therapy training was based on theory, rather than hard evidence. I had my doubts even back then, and even if a theory made sense, resonated with me emotionally, hung together as a coherent story, I was never convinced it was truly helpful. Take the 18-year-old woman I was seeing each week who couldn't manage to get up in time to attend a single one of her classes and was now on academic probation. She was depressed, she felt useless and alienated. She hadn't made friends, as she was on a different time clock to everyone else and hadn't met people in class or the library. But she was baffled, too, bemused by how much she was stumbling: this wasn't the person she'd thought she was! She wasn't the problem child in her large,

Latinx family. She was the good and studious one. She was the smart, obedient one; the one whose nursing assistant, single-parent mother had always made sure she got up in time for school, got out the door with all her books, sent her off with lunch made and packed. She was the daughter whose mother shone with pride when she got a full scholarship. She was the good daughter, the first in her family to go to university, and to a prestigious one at that. And now she couldn't even get herself up to go to class.

Yes, it was important to find out why she felt so overwhelmed. If she understood that, she'd be more likely to adopt a change in behaviour. But it was also crucial to learn that she'd never had to get herself out of bed, make her own lunch, or think about how to feed herself. She was completely ignorant about how to look after herself. I asked her if she had a watch. She shook her head. I asked her if she had an alarm clock – it was in the days before smart phones. She shook her head. 'Before our next session I want you to get an alarm clock. That's a first step,' I said.

When I ran this by my supervisor, I was scolded. This wasn't the point of therapy, she told me. In her view the point of therapy was insight, not behaviour change. Presumably, I guess, insight would automatically lead to behaviour change if the insight were deep enough. We now know that just isn't so. According to my supervisor, achieving insight meant making the patient focus on the distortions she was experiencing in her life. The particular distortion here, as ever, was around her parents, particularly her mother. Was she angry at her mother, envious of her mother, punishing her mother by enslaving the mother to her? I was the mother substitute – what was she projecting on to me?

Even if I bought into this interpretation – that it was about her feelings for her parents, an as-yet unscientifically tested story very much taken as truth in the clinic in which I then worked – to me the more pressing goal was to change the way she behaved, to make her more 'able'. It was to make her grow into life as a young adult; to get her to be more functional; to get her to class and to help her make friends; to get her up and out of her room. She needed to start with getting an alarm clock so she could learn to get herself up, not rely on her mother. These days I would also try to work on how she related to her mother. I think that would have done them both a world of good.

The studies of John Bowlby, a psychiatrist and researcher working on parents and babies, started this all off. He identified that each person influences the other and how they behave together is key. He showed how important feedback loops are and how each person is just as important in making this loop go positively. The baby coos in satisfaction and the mother knows she has understood the signal correctly. The mother feeds the baby and the baby gets the message that crying when hungry produces the right response. As you'll see in a moment, some babies learn the futility of crying when that doesn't happen.

Starting in the late 1950s, Bowlby observed babies and mothers. He watched how, in order to survive, babies seem to instinctively 'know' how to signal what they need and their mothers seem to 'know' how to respond so that their babies thrive. He proposed that human babies and their mothers have instincts, just like other species. Babies seek the security of knowing their carers will respond and keep them safe from threat; that they are, in consequence, able to develop, to grow, to thrive. The right interactions between mother and baby form the baseline.

Trusting your important caregiver means a relationship develops and creates a system of 'attachments', as Bowlby called them. According to his 'attachment theory' humans need to feel secure, so they can develop well and avoid threat. That strong emotional connection is what we would call 'love'.

But what about when this love and care isn't there – when a baby isn't nurtured? Babies in orphanages Bowlby visited couldn't depend on a safe carer and they showed stunted development. He observed young children separated from their caregivers – children in hospital in an era when parents weren't allowed to stay with them – and saw that, over time away from people with whom they felt secure, the children became distressed, depressed and regressed. These findings are fundamental to understanding how human beings develop and what he observed about needing security within relationships is true all across the life cycle.

So that's the template – security versus threat. We seek security and we're on the alert to avoid threats. As we get older we're no longer in the same scenarios – we're not babies seeking to be fed. Instead, it's about how safe you feel to try out being 'you'. In whose presence are you secure enough to try out thoughts and behaviours? Are you valued and understood. Are you safe? Can you trust? When you're interacting with someone, you're both on the alert for this innate 'threat'. Are they safe? Can I trust they'll understand me? You're also seeking to be in alliance, because if you are you relax and don't worry about threat.

Relaxing around someone is crucial. Your 'primitive' brain is the one that's concerned with your safety. If you sniff threat adrenaline floods your body and all you're concerned with is fighting or fleeing. If you feel safe, you're operating from the rational part of your brain. You're free to roam and explore; you develop. You can discover, think and engage with the world, including the other person. Who is this interesting being who is also interested in me? Are they an ally or an enemy? To erase the threat that is always there, just beneath the surface, we need allies, so we seek them out, but if we have a breakdown in communication with someone, we instantly feel that threat. Repairing the relationship banishes that threat – we have an ally again and feel safe.

Our emotional life is underpinned by these two instincts – to sense threat and to try to be in an alliance that makes us feel secure. Behaviours grow out of one or the other of these fundamental emotional states. Am I secure? Am I threatened? What you do in interactions – your behaviours in them – can be reduced to creating alliances when possible and managing threats if they are present, so becoming skilled in interactions helps us feel more secure.

From all the evidence, I can say with conviction that good interactions are the pathway to wellbeing; that it's about how people respond to you and how you can get them to respond positively. When the balance leans towards positive, you're going to feel good, because it's then you'll feel secure and safe, and those are the conditions in which you'll thrive.

The behaviours in between

So now you know that all our human emotions are based on these two primitive, basic instincts – to seek security and to avoid threat – and because emotions and behaviours are linked, if we change our behaviour we can influence our emotions.

Let's look at the link between the behaviours we observe in others and what might be going on behind them. Think about the last time you had an argument with someone, especially with someone you don't know that well. If you're typical you probably didn't make a conscious link between their behaviour and their emotional state. Much of the time we just react to behaviour without thinking. Even within the world of therapy it took a long time to separate out thinking, feeling and behaving, and make the links between them clear.

A psychiatrist called Aaron Beck realised that the people he was seeing in his clinic were feeling, thinking and behaving in ways that were linked. He realised that working on changing the thoughts and feelings behind the behaviours would help people change their behaviours, and make them feel better. His method was what became called cognitive behaviour therapy or CBT. This was a new and powerful route to change. As we know, feelings are linked to behaviours, with their accompanying thoughts or beliefs. Behaviours are like their outer coat.

Like the Wizard of Oz pulling levers unseen behind the curtain, feelings operate behind that curtain and are the motivators of behaviours. If you can decode what the feelings are likely to be, it can help you figure out what your own behaviours should be when you're in an interaction. Is the other person defending? Maybe being aggressive or withdrawn? If so, why? And are you?

Emotions, the feelings behind behaviours are basically all about seeking security and avoiding threat. They come in various shades, but the bottom line is this. Emotions are either hard – they are the ones that grow from a sense of threat – or soft. Soft emotions are about a wish for security, to be in alliance with the other person, but they make you vulnerable. Soft emotions connect. Hard emotions cover over soft, defending us against revealing vulnerability. Seeking security comes first and hard emotions follow, to protect our softer emotions.

Hard emotions might include resentment, irritation, envy, anxiety, frustration, aggression, anger and annoyance. Behaviours that act these out are such things as physical fighting, abusive language, sulking, tenseness and withdrawal.

Soft emotions – the ones that come out in behaviour during safety – are when you feel caring, compassion, kindness, understanding, affection, mutuality, loving, appreciating, gratefulness, relief and mirroring. Behaviours that show these are actions such as smiling, friendliness, embracing, caressing, and other physically loving gestures and actions.

Interactions are the crucible; the stage for negotiating how safe you feel with the other person; the vessel in which you are sniffing out safety and trust. Each moment-to-moment interplay is a series of trust negotiations. Misunderstandings and hurts mean the sequence following can build to mistrust – or be repaired back to security.

Making meanings

So, how do you know what a behaviour, with its emotion behind it, means? With newborns it's easy: hunger, safety, comfort. There's not much to interpret, but think about the last time you had an awkward interchange with a friend, when you weren't sure if the friend was angry with you or just joking. Their words weren't clear, their tone was ambiguous. How do you know if someone's on your side? And whether they think you're on theirs or not? This is where we get to the important bit of how you know whether to trust or not: *meanings*. Are you understood? Do you understand?

Here's an example. You remember I told you about the time I was in a restaurant with an Italian friend with little English. The waiter rapidly rattled off a florid description of the specials, and my friend registered bemusement. So, the waiter just repeated himself, aggressively and loudly, as if the problem between them was my friend's deafness. I was startled. In return I felt aggressive. I imagined my friend felt the same. If we'd responded aggressively, we'd have done the fight-or-flight response to the threat of the waiter's aggression. But we didn't. We calmed. I formed a hypothesis that stilled my anger. I mentalised. I hypothesised that the waiter felt out of his depth, threatened by his own ignorance of how to conduct himself with someone who didn't speak his language. He, himself did not feel 'secure'. Maybe in some way he imagined my friend as an aggressor. Maybe his foreignness itself felt like an aggression, a challenge. I don't know what my friend did to help himself, but his behaviour showed he'd done some rapid thinking, too: he smiled. The waiter, surprised, caught himself for a split second and smiled back. The whole mood felt safe again.

If missed meanings are the problem, as they were in that episode, going on the offensive doesn't address it, of course. Instead, hard emotions create a new problem: a rift and then mistrust. Who knows what might have ensued if we had met aggression with aggression. He might have spat in our soup!

Meanings people give to things are the ways in which they bond. Carers 'get' the meaning of babies' cries and smiles. In the UN, translators are used to get close to shared 'meanings' through shared words. Shared deep meanings bond you deeply. Think about how you made your best friends: wasn't it that you found the same things funny or shared similar memories, with certain words, say to a particular song, that set off the same feelings in each other? Shared meanings fire up those mirror neurons: you're like me! I'm like you! I'm understood! They glue you together. Shared meanings create trust. You 'get' each other. Communication flows and interactions are easy when that happens. Connections in understanding – shared meanings – are moments in which you feel safe and have an ally.

So meanings are important, but here's the rub: you can't always be sure you share meanings, even when you've known someone forever and even when you live together intimately. You make assumptions, based on your past together. Those assumptions could be wrong. The process of bonding is a process of discovering how much you share meanings and everyone has their own individual shapers of meanings; their own particular families and childhoods; their particular cultures; their particular relationship histories; the histories they have with particular people. Not even identical twins live exactly the same day-to-day lives and every day we accumulate experiences that shape meanings.

So, everyone has to negotiate around everyone else's particular meanings. Especially in ongoing relationships. To do that you have to *keep* learning about the other person and how they got to think and feel the way they do. You have to guard against making the wrong assumptions. You've got to be prepared to keep being surprised at what you thought you knew about someone, but don't. There are so many ways to 'read' things incorrectly that it's really important to think, 'Maybe I'm wrong.' It's safer than 'I'm probably right.'

When meanings aren't shared there are ruptures. Sometimes these go unnoticed, because you assume you mean the same thing as the other person, but you may not. Multiple misunderstandings can easily occur, primarily because not only do people make assumptions about the meaning of actions or words, but also because of their – often mistaken – conviction that their own meanings are absolutely clear.

I remember one exchange in a therapy session with a couple, discussing a recent event. 'I told her that I didn't want to go out on my birthday and she arranged a big dinner with a bunch of friends. I couldn't have been clearer!' said one partner, in exasperation. The other partner, on the backfoot answered, defensively, 'But it was said with a laugh. And I know how awful it would have been not to have had those friends around on the birthday, because last year they weren't and it was remarked on how much they were missed!'

If you get it wrong and respond on the basis of a misreading, the next response to the one you've just made is also likely to go wrong – and so on. So, it's critical to repair or to be sure you do share meanings; to be sure that you understand and are understood.

Safe and secure

Try and think of an awkward conversation with a friend, when you weren't sure of their meaning, but you recovered. How did that happen? You're an 'animal' so you must have been poised to be in 'threat' rather than 'secure' mode. How did you and your friend become 'secure' again? You will have done so because you aren't just an 'animal.' You've got a really big and agile brain. You're capable of higher-order thinking. You can learn and your capacity for learning is vast.

We can learn behaviours to control our primitive brain and use our rational one. You can learn skills to take you to the rational place. You can learn what the skill looks like, the sort of situation in which you need to use it, and then you can practise it in that sort of situation again and again. The skill then becomes habit.

The first crucial skill in good relating is emotional regulation. Without it your primitive brain rules. Thinking about the meanings of your interactional behaviour, yours and the other person's, won't follow until that part of your brain – when you're tense, angry, whatever – is no longer in charge.

A famous experiment showed just how crucial emotional regulation is for success in life. The Marshmallow Experiment, conducted at Stanford University by Walter Mischel and colleagues, showed that self-control, or emotional regulation, has considerable advantages and that some very young children are already able to find ways towards achieving it. It showed that having strategies to delay gratification – that is to override our first emotional impulses – is a good thing for lots of things in life. In the first version of this experiment, 32 young children, aged between three and a half and just over five and a half, and only those who understood the terms of the experiment, were offered a treat, either a marshmallow or a pretzel. They were told they could eat the treat, but if they waited 15 minutes they'd have two treats. The researchers observed children showing skilful ways to get through the difficult waiting time and managing their instinct to grab the sweets. Some children covered their eyes, rested their heads on their arms or found other ways not to look at the treat. Others talked or sang to themselves, invented their own games or tried to fall asleep while waiting - as one successfully did. Those strategies and techniques for calming enabled those children to make the better choice.

Here's the bottom line: in follow-up studies with these children, when they'd grown up, the ones who'd postponed gratification, who'd learned how to calm themselves, to think their way through to getting the doubled reward – who'd tamed the primitive brain and let the thinking one out – were more successful in life on a number of measures than the others.

It's true that it's easier to calm the primitive brain and think more clearly when you feel less is at stake. It wasn't a stretch for my Italian friend and I to do what we did. It was a tiny interaction. Relationships exist on a scale of intimacy, with family and loved ones normally at the very top and close friendships nearby. Other relationships, such as some work ones, can be loaded with emotion as well, but intimate relationships can pose the greatest risk and feel the scariest, because more is at stake.

In intimate relationships you are most naked and vulnerable. Bleakly, more deaths, abuse and violence occur within families than anywhere else, but putting those extremes aside, if your partners, parents or most trusted friends keep misunderstanding you, you're likely to feel consistently more hurt. Just as in such relationships there are more possibilities for good alliances, because the more intimate you are, the more your lives are intertwined, there are also more possibilities for loops that go wrong, for missed meanings and missed understandings to build, and for you to feel much more let down, much more unprotected. There's lots more scope for deep anger, disappointment and resentment, for a build-up of things being misconstrued and misunderstood.

That brings us to the pivotal importance of both mentalising and clear, concise, collaborative communication. They are the building blocks of trying to assure you are on the same page, that you share meanings. A host of studies, from therapy research to research on 'normal' family development, to studies of communication within couples and how people function together within organisations and businesses, underscore the significance of learning how to communicate precisely to ensure shared understanding.

A few years ago, I was part of a research and development team put together to help warring separated parents learn the same skills as the ones in this book. We developed a series of programmes that coached people first in emotional regulation (that self-control the children in the Marshmallow Experiment showed), which then opened them up to being coached in turning their minds to mentalising about differences between them and their ex-partner, and their different states of mind. Learning those first two prepared them for the last set of skills: being clear, concise and courteous, using invitational language and 'I' statements. Those who completed the training reported that these skills helped them collaborate over their children's best interests.

Another programme was designed for separated couples who claimed they couldn't sit in the same room together, but were being required to do so by the courts for mediation meetings. The exercise was about making sure they shared meanings, because if they didn't, they wouldn't be able to do what the courts were asking them to do for the welfare of their children. The team developed coaching for these couples based on a simple listening and communication exercise called Active Listening. This trains you to be concise and clear, punctuating the action at the end of each brief utterance to check out whether the other person has understood.

The first person makes the first statement – in the case of the divorcing couples it was a very simple statement of 'how I got to the appointment.' You don't carry on to the next utterance until that has been established. In the exercise the listener had to say back what they had heard. The first speaker either agreed that the listener had got the whole gist of it, or not, pointing out what part they'd got right, if at all, and what they might have missed. The listener then tried again, stating what they'd understood they'd heard. When the first speaker was satisfied that what they'd tried to communicate had been properly understood, it was the other person's turn to respond. They might have had a question, for instance. Or they would just go on to say how they had got there. The same procedure followed. This was an exercise in people both listening and understanding, but also in trusting that they would be understood. It established ground rules for how communication had to proceed. But more importantly, perhaps, the warring couples, having been terrified beforehand of being in the same room together, were, through this exercise, calm enough then to go on to the more substantial business that the meeting was convened for. Data from the programme suggested that, to their astonishment, many of those couples felt able to take the next steps, because they'd discovered they'd been able to share meanings, and even felt emotionally safe.

Learning skills

Before I teach you the crucial skills, let's look at how skills are learned. In the psychology labs of Stanford University in the 1970s Professor Albert Bandura laid down some principles of how we learn things and, more fundamentally for this book, how we can change our behaviour through learning skills.

When you're learning a skill, at first you don't do it well – you keep getting it wrong. You know you're doing it wrong, but you

44

don't know how to get it right. What Bandura found is that you need to define the skill. Then you need to see it in action in a similar situation to the one in which you'll need it – you need an example. Then you should try it out in your own life, as many times as you can in as many similar situations as possible. Your habits will gradually alter and the new skill will become your new normal. This is the learning principle used in programmes designed to teach separating couples not to fight in front of their children and that's the model for this book.

In chapter 2 we defined the skills needed for good relations: emotional management, mentalising, collaborative communication, and repairs. In chapter 3 we've started to look at why they are fundamental; how you might develop them; and see how they might be used. They're certainly skills that you need to learn and the key now is to just keep trying them out yourself. In the following chapters you'll see them in action.

4

Parents and children: Generation games

Dan and Louisa are parents of a toddler, Alfie, whose tantrums rule them. What is the line between being too strict and too lax? Between letting your child be 'who he is' and having to decide things for their welfare as a parent, especially when your child is too young to reason with?

Then there's Katie, an eight-year-old whose friend is introducing her to things Katie's mother, Harriet, feels are 'inappropriate'. Harriet tries to close down that friendship, but feels desperate, guilty and out of her depth. What do you do with a child who's still a child, but claims to 'know' what she wants?

Or there are 14-year-old Carrie's parents, who, at their initial family therapy session, claimed half-jokingly that an alien had replaced their once sweet child. At first, she only broke school rules and hung out with kids who were perennially in trouble, but what do you do when, like Carrie's parents, who suspected she was involved in dubious online relationships, you worry your child is at risk? What do you do, if, like Carrie's parents, you don't know how, or even whether it's right, to control your child?

This chapter is about how you can parent better and have good interactions with your child. As a parent you're handed the most difficult task you'll ever have: to rear a child to become a functioning, happy member of society. To fail is a parent's worst nightmare; to succeed their greatest reward. To become the well-adjusted, happy citizens you want them to become, children need love and security. These are best nurtured if childrearing is guided by two key factors: *respect* and *power*. In this chapter you'll see why this is so, and how, when there are struggles between you and your child, if you take note of those two elements you will help yourself to manage the problematic interactions that arise as you move through life raising your children.

Imagine your eight-month-old baby, newly adept at crawling, is exploring his environment. You are enjoying his new skills and his new discoveries with him as he encounters chair legs, the rug, the feel of wooden floors. And then he heads towards an electrical socket. Do you scoop him up and whisk him away? If you do, he will protest, cry, be angry. You've delighted in his achievements: you've respected him for who he's becoming. Now you're stopping him literally in his tracks: you're exerting power over him, which frustrates his power of discovery but is in fact necessary. And the truth is your delight and your censure will be creating a sense of your love and giving him security.

Or imagine you have a six-year-old, now dressing herself. That's great! She's becoming competent, so competent she wants to show she's even more adept: please, she asks, let her do it all by herself, without you watching. So, you leave her alone and she does. She comes down ready for school, but while she's done up the fastenings correctly and put her clothes on the right way around, she's appeared in a summer party dress, totally improper both for school and the wintry weather. You want to praise, but you want to undo the achievement she's just displayed: you have respected her achievement, but if you exert your power as a parent and overrule her, you frustrate her power to choose.

Or imagine you discover that your young teenager, much more adept and au fait with all things technological than you, which is something you've admired – and respected – about him, has been immersed in what you suspect is an internet communication that might be inappropriately sexualised. Is he doing something that could get him into trouble? Are you overstepping privacy boundaries if you try to find out? You doubt his judgement: he might know about the tech, but he doesn't really understand about people or, you guess, sex yet. Should you intercede? Should you stop him?

While there are many ways to slice up the metaphorical theory cake that tells you kids need love and security, after many years of working in this area I believe the key ingredients in that cake are respect and power. As a parent, you communicate love best when you respect what's unique about your child, but use the power of your wisdom and experience to identify what they need at their developmental stage. So the respect part is about understanding and appreciating their individuality, what makes them who they are, and the power part is about acting on what, in your parental estimation, they need for their benefit. When your child knows you get them, they feel loved for themselves, and they can trust and feel secure that you will tune in, support and steer them in ways that will help them develop.

As a parent you do your job well when you show you understand who your child is, but remain clear that your bottom line is using your judgement and authority as a parent wisely. Think about how power feels when you encounter it as an adult: you do better with a boss or a team leader who not only shows you respect, but whom you trust to direct you towards safe tasks that will enlarge your abilities. Or, put another way, will direct you away from danger and self-defeat. That's true for kids, too. Power and respect, therefore, work in tandem. When power feels arbitrary, that it's being wielded without reference to what you can or want to do, you feel disrespected and you want to kick against it. Again, that's true for kids, too.

Especially as your children get older and become better at making their own judgements, their respect for you and the judgements you make on their behalf will be influenced by how much they feel you have respected, continue to respect and have understood them, as well as how much you have shown good and sensitive parental power in decisions for and about them. As your child grows, tussles will also grow over power and respect between you. There will be struggles over just how much respect you seem to be showing them: they'll want to make their own decisions and judge what's 'best' for them, in line with their increasing range of abilities. Meanwhile you, as a parent, will have been taking on board their new abilities, their changing desires, but will still have to judge if it's wise, safe or healthy for them to do what they want to do. You'll also want them to continue to respect your judgement.

The tussles will be about respect, on the one hand – 'You really don't get who I am now, Mum and Dad!' – and power on the other – 'I don't want to do what you tell me to do, Mum and Dad!' For you, as a parent, the two are combined – 'I expect you to respect me when I put my foot down!' As children get older and more capable, most especially in adolescence, struggles over power and respect mount. Adolescents can sometimes make good judgements, but usually not as often as they think they can and they always expect you to respect how competent they've become, even if their judgement about their own capacities is askew.

Authoritative power

A parent will have more social, not to mention economic, power and, of course, the power of more wisdom and experience backing parental decisions and judgement. However, if you're wondering about how much power you ought to exert, there are no strict guidelines, but here's a steer. Studies of what makes for good parenting divide parenting styles into power categories. The ones that are 'authoritarian' at one end, or 'permissive' and 'uninvolved' at the other end, are the ones to avoid. The first breeds aggression, the other two seem to lead to chaotic lifestyles at the very least, and, at their worst, studies show they can be associated with imprisonment and mental illness in adulthood. Something called 'authoritative' seems to work and that is best described as parenting with a 'respectful use of power'. If you're respectful – trying to 'get' your child as they evolve – you employ your power in the service of helping them adjust to, as best they can, the needs and norms of places they're going to have to live within, places like school or playgrounds. You try to explain your decisions when you limit their freedoms. You try to let them make decisions as befits their growing abilities, but guided by you. You modify your language as their capacity to understand concepts develops, so they can get their heads around your explanations about rules, limits, power: why the school might make such a rule as getting there on time or why you might insist on them doing homework when they get home, even though they want to watch something on their tablets instead and claim they'll get around to it later, when you know from experience they'll be too tired.

Authoritative, not authoritarian, parenting sets boundaries around behaviour and teaches rules, but also tries to show as best as possible why limits need to be there. As a parent, for the most part even when your children are adolescent, you do get to say, in the end, what's for dinner, when bedtimes are, what's acceptable behaviour – you've still got the balance of power – but the good kind of parent explains why and tries to get their child to understand.

So, let's go back to that crawling baby. You're his parent, respecting, enjoying his development, yet your worldly wisdom, something he pointedly does not have, says that socket is dangerous. Yes, the child needs to exercise his crawling and investigation abilities, but the parent needs to exercise the power of judgement. You remove your baby from the path of the electrical outlet. That one's a no-brainer.

What about that six-year-old who has dressed herself and done so, without supervision, successfully. It's wintry outside and she's wearing her favourite summer dress, plus it doesn't conform to the school dress code. When you point this out, she responds that, 'Betty wore funny socks yesterday and she didn't get into trouble.' You and she are having a power struggle. She doesn't yet have the sophistication to get the nuances of rules, nor the foresight to imagine how cold she will be, but you do. You put your foot down. She takes off the dress and you explain those nuances. You predict for her the cold. You're helping her learn. If you do this, you're taking an executive decision that is actually about respecting the needs of a six-year-old to learn a bit more about how to dress sensibly, building on the respect you've shown her for her ability to get clothes on by herself; to protect her and her health. You'll have made her feel loved in the moment when you've praised her achievement and secure in the long run by exercising parental power judiciously.

Evolving respect

But the power balance changes as children grow older and it changes because of respect. Watching, taking in and changing your notions of your child as they evolve – how competent they are about their environment, what their talents are turning out to be as they develop – guides you as a parent about how much power you should exert over decisions regarding your child. You watch and see what they grow into and seem to be able to do.

What about that teenager possibly engaging in worrying online behaviour? He's capable of many things technical, but he's not yet shrewd about people. When we look at the dilemma of being an adolescent you'll see that part and parcel of adolescence is that their cognitive abilities, growing at a rapid pace, can be alarmingly unstable, with good judgement one moment and appalling judgement the next. Trusting in your child's judgement is a risky business for you. Later in this chapter we'll look at how to use the core skills in this book to exercise appropriate parental judgement, and resolve a parent-child power struggle with respect.

The elements of respect and power within parent-child relating stem from a primal and desperate love on both sides, operating way out of your consciousness. That means you've got to dig them up and make them conscious, to recognise that this love is at the heart of it and will be at play when you have parent-child struggles or misunderstandings. You need to do this if you want to get that momentous task – rearing your child – right. But these are big issues: they can erupt. Unsettle. Wreak havoc. So that's why you need the core communication skills when there's conflict and potential negative spirals. The skills we're learning in this book will interact with those two elements: power and respect. When there's conflict, misunderstanding or discomfort I always tell my clients to remind themselves that those two things are probably at the root of it all.

And then you use your core skills. First you emotionally manage yourself. Then you mentalise, keeping in mind as you do that the power and respect elements are probably at play. Then you shape what you say and do with that in mind, and you're collaborative and inviting. You are not combative. If you get things wrong, you repair. You apologise and seek to try to understand, to unearth the misunderstandings, so you can find a shared one.

In the rest of this chapter, we're going to look at some examples. First, with a newborn. Then you'll see, through the example of Alfie, the toddler, and his parents, how to use the core skills to manage struggles with respect and power in that next stage of parent-child life. Then we have an example from middle childhood of conflict between Katie and her mother, Harriet. Finally, we'll look at how to use these skills with a difficult teenager like Carrie.

Newborns

Marc and Holly, new parents of five-month-old Emily, meet up in a park with their friends, Peter and David, parents of somewhat older children. 'God, you look like death warmed up,' David remarks sympathetically, noting their hollow-eyed looks and heavy footsteps, and having already experienced Marc's inability to finish a simple sentence.

'You think?' Holly retorts, with a sleeping Emily in a sling on her front. 'The past week has been hell. The longest she's gone has been two hours at night and then she's up, and crying, and we just aren't able to comfort her. Somehow, after a while of us walking around and cooing to her, she stops. Then we try to sleep and then it starts again.'

'We know, we know,' both David and Peter soothe. 'We've been there, ourselves. It's hell. What have you done?' Marc sighs. 'We pick her up. We think it can't be that she's hungry, because she's just had a feed. So maybe it's a bad dream, if babies have such things, so we walk her around and then when that doesn't work, we think, maybe it's her nappy, even though we just changed it, so we check and do that, and then when that doesn't seem to be it, we just keep walking around and trying to relax her. . .'

Holly continues, 'And then I'll try to feed her again, because maybe she's having a growth spurt. We feel her gums. It's early, but maybe she's teething. If that seems to make a difference we rub something on them, but, well . . .' The parents sigh and look bemused. 'We do it by trial and error. If she settles, we know we've got it right for her.'

With newborns, the power issue is not the hot one. You've got the power – you decide. At this stage the theme that emerges and helps you wield your power is about 'respect' – who is this baby? You're trying to learn about them. In doing that, you're using the skill of mentalising. The parents in the example above are showing good skills and navigating the themes of power and respect in responding to their baby. They're managing their emotional states, even through sleep deprivation, and tuning in to their baby Emily's (non-verbal) behaviour, responding with their best guesses, then using feedback from trial and error about which of their guesses are right. They try out their mentalising – could she be teething, wet or in pain? – and then they decide what's 'right' for their child: they employ parental power. That decision – the power to decide what to do for their child, such as how long to let her cry, what intervention to make when she does – is informed by who Emily is. They have respect for her.

When John Bowlby studied babies in orphanages, he saw that, in some, babies were not responded to on the basis of their distress, but left just to cry. Those babies eventually went silent: no one listened to who they were. The carers weren't interested in learning about the baby. And those babies' development was severely affected as a result. Those babies, as individuals with needs and wants, were *dis*respected, their individualities dismissed. Whereas Marc and Holly are showing interest in

Emily as an individual. Is she distressed because she is getting a tooth? If so, that will inform what they do to alleviate her distress.

Toddlers

Research on small children has established that they are, indeed, born with particular temperaments and to know that is helpful for you as a parent. Helpful, that is, in part. It's normal to begin to 'label' your child: you want to be able to predict things, but also to think you're really getting to know them. You'll think you've got their number, that there will be certain characteristic responses to things, and if you can recognise what sets your child off, what will calm them, what food they like, you're helping make them feel happy and loved: respected. But *respectful* parents also remain curious, watching how their child develops, because it turns out 'temperament' is a pretty nuanced thing, very dependent on circumstances. Change the context and your child can really surprise you. You might think you've got a 'timid' child and then there he is up on a stage, singing that song you taught him with all his heart. As a parent, helping your child to mature means you need to be tuned in to the differences in that child as he grows, and respectful of these as you make decisions about what he can and cannot do – what you'll permit him to try out and what you won't as he grows.

A tiny child does not have a sense of their parent as a person other than you're the one who's their safe base and – normally – that they like, indeed love, you best of all the other grown-ups. However, the ability of a child to develop respect for you as an individual grows along with their social and cognitive capacities. Toddlers begin to formulate things about their parents as separate beings, with characteristics that define them, so for instance Mummy is stricter than Daddy or Daddy is the one who plays harder than Mummy, but these are broad categories.

The fine distinctions that show they are learning about who you are, and giving you respect for who you are back, develop over their childhood. In fact, some psychological theories frame the development of the capacity to see yourself as distinct from your parent, and so them as distinct from you, as the main marker of development to maturity. For very young children you are like an extension of the 'big world'. You are the thing that brings them into interaction with that world and, in consequence, you help regulate their behaviour in it, so you become the thing that must 'regulate' them when the world is too much for them, when they're out of control in it.

As a parent of a very young child, you actually have to exert the power of judgement for them, even if, as in the example below of little Alfie, your child protests. Your child's 'respect' for you is total: you are their capable brain. It's sort of like when an expert solves your tech problems by taking remote control of your laptop. In the end, respect comes into play and your child lets you take over. In the example below Louisa and Dan, parents of Alfie, show how they employ these skills while wrestling with the issues of respect and power with their toddler.

Louisa is a costume designer I saw with her husband, Dan, a carpenter, for marital therapy. In the two years since the birth of their son, Alfie, their relationship had been plagued by arguments, an absence of sex and building mutual resentment, but it had improved tremendously with just one remaining problem: how to manage Alfie. This was a potentially combustible area, threatening to divide them once again. They understood this, and agreed they needed help specifically with how to understand his difficult behaviour and how to respond to it.

The 'terrible twos' was how they described their problems with Alfie. Terrible twos often means opposition culminating in tantrums, and so it did in their case. Tantrums are the universal way a small, especially preverbal, child can exert power. If tantrums are successful the child wins, whether their desires are reasonable or not. Alfie's parents felt they were successfully mentalising about him by thinking that what he wanted was to feel free, which would mean he'd feel loved. However, when they let Alfie have his way, showing, they felt, 'love', they weren't actually respecting who he, as a two-year-old, was. He wasn't capable of good judgement, as the tantrum episodes showed. They needed to respect his actual capacity and use a bit more power to keep him safe and secure. That would be real 'love' from his parents.

The example of the tantrum that Dan and Louisa brought along mainly involved Louisa, but Dan had made his own significant contribution. It was 4:30pm. Two hours earlier Alfie had had his short afternoon nap and was playing happily in the park across from their house. Everything went well until it was time to come in for winding down, then supper, then bedtime, then a snatched hour for some work for Louisa until dinnertime with Dan. Bored by the constant swinging, her mind had indeed turned to work. She'd felt guilty for not thinking about Alfie even before the tantrum, worried she had already been 'unloving' with her mind half on her emails. He kicked off almost immediately on her saying, 'Time to go home, Alfie,' clinging heavily to the swing, refusing to budge when she tried to lift him off and crying. Feeling embarrassed in front of other mothers, Louisa relented. Time marched on; he'd be put to bed later than usual if she did not get him home soon and she wouldn't have time for any work.

Louisa got twitchy, made feeble efforts to lift her son again, then felt guilty as he again resisted, this time chortling like it was a game, and she lost heart in the face of his pleasure. Finally, as she saw Alfie getting visibly tired and fractious, Louisa was reduced to forcing him out, wedging his unyielding, protesting, angry body into his buggy, intensifying his protests and tears.

At their door she noticed the neighbour, peering through her curtains. Louisa, rattled, drained, humiliated, near tears herself, was certain she'd thought, Bad mother.

Inside, still screaming, Alfie demanded to watch cartoons on the tablet, but it was too late for them and he'd already had screen time that day, and the couple had read too much screen time was bad for young children. On this Louisa was firm and so the thwarted tantrum turned physical, a kick landing on his now frightened mother. Louisa then 'lost it' – she scooped Alfie up angrily and deposited him in his cot, putting a pillow over her head to deafen the sounds. The sobbing eventually ebbed and a whimpering Alfie called, 'Mama!' Louisa's heart melted, her guilt sharp, and she gathered her child tenderly into her arms. All was okay until the next time this sort of thing happened.

So, what went wrong? What could be fixed? Well, a two-year-old needs to be seen – respected – for being a two-year-old, rather than stretched to things he cannot yet do. A two-year-old needs the safety of a parent's better judgement about his basic needs, in this case, about the function of a predictable routine to guarantee the sleeping and feeding patterns he needs to expect to feel secure. He also needs the safety of knowing something can calm him down: intense negative feelings out of control are frightening and very young children have both no understanding of them or skills to manage them. Parents need to manage those explosions for them. You're respecting your child, as a two-year-old in a particular stage of preverbal development, when you respond with something that communicates, 'I hear your crying as proof you're tired, need food and winding down.'

Louisa came from a rigidly controlling family in which she'd felt unloved. She'd been disrespected, controlled by arbitrary rules regardless of her abilities or desires. She was doing what some therapists call 'correcting her family script', but going too far the other way, without reference to the particulars of the child. Dan had been brought up in a warm family with loose rules and boundaries. Louisa's 'correction' didn't seem a million miles from the childhood that had roughly worked for him, so it had felt reasonable to him.

This couple had already learned the value of using skilful interactional behaviours between themselves. The skills in this book apply just as much to how you interact with your two-year-old as with your partner. We replayed the scene in the park to imagine how things could go differently from the start.

The first lesson was that those first interactions set off the sequence of loops upon loops that had ended up so badly. By working through what happened, they'd know that next time it would be their responsibility to monitor their emotional responses to Alfie's resistance, so they could emotionally manage themselves if he threatened to act up. For instance, the other mothers and the neighbour probably weren't judging, but instead sympathising with her. Louisa and Dan would remind themselves that Alfie needed their brains to make decisions for his benefit. They could soothe and calm themselves. I taught them to think of the airline principle: put your own mask on first before you put on your child's or you won't be able to help him. Manage yourself to manage helping him.

Then, mentalising Alfie, they realised that they needed to take in his developmental context. He's a two-year-old who gets tired at the end of the day and he doesn't know he needs to unwind, but they do and he needs them to be his brain. He might protest, but the parental brain takes him from exciting swings, to gentle play, to being fed, to the end of the day and finally to bed. He's learned up to then that carrying on protesting means he'll get what he wants, but if they are consistent in their new approach he can unlearn that and understand that his parents make the decisions and when they call time on the park it's for his benefit.

Having mentalised, they then needed to find a way of communicating with their still pretty much pre-verbal two-year-old. They needed to do this in a way that showed 'respect' — that they knew how he felt but they also knew he was out of his depth. That would be communicating empathy with understanding of him. Their authority, or power to make sensible decisions for Alfie, had to be communicated in a way that showed that empathy and understanding while making their authority clear. He'd show that by truncating his tantrums, perhaps eventually complying right away. Even with preverbal children you communicate that you're on their side, that you're being collaborative. You do that by using language and tone that shows respect for and understanding of why they have the wishes that they do: 'No, no, that's interesting but don't touch – it will be ouchy!' to a baby reaching for something dangerous or 'I know you don't want to leave – it's fun – but I also know you will be tired and we need to go now' to a toddler.

Dan and Louisa described cooing and soothing sounds, and imagined phrases their son would find comforting: 'It's okay, sweetie . . . We'll come back to the swings tomorrow and you can play then, but now it's time to go home.' And to validate, rather than dismiss, feelings: 'We know you want to stay for more fun and there will be more tomorrow.' They agreed they could picture chanting these, as they also pictured fitting a struggling, even crying, Alfie into his buggy and on home. They recognised that was about being loving parents just as much as letting him play with finger paints, and they could delight in observing how he was expressing himself just as much as how he was adapting to facing limits imposed by the world – in this case, by them.

Middle childhood

Children in middle years show growing, if limited, abilities to make judgements about what's safe and appropriate to do, ranging from, for example, food and dress choices, to acceptable behaviour towards others, to what's safe. They start to make leaps from small categories in their thinking to large ones. They want to try out new things that they think they are just beginning to understand, but that's where parental respect for where they are developmentally and how cognitively sophisticated they are comes in. In the example below Harriet, mother of Katie, grapples with her own problem of respecting Katie's differences from her and learned to curb her authoritarian power over her, moving into a more authoritative space, while using her skill of mentalising most of all.

I'd seen Harriet and her former husband, Stuart, before they'd split up just after their second daughter, Melanie, was born. Their elder daughter, Katie, was then four. Stuart left Harriet for the young assistant he was having an affair with and Harriet carried on seeing me. She was, at first, depressed, then angry and, finally, settled and happy about running her single parent household in the way in which she wished; we ended therapy. But three years later, when Katie was almost nine, she returned. She and Katie were clashing: Harriet found her exasperating, pugnacious and 'unloving' – which I thought was an interesting description. She did not say 'unlovable'. Katie, it seemed, got on well with everyone but Harriet, something that, on probing, seemed to be also true of Harriet: she got on well with everyone except Katie. Their combination was 'toxic', Harriet had decided.

What irked Harriet about Katie, above all, was how different she was to Melanie. Melanie was pliable, sweet-tempered and had tastes Harriet could understand. The latest complaint, the breaking point for Harriet, had been discovering Katie dressed up in what Harriet called 'tarty' clothing, an outfit which she'd borrowed from the friend at school Harriet most disliked. She deeply disapproved of the girl's family, and their lax and tasteless 'lifestyle'. Then she found Katie had somehow figured out how to access her Spotify account and play music Harriet thought entirely too old for an eight-year-old to be listening to.

She realised that Katie must have picked up from that friend how to dance in what Harriet called a 'ridiculously suggestive' way.

Katie had protested loudly and rudely to Harriet that she was 'nearly nine!' and it was 'normal' to do what she had been doing. Harriet, incandescent – not emotionally regulating, mentalising or communicating in any collaborative fashion – was exercising unlimited parental power, without respect. She didn't have any regard or curiosity about what Katie's angry protests might have been about and had confiscated the clothing. She then removed all devices that could access Spotify and forbade Katie, as a two-week 'punishment', from seeing that friend. Katie, wailing, her tears a clue about the wounded state behind the aggression, which was all Harriet saw, shouted, in front of a wide-eyed Melanie, that Harriet was 'Crazy!' and 'A bad mother so you can't tell me what to do!' and that her friends' mothers would all agree, because none of them would have thought what Katie was doing was wrong. Was she all wrong and 'crazy'? Was she really so oddly different from all the other mothers? Harriet wanted to know.

Harriet was riled, not crazy. She had been upset and frightened, rather than respectful; her power authoritarian, rather than authoritative, dictating what Katie should and shouldn't do, and dismissing any signs of Katie being different to her. No wonder Katie had fought back: she'd felt disrespected. Harriet wasn't trying to mentalise about her daughter, and part of that was her refusal to entertain what was different and unique about her. Her efforts to socialise Katie into being the kind of girl she thought she ought to be were, in fact, making Katie, towards her mother at least, uncivil, unkind and, in the end, untrusting. 'You're crazy!' doesn't sound like she feels safe and secure with her own mother, and certainly shows disrespect for her power. Harriet's authoritarian pronouncements were hardly collaborative and, issued like diktats, produced resistance which would only get worse. They were in a power struggle, leaving Katie fighting her mother as if she were an equal, rejecting parental judgement. It didn't seem that Katie felt very loved and Harriet confessed, 'It feels hard to love Katie because Katie is so unloving to me.' The problem, Harriet also admitted, lay in how they related. Since she felt she was failing Katie some of it had to be down to her, so maybe if she were more skilful in her interactions with her, she could turn their vicious cycles into virtuous ones.

As with Louisa and Dan, Harriet had beliefs about raising children stemming from her own childhood that were stopping her from listening and learning about her own child. Fears and rigid beliefs from her own experience as a child were overriding her ability to remain curious, to be respectful and tuned in to her daughter, preventing her from mentalising Katie's state in those moments of discord between them. In those moments she dismissed how Katie was feeling: she immediately panicked that it was 'wrong' for her daughter to be how she was. Yet, from a developmental perspective, it is entirely appropriate for a 'nearly nine-year-old' to have her own preferences, to develop her own tastes that could be different from her mother and her sister's. Harriet's old, past issues had been triggered by Katie's dress and musical tastes. Katie, feeling injured, disdained, her joy cancelled out, had consequently attacked Harriet. They'd established and were continually reinforcing their vicious cycle.

What had been getting in the way of Harriet parenting well? 'Tarty' was possibly the worst thing Harriet could imagine for her daughter: her own parents had been strait-laced, prim and judgemental. They'd closely monitored Harriet's dress and demeanour; it was of the utmost importance to them that she be 'proper'. Sex remained, in fact, an area of profound discomfort for Harriet, her embarrassment around it being the biggest, ultimately unsolvable, problem in her marriage. In fact, she sighed with relief when, with divorce, it was no longer a requirement for her. On top of that she had a fixed idea of what a mother-daughter relationship should be. Hers with her own mother was close, but 'top-down', with her mother still holding the balance of power. One of five children and the only girl, she'd been and remained her mother's confidante, her mother's friends to this day comprising her own inner circle, her mother's tastes dictating her own. That her own eight-year-old disliked the classical music Harriet played as background to their lives, as her own mother had to hers, both baffled and angered her: Katie should like – and accept – what Harriet decreed was 'good'. That Melanie complied with Harriet was proof positive of her position.

Harriet's great fears were two-fold. First, that if her child were too different from her Harriet would both be out of her depth – that wasn't the way mothers and daughters were meant to be – and it would signify she was not loved. Second, that a daughter of hers could be 'tarty', somehow lured into a world that hinted at sex, the very thing Harriet feared.

In teasing out these themes Harriet admitted that she was imposing things on Katie, things that needed questioning. She dimly remembered being the same age, and having questions and wishes that her own parents censored, and resenting them for doing so. We gently started to probe, and I encouraged Harriet to mentalise and to work on the respect side of their relationship. Who was Katie? From babyhood, Katie had been a child who pushed boundaries, who questioned and explored, unlike the more placid Melanie and unlike Harriet herself. Now Harriet considered those qualities in a new light: that Katie's enquiring mind was a good thing. It was a relief to think of Katie having a gift, a gift that was developing, and that that was a good thing, too.

Harriet realised that a daughter doesn't have to be a clone of her mother to show proof of love. Should cloning be what you strive for when you're bringing up children? Is 'tarty' something everyone agrees on or was its definition coming from her own mother? Could her admitted fear of the world of sex be about to infect her daughter – and is that what she wanted, for either of them? In fact, knowing what a struggle it represented for her, she very much didn't want to pass that on to either daughter. These questions felt liberating to Harriet. She was being released from her own childhood and she had the power to liberate rather than stifle her own children.

Ultimately, she realised sadly, she did not know her daughter and she'd lost the crucial thing she had with Melanie: respect. She wasn't afraid of Melanie, so she was delighting in her as she grew and changed. Katie's difference frightened her, so she'd tuned her out, rather than appreciated her. Katie was a girl, soon to become a woman, and through her 'tarty' clothes, suggestive dancing and too sophisticated music, she was looking for answers about what that means. By closing the door on her when it came to her awakening sexual feelings and questions, Harriet was denying who Katie was at that moment in her life. For Harriet, without experience of her own mother doing it for her, even to speculate about Katie in that way was hard. To parent well means helping your child at this stage of life prepare for the next stage. This idea was already enabling Harriet to become more respectful of Katie's needs, to see her as the particular eight-year-old she'd become. That helped her to mentalise into Katie's world of dancing and singing, and realise those things weren't about defying Harriet and that to think that way wasn't defying her own mother, either.

Armed with this insight how could Harriet improve her next tricky interaction with her daughter? From learning the skills with me at previous sessions Harriet knew that if she was triggered by something Katie did, she'd first make sure to regulate her emotions; to take a step back and calm herself.

Then the mentalising could happen – she'd already started to think more about Katie as a different person, with different likes, dislikes, hobbies, interests. Katie is exuberant, questioning, and starting to enjoy her body and how it moves. She'd keep in mind, she said, 'This is Katie. She is eight. She isn't me.' And then she'd also know that being Katie at eight, because she is only eight, means she needs guidance – the exercise of wise parental power to think about that body, its movement and what dressing it in a certain way can mean to people. It would be helpful if she could use the language of collaboration with Katie; to invite her to think about it. Because she is 'nearly nine' and a questioning child, Katie might have her own ideas about what it means, so how could she use collaborative language to show respect for Katie, yet ultimately that she has the power?

'As her mother I can talk to her, to help her ask me questions about it further. I probably could have used that when I was her age,' Harriet offered. She was already moving towards thinking about how to formulate her communication now that she'd done the mentalising. 'You get joy from dancing – I see that and I like to watch your joy!' she thought she could start with. Or, in a warm and curious tone, 'Tell me about that song and why you like it.' That would invite Katie to open up. Or, self-deprecatingly, 'I don't get it and it seems to me like it's for someone older, but, like I say, I probably don't get it. Tell me about it so I can try?' would be another approach. That would be about how it feels to Harriet, rather than telling Katie it is wrong. She thought she might ask where Katie got the dancing and the clothes, and what she liked about them. She might say that her own first thought about them had been they were for a much older girl, but maybe she'd got that wrong. Here's why she thought that – what does Katie think about why Harriet might have thought that and did she agree? These would be inviting phrases, trying to gauge Katie, as well as gently introducing concerns.

To remember that your children are developing is part of your job in managing them as you parent, and it underlies the essence of positive interactions with them. In fact, coaching Harriet to mentalise into Katie's world, to keep respectful and to hold back from wielding power automatically, also helped Katie, herself, when Harriet was able to communicate successfully to her, to feel safe to show Harriet who she was. It opened her up to Harriet. She could start thinking positively about who her mum was rather than defensively and defiantly shutting her mother down. 'You can't tell me what to be! You are crazy!' were defences, walling Harriet off. With them down, respect could grow for Harriet towards Katie and in Katie towards her, in return.

Harriet told me about a small incident a few weeks later which showed their growing relationship together.

'I know you don't like Andrea, Mum, because she's a little bit loud, but she was really funny today,' began a story from Katie that Harriet, beaming, reported to me. Not only was Katie thinking about who Harriet might be, but she now wished to share more of herself with Harriet. Katie was bringing stories, as if gifts. Harriet began to take pleasure in seeing what Katie was really like: sparky, funny, observant. In fact, even more impressively, Katie was observant of who her mother was, I pointed out. She had stepped into Harriet's shoes, as a step towards being able to mentalise, thinking about who 'Harriet' was: 'I know you don't like Andrea . . . she's a little bit loud.'

Adolescence

It's in adolescence, however, that power and respect between parent and child, both ways, normally rear their heads and where most parents will find the navigating most tricky. Adolescence heralds the fastest growth change in life apart from early infancy, and with those physical changes come cognitive, social and psychological ones. With that sudden surge of hormones that induce physical growth and pubertal changes comes a growth in cognitive capabilities: there's a rapid increase in the adolescent child's brain capacity along with other rapid growth. The influx of hormones also destabilises mood. With all that drama going on inside an adolescent child it's no wonder adolescence is the crux period for struggles over power and respect. By this stage in your child's life most parents are fairly practised in trying to crack the code of their child. They're on the lookout for their changing interests and passions, and have figured out how to communicate pretty well over the years, but even if you're good at parenting, adolescence can throw you a curve ball. It's too much all at once and the instability that comes from all these changes means there's a paradox for everyone: is this an instance when I trust my child's judgement as that child is now demanding I do? Have I kept up with all the changes in that child so I'm not so caught off guard by requests about what they wish to do? Even though an adolescent can make better judgements, they're not stable. Meanwhile, the mood surges create a shifting sand around your child's own ability to judge what they want, can and should do.

Sometimes their judgement looks good, sometimes it's terrible. They fluctuate between grandiosity and insecurity about their own abilities, and one moment they want you to respect those abilities totally and then the next expect you to take over things as you did when they were small.

Even if you don't have a teenager yet, you'll probably sheepishly remember that's what it was like for you when you were one. In some ways teenage children actually need to try out making their own decisions about things, experiment with new experiences, otherwise their capacity to think clearly to make good judgements won't develop. In order to be able to make good judgements and have confidence in your abilities, the science of cognitive development tells us you need increasing experience;

trying out things makes you better at being able to predict your effect on them and what's likely to happen. But young teenagers can't yet do that stably. As a parent guiding them into the world of adulthood you need to give them some power to do so, but it's unclear when, over what and how much: it's trial and error and the errors can be really dangerous, as it was for Carrie, in the example below. Or small. That's part of why this is such a turbulent period for parent-child relationships.

———

Carrie came late to puberty, but when it hit, her mother, Kirsty, described it as having 'stolen my child and replaced her with an alien.' Formerly acerbic but manageable, 14-year-old Carrie became the classic tearaway. Her two older, apparently well-behaved, sisters had both left home, the second sister just a year previously. Kirsty and her husband, Lee, had never once before been called to the school to sort out a daughter's disciplinary problems, but they now found themselves becoming very familiar with the pastoral and disciplinary team at Carrie's school. Carrie truanted, hung out with the 'bad kids', didn't hand in assignments, cut classes and was caught numerous times smoking on school grounds.

Her parents felt out of their depth. They'd tried authoritarian parenting, since authoritative had failed. That, with its strict discipline and punishments failed, too. Carrie took her own power to new levels, finding ingenious ways to subvert rules and limitations. Then they as parents would veer to the scary other extreme – hands off and 'lax' – giving Carrie all the power to decide and let the consequences fall where they may. That failed, too: more than once the police were called when Carrie disappeared. Respect had become irrelevant. She was an enemy presence in the house. They certainly weren't mentalising and they were way past trying to manage their emotions. They were angry and frightened.

Referred for family therapy, the parents were keen, but Carrie resisted until she was caught in a tangle that terrified even her, as she and two friends were catfished online by a paedophile posing as a teenage boy. When I met Carrie and her parents, she was rude and uncommunicative, but I modelled respect, respecting her, waiting for her responses and responding warmly and supportively when she did. Gradually I drew out Carrie's version of why she'd become the person she had at reaching puberty and since her sisters had left home. Forced by the structure of therapy to listen, over the sessions her parents gained knowledge of the teenager she was rather than the child they'd remembered. Similarly, Carrie was forced to hear their anxieties over her misjudgements when her safety and welfare had been at stake and to consider the wisdom of their guidance.

The departure of the older girls had shaken the family without any of them preparing for it or noticing it. Kirsty and Lee had still absolutely considered themselves parents to a young child, Carrie. Complicating this was that puberty had arrived late for Carrie. But by the summer before the last sister left Carrie had not only had her period, she had also had her first boyfriend. 'I really loved him,' Carrie said at one early session, while her parents had thought it was just a 'cute' way of describing a flirty friendship. 'They wanted me to stay the baby and I wasn't a baby anymore.'

Complicating the transition to her new persona was that her nickname, given to her by her sisters, was 'Baby'. Babies don't have breasts and bleed each month, nor do they feel 'love' for a boy. What could Carrie do to show she was no longer the baby? Telling her parents she was in love didn't do it. They didn't take it seriously, as she felt they should have. More than that, how could she show them all that she was her own person in a family of three girls, where her allotted role up to then had been to be the 'baby'? She was not a baby and she was different

71

from the sisters who'd just left. Now there was an open space in which to be who she was. The first thing was she wasn't her sisters, good at school, dependable at home. She loved them, but they were 'boring'. She wasn't so good at school, but she was good at art and knew what songs were popular, and how to do the latest moves, and those kids at her new secondary school who were like that weren't the 'good', 'boring' ones. She was like them. That's who she was. They were exciting. They broke rules because they were brave and creative. That story of who Carrie was trickled out in angry, emotional spurts.

Her parents listened and learned. They hadn't really listened before, in part because her anger and defiance had disarmed them and they had finally given up: she was 'alien'. When she was angry in the sessions, they either retaliated, justifying themselves, or shrank back fearfully. I managed Carrie's anger, soothing her so she could say things calmly, asking her to try to phrase things so her parents could hear, so the attack in her words would diminish, and perhaps she would show some regard for how they might be feeling. When these efforts to give Carrie interactional skills succeeded, her parents listened and learned.

As they did, they began to be curious, even respectful about Carrie as a teenager. They began to see that since her sisters' departure and her change from babyhood to womanhood, she was looking for some respect for this emerging status. I helped them to use this new ability to mentalise about her, to use calming techniques when her defiance triggered them, and to try out how to ask her to help them think about managing the dilemmas she kept coming up against. And she saw these dilemmas, too. How could she could stay friends with those friends she liked without endangering herself? How could she make wise decisions that both helped her to feel good about who she was – 'creative', 'not boring' – but also be prudent and safe? Could the three of them

72

learn to collaborate, with Carrie trusting that they respected her emerging ability to think, but also trusting her parents' ability to be wise in ways she, as still only a young teenager, could not yet be?

At one point, her mum demonstrated to Carrie her growing understanding of who Carrie now was, as well as her desire to learn more. 'You know, Carrie', her mother wondered, 'did you think that we only thought of your sisters as "good girls" and that we only loved "good girls". Would I be right?' and Carrie nodded, relieved that her mother 'got' something profound about her.

Having got her mentalising right, Kirsty then went on, using collaborative communication, to ask Carrie to help her think further: 'So, I'm thinking that maybe you forgot or maybe didn't even realise that, for one thing, we delighted in you as a funny, spiky little girl? Maybe we didn't show that enough?' Carrie had smiled at that and grew thoughtful. 'I do remember that. But I was a baby then, wasn't I? How could you find me funny anymore?' Carrie was showing interest in learning about her mother's internal processes. She was entering into the shoes and mind of a parent who had to make a transition from having a 'baby' child to a more grown-up one. This was a step towards being able to mentalise herself. This was a collaborative conversation, with interest on both sides to gain understanding.

Lee joined in at that point. 'We didn't love you for being a baby. We loved you because you were a funny, sharp kid, who had a real gift with animals, who was creative and artistic, good at making things. And, by the way, I think you think we only loved your sisters because they were "good", but, you know, first of all, they weren't just "good". They were easier, they listened, but they didn't surprise us with things they'd gone off to their rooms and made. They were other things and we loved them for all of them, for lots of other things, not for "being good" ... I want you to know that so you know what it's like for me. But really I want to know does that make sense to you?' Lee was phrasing things collaboratively, too: speaking from his heart, inviting Carrie to join him in thinking about their relationship: 'Does that make sense to you?'

As they started to repair their relationship, we all started to see results. We saw changes in Carrie's demeanour over the sessions. She said more, smiled more. And, indeed, she began to dress with flair and care: her hair styled, her usual jeans and sweatshirt traded in for flowing dresses and pantaloons, swathing herself in scarves and quirky jewellery. Respect on both sides increased, guiding Carrie's transitioning from baby to someone with a distinct role and identity she could develop within the family. As understanding of Carrie grew, as her behaviour demonstrated more maturity, Kirsty and Lee gingerly trusted her a bit more: that showed an increased ability to mentalise who Carrie was now and who she had been, and why. Eventually they aimed to get back to authoritative parenting: give Carrie some power to decide over, for instance, her social life, but retaining judgement for safety and security reasons.

Carrie, herself, stopped resisting restrictions, while bargaining reasonably with them on what easing them might look like. That showed mentalising on her part. To be able to negotiate around such an emotionally hot area meant they were, on both sides, able to utilise the other skills: emotional regulation (communicating calmly, without outbursts) as well as collaborative language. Restrictions on Carrie gently eased. She could go out on one evening a week, if she phoned to let them know where she was, who she was with and was back by a set time. She complied. As a result of her traumatic experience, Carrie had also learned that boundaries kept her safe and now she felt for her parents, too, and did not want them to worry.

Parents and young adult children

So, you've raised an adult. They've had your love and security, and they're on the road to personal happiness and satisfaction. They respect and love you, and you respect and love them. And as long as you keep an eye on the respect and power balance, which is now equal, everything should be fine now, shouldn't it?

A study in Japan on university and post-graduate-aged students showed that parental acceptance was incredibly important for students' psychological wellbeing. These younger adults were on the road to good adult adjustment, helped on that road by parental respect: they'd gained a sense from their parents that they were okay to be who they were. Another recent study found that parent-child relationships are important for psychological wellbeing all across the life course: you mean so much to each other that it helps to know that your parents respect and like you. Meanwhile, yet another study found that elderly parents had higher levels of life satisfaction when they had higher levels of relationship satisfaction in their parent-child relationships. Knowing you're liked, respected, thought about goes both ways.

Moreover, numerous studies over the years keep finding that practical and financial support goes two ways between parents and adult children. If you've managed both themes well, you can expect balanced support from and to each other. A study on parents and children at a late life stage went further: a two-way emotional support system, not just practical and financial, characterises good relationships. Elderly parents do support adult children with life problems, but they also receive similar support back from them: you are both adults, and respect and power even out. The elderly parents reported that they felt in a better mood on the days when they'd provided support to their adult children. It's more than just 'good vibes' from an ego boost, it's about behaviours; it's about respect and the judicious handing over of power. It's about the safety and security those build and which are communicated in good relating; in skilful relating when there have been ruptures; the flow of love and care that has grown up between parents and children, laid down early and maintained over the years. That, at least, is the ideal.

5

Siblings: Shared values and rivalry

Let me share four conversations I had with people connected to my therapy practice about siblings, all over a two-day period:

+ With Elizabeth, a 50-year-old married mother of three: 'I have a lot of friends – lovely friends – but I have never needed a best friend because Lisa, my sister, is my best friend. She knows me, understands me, better than anyone else in the world. I don't have to explain anything to her.'

+ With Tom, a 28-year-old single writer: 'The single formative experience of my life was the birth of my brother when I was 10. I was a single child till then. I didn't understand why my parents needed anyone else. We were very happy, just the three of us. My brother and I aren't close. He definitely looks up to me and that's annoying. I try to have nothing to do with him.'

+ Two-year-old Amelia very proudly pointing to her four-year-old brother, who is playing on his own and looking away, impassive and possibly stumped: 'This is my *brother!* I love my brother!'

+ With 84-year-old Stella, at her twin sister's hospital bedside: 'I have to do all the stuff to prepare for the end – I just met with the hospice people – and, of course, I am heartbroken. She's been with me my whole life.'

It seems you can find your relationship with a sibling one of the most meaningful and rewarding of your life. Or you can feel your sibling thwarts your happiness. Or both. You can feel as deeply allied, twinned even, as Stella or Elizabeth have felt about their respective siblings. You might feel alienated from them, as Tom does. Or, like Amelia's bigger brother, caught somewhere in the middle, perhaps feeling like Elizabeth one minute and Tom the next.

The first thing to acknowledge is that, unlike friends and lovers, siblings are family. Everything about them is linked to the meaningfulness of family for each of you – how you were brought up together or not; whose love you shared or not; and how over your lifetimes the meanings of family shape and shade the meanings you continue to have for each other. Siblings are a family phenomenon. In this chapter we'll look at the good and bad of sibling relationships and how different family transition points can be potential triggers and typically throw up tests for sibling relationships. First, we take a look at why sibling relationships are inherently meaningful, but why they can both bind and split.

Love, hate and learning about love

From the outset brothers and sisters pose an existential problem. Every sibling means you are replaceable: first-borns wonder why they weren't enough, while second- and further-borns know there were always others there before them. But siblings are, profoundly, links in the chain of human connection. You share genes, physical space in the home, daily experiences; family fortunes and misfortunes; and an idiosyncratic family script of practices, beliefs and stories that tell you how to be in the world. You also share resources: parental love, attention and time, food, family friends and relatives, bedrooms, schools, pets, clothing. Often you share physical features and your siblings will look and sound like you.

As a sibling you confront two inevitable existential truths. First, the world must be shared. In contrast to only children, siblings confront this every waking moment. Second, siblings hasten the need to face the notion 'How am I unique?', an early form of 'Who am I?' You need to know what's unique about you to feel sure you have a distinct, irreplaceable position in your family. Siblings start to form part of the answer to that because families usually define children in contrast to their siblings: 'You're the naughty one . . . you're the shy one . . . you're the brainy one . . . you're the popular one.'

To have a sibling means you experience, and hopefully learn to tolerate, ambivalence. The psychologist, Terri Apter, describes the guilt a sibling feels for that ambivalence: you love them but hate them, you feel envy and anger for both displacing you as your parents' focal centre (this occurs no matter the birth order, as newborns in any birth position are necessarily the centre of attention for a certain period) and for forcing the question of uniqueness upon you. Siblings also love and are loyal, stemming from their connection and identification with each other, but with that comes guilt, because of the envy and anger.

However, having siblings opens a pathway to learn a profound truth about loving real, not idealised, people. Real people have things that you dislike and things that you adore, and love contains those mixed feelings yet remains love. It's always adulterated, and impatience, resentment, anger and frustration, to name just a few negative feelings, can infuse it. That's true even in its purest forms: even parents of newborns find the ecstasy of love shot through with moments of perhaps irrational resentment for broken nights or colicky episodes. Yet they find that moments later adoration springs back whole – if with a legacy of guilt for love's apparent lapse. Through being siblings, we are forced to confront such feelings. If conditions are right – and we'll see, in a moment, what these can be – through

79

being a sibling, with its continual confrontation with hate and envy as well as deep identification, we can learn to tolerate and expect love's ambivalence. Being a sibling also gives you a head start in developing empathy: connecting up close on a daily basis with another person, a peer, often very like you, having to trade with and hustle against each other, means you know what you both have to go through. One study of toddlers indicated that siblings positively contribute to empathy development in babies even as young as 18 months. Indeed, having a sibling worked better than positive parenting practices specifically designed to inculcate empathy.

So having a sibling can give you a developmental advantage in defining who you are and want to be; in making friends and trusting allies; in sharing resources and trusting in fairness; and in validating your expectations as well as the beliefs and practices that have been learned through your particular family experiences, because siblings too have been shaped by them. If you have a sibling maybe you were lucky enough to have been helped by your parents to manage your ambivalence about them so your relationship took a mostly positive course, with, ultimately, a beneficial outcome. And if you were lucky enough as a child to have had good moments, even periods, with a sibling, perhaps you can identify with the idea that you had an advantage by having one. Having a sibling with whom you got along will have given you, in contrast to children who didn't, a better ability to solve problems. That study I mentioned also found, unsurprisingly, that siblings who got along well experienced a generally greater sense of warmth and closeness in their lives, coupled with lower levels of antagonism.

If being a sibling works out well over your childhood, then as you get older siblings can be great resources for you. Some might become your best friends. You'll know that if you have a good relationship with a sibling and you've experienced a death in the family, for instance, they can be a source of exquisite support, solace, humour and understanding because siblings share meanings and experiences. You literally speak the same language. Another study pointed out that siblings share language patterns and vocabulary. As Elizabeth, the woman whose sister is her best friend, said, 'I don't have to explain myself.' Among siblings there's an economy not just of shared understanding but also of expressions and words.

But being a sibling can stymie your own or a sibling's growth, because you and your sibling or siblings may have failed to negotiate what Apter has called 'the sibling trauma' – you haven't dealt with the ambivalence siblings feel or accepted that you must share, and you don't value your connection to each other. Failure to negotiate it yields an unhappy sibling relationship in which siblings can't act as mutual resources and are stuck in rivalry and hostility. In extreme cases it might result in a cut-off: a brother or sister not seen or spoken to in years. Cut-offs aren't the norm, but they happen.

Sometimes, as Tom, who resents his younger brother, says, they usurp your place in the world and you have to figure out a satisfactory way to make a new one. Sometimes they are, as Amelia the toddler innocently proclaims, a source of love, pride and admiration, but, as her brother shows, exaltation can evoke uncertainty and mystify you.

Living within the 'twin poles'

So, sibling relationships are all about the twin poles of love and hate, with 'ambivalence' holding both in tension, and this defines sibling patterns throughout the life cycle. Learning to tolerate this middle ground of ambivalence means a healthy sibship that will be generally supportive and satisfying, with love dominating.

Normally throughout childhood, closeness and affection will be strong during some periods or when you're involved in specific activities, while at other times envy, hostility or estrangement will dominate. Ultimately, such fluctuation smooths as siblings mature and competition recedes as they become comfortable in their own skin. You don't have to compete, to measure who and how good you are against each other if you're happy in yourself. By your teenage years it will be your friends against whom you tend to measure yourself. A study of undergraduates – people who have largely recently left their siblings, because they've left home – found that most felt positively as they thought about them, indicating that by then, perhaps, most had swung to the positive pole of feeling, if they hadn't already got there beforehand. In fact, many studies suggest that most sibling ties are affectionate, supportive and remain so on into and throughout adulthood.

Being able to have good sibling relationships is particularly important in childhood. One study showed that siblings spend more time interacting with each other than with other family members. If you can get along well with the people you spend most time within your life, of course that will feel that much better. The reverse is also true: a mostly aggressive relationship with siblings can be deleterious to your mental health. One study showed that children with aggressive sibling relationships are at risk of lower self-worth. There is evidence, in fact, of links between childhood sibling violence, aggression and anxiety and criminal behaviour in adulthood. However, it is unclear whether such high levels of violence, aggression and anxiety might be more reflective of larger family dysfunction, as sibling aggression probably occurs more frequently in families that are out of control themselves. Nevertheless, a violent or aggressive sibling relationship, in itself, can contribute to damage, underscoring the significance siblings do have in our development.

But even if you've emerged, as most do, with good sibling ties, as your lives unfold the negative pole of envy and anger can be stimulated by events that bring up potentially rivalrous situations. Transitions – comings and goings into the family, such as marriages, births, deaths, or illnesses; celebrations of meaningful moments, for instance launching moments such as graduations, job changes, successes or failures – can be particular sources of such triggers. You'll be tested. How loyal are you to your siblings and how loyal to you are they? Are you 'split' or 'allied'? How much rivalry and envy gets triggered versus how much pride you have in them should they outstrip you (or vice-versa)?

To maintain good sibling relationships, keeping this in mind helps you navigate eruptions of envy or 'hate', the negative pole. Skilfulness in how you relate during these sensitive episodes is paramount. This chapter will reflect on navigating these, using the core skills to help you maintain the 'love' and 'ally' positive pole of sibship. But first let's consider what the conditions are for nurturing the potential for having good sibling relationships. Were they there as you grew up? Are you helping to create them if you are a parent of siblings now?

Fostering good sibling relationships

As you grow up, what helps you forge good sibling relationships? Research validates what intuitively makes sense: specific factors in family life will profoundly shape whether you emerge with a good relationship with your siblings. Most importantly, how well you do as siblings emerges out of the larger family dynamic: what your family atmosphere has been like.

So, unsurprisingly, a mostly positive emotional climate between parents, a general climate of family warmth that includes openness and positivity, and being in a family that values maintaining good relations all foster sibling harmony, and that harmony continues into adulthood. If your parents co-parent well you're also more likely to develop good sibling relationships. That particular finding suggests, among other things, that such parents model cooperation, showing siblings that cooperation can work despite competition. Having a good relationship with your parents yourself also makes you likely to develop good relating with your siblings. It's been found that if your own parents – particularly your mother – have had siblings they're more likely to nurture good relationships between you and your brothers and sisters. That may be related to them having experienced both the value of having siblings but also recognising and knowing how to manage the inevitable negative emotions when these emerge in their own children.

It should also be said that sometimes sibling relationships themselves are the key to being okay. In families in which there is conflict, sibling relationships can be protective. Strong sibling bonds can, in fact, neutralise interparental conflict: you can, with your siblings, form a protective alliance, even a coalition together, to fight off the effects of your parents' conflict. If you don't have a strong sibling bond, you're more likely to be vulnerable to its negative impact. That's been shown to include insecurity, in particular, but also a range of psychological problems during childhood. Good sibling relations can offset these.

That was the case with Elizabeth, the woman who identified her sister, Lisa, as the only best friend she needs. They came from a family of high parental conflict. Their biological father – who in family lore was the source of both the tragedy, because he abandoned her, and the love of their mother's life – left them when Lisa was born and Elizabeth was 18 months old. While such closeness in age can, in theory, create deep rivalry, as babies need and claim parental attention, it can also lead to an unusual closeness and early sharing behaviour. Elizabeth and Lisa were like twins, sharing equally. And, as studies of twins have found, Elizabeth and Lisa created a specific, strong bond. In fact, Elizabeth and Lisa, as has been found with twins, developed into each other's attachment figure – the person who you feel 'gets' and mirrors you, responds protectively and builds a sense of security and predictability for you. Always there, always understanding the other so exquisitely, they were that for each other, together with their adult attachment figures: their mother, their grandmother and finally their stepfather. When they were still toddlers their mother remarried a genial but distant man. Easy-going, well-meaning, but emotionally remote, this second husband became a whipping post for the defects of men in general, and most pertinently and specifically, for not dispelling their mother's grief over the loss of her first husband. It is difficult for the sisters to pinpoint a night free of arguments, usually erupting randomly, never resolved. Each other's bulwarks against distress in childhood, they remain so today, joined still as middlemen in their parents' ongoing drama.

Gender also shapes how you do as a sibling. Girls still tend to do more emotional caretaking of younger siblings than boys do, no doubt because of social training within their families, being assigned 'female' caretaking tasks more often than boys. Sisters also report being closer to each other than brothers. Again, this is something likely to be reinforced on the playground and by observed gendered behaviour, whether in the family or the world outside: having best friends, pairing off, chattering and sharing gossip together. Birth order combined with gender also affects who does the caretaking and what sort of caretaking occurs among siblings, with caretaking divided along fairly conventional gender lines: boys teaching and assisting in the more masculine areas – for instance, teaching younger siblings sports – and girls taking over the more conventionally maternal roles – helping prepare meals or more commonly babysitting younger brothers and sisters. I think we can expect some of this to change over the years as we witness, as we are doing, the whole definition of 'gender' and what defines it being questioned and changed.

And birth order comes into play again in another way, this time as a source of guilt. Toddler Amelia's admiration of her older brother provokes his potential guilt. Her pride in him, as an older sibling, poses a unique burden: shame for unrequited admiration. Younger siblings admire older siblings. They're models and this can continue as an expectation through life: you got there first; show me the way. But it can create an imbalance: while there may be much to like and enjoy, when you're a child there's not much to look up to in a younger sibling. I distinctly remember, particularly when we were pre-school, the discomfort of my next youngest brother's admiration. It suggested a love from him unmixed by the hostility I felt towards him. I also remember the guilt-free love I felt for my two next younger brothers. They posed no real competition; I'd got used to the notion of sharing, and my role with them was distinct. I could be a second mum to them, but I was too close in age to my first brother to be that to him. In fact, he told me when we were adults that when he would hear my parents' departing words, 'Janet's in charge!', leaving me as babysitter, his heart would sink. Unlike the docile younger ones, he resisted my authority. Our roles as quasi-authorities were competitive, not distinct: his was oldest brother, mine was oldest sibling.

So, while gender and birth order affect the way in which the sibling relationship is performed, most siblings plough through the childhood years mostly benefitting from good, affectionate, supportive relationships. These are bound more by loyalty, identification and similarity of experiences than by the negative feelings of envy, rivalry and resentment, although these do teach them valuable lessons in relating. Siblings can remain uniquely supportive and validating, so it makes sense, if you can, to try to get things right should your relationship with your siblings be tested.

Now you've got a handle on those twin poles and how they might fluctuate – and have also thought about your own family climate, your gender, your birth order and how they've contributed to the health or not of your own sibling relationships, or your children's if you have them – we'll consider how to try to make those relationships go smoothly as they play out across life and certain significant transition points.

Graduation

The lessons you learn from being a sibling are tested at points your family considers significant. The first challenge can arrive when one sibling achieves an expected and valued milestone that the others either have not yet reached, either because of age and life stage, or because they have not managed to achieve it despite being 'ready' – sometimes because of failure to achieve and sometimes because they eschew it. Milestones comprise events like graduations; attaining jobs, promotions or other occupational successes; marriages; or births. But in any case, marking the milestone can summon past rivalries. Do parents, as well as other family members, not to mention the world, admire the sibling in the limelight more?

Sarah was 28 when her younger brother, Ben, graduated from university. Sarah, 'second mum,' and Ben, 'cute little brother', had mutually adored each other. Sarah's evident success – she'd done theatre arts at university, starred in many productions, gained an agent right away, appeared in a well-received independent film within two years after graduation – had earned Ben bragging rights among his peers. He'd been assigned the role of 'serious, academic' child and when he'd graduated with first class honours in biochemistry from a top university Sarah had come along to share the celebration and dinner out with their parents. But her joy had seemed forced, her mood distracted and when her father had offered a toast to Ben, she'd fidgeted, limply raised her glass and then turned on her parents. 'I don't recall you taking me out to dinner when I graduated!' she accused. Then she got up, excused herself and left.

What had been provoked was envy, the first time she'd admitted ever feeling it towards him. At the time of his graduation dinner Sarah had been feeling that she'd sunk. She'd hit a wall professionally, repeatedly failing auditions; she'd recently broken up with a lover; and, having had no acting jobs for months, had had to ask their parents for a loan. For the first time she'd had regrets: why was she chasing an artistic dream? For the first time she eyed Ben's more practical abilities with envy. And as she did so, flickers of memories of resentment over his academic prowess and their parents' pleasure in it contrasted with memories of her own comparative academic struggle and their disappointment, which till recently had been offset by her artistic success. For the first time she felt displaced. Ben seemed 'admirable'; Sarah, in comparison, pitiable. Later in the week Sarah wrote him a note: she felt guilty and embarrassed, apologised for tarnishing his big day, but, afraid and embarrassed by her envy, hoped he'd understand that she needed distance.

When Ben told me this story the incident was still fresh, upsetting and unhealed. So, I asked him what he thought should happen. 'I want to make it okay for her. And me. I want to be able to see her and for her not to feel guilty,' he said.

Ben was primed by Sarah's admission that sibling issues are likely to be around envy and competition, and that because of her sinking fortunes while his stock rose she was vulnerable: sibling success felt like a zero-sum game at this point in Sarah's life. In terms of 'mentalising', if he was going to try to make it right with her what he needed to know was how to normalise this, both for himself, to understand and put in perspective his own shock and hurt, and his sister, and what she might be feeling.

He said, 'I'm going to get in touch. I'm going to say, "Sarah, first of all, I love you and I thank you for being generous enough to take pleasure, in the past, as I always felt you did, in what I do. And I am so proud about what you do, things I really can't do. I'm in awe of how easy you are, socially, with other people and when you're on stage I am bursting. I think you've forgotten just how special you are, for all of us."'

While I thought that was something Sarah should hear, I wondered if, receiving this gift, she might feel even guiltier, more competitive – in hearing that his love was pure, she might feel hers was not. And that is part of the problem for siblings, in a normal, inescapable way: they love and they resent, and then they feel guilty. This was hard for Ben to hear. He was anxious to get his relationship with his sister back on track, and his words were genuinely generous, but his anxiety and eagerness were overwhelming his ability to put himself in Sarah's place, actually undermining his mentalising about her. Instead he was thinking about his own wishes and how they might be getting in the way for her. He could accept that and he calmed himself down.

Seeing that he had to think differently about her, he turned to the next step: how to shape what he could say? How was he going to say what he wanted to so she'd hear it properly? We worked on telling it from the heart: his feelings, his take on it. If he was describing his experience, rather than assuming hers, she couldn't dismiss it. Then she might listen. His own words, as it happened, seemed to validate what he thought her feelings might have been, but I suggested that perhaps he ought to be prepared to feel trepidation, because he was going to bring up the part of their relationship they'd never admitted to existing before. She might attack, he might feel rejected, especially as, Garbo-like, she had already pushed him away with her 'I want to be alone!'

'Oh! I see what you mean,' Ben replied. He thought for a bit. 'So, I'm going to tell her that she's not the only one. What she said made me remember things. That sometimes when I would see her on stage, getting applause and me looking over at my parents' eyes tearing up with pride, I'd be jealous. I'd be thinking, Wow! If only I could do that! Look at what she makes people feel!'

The next time I saw Ben his mood was lighter; he reported that he'd had a dinner with his sister. And it had gone something like this:

Sarah, sullenly: 'All right, you've got me here, even though I asked you to give me space . . .'

Ben, emotionally regulating and calming himself from being upset at her opening attack, by taking both a moment and deep breaths: 'I'm sorry. I know you didn't feel ready and maybe I should have waited, but that wasn't so simple. I found waiting really hard. I missed you. I was worried. So, here's the thing: I've talked to someone about sibling relationships, because that was really the first time you and I have had anything like that happen and I wanted to understand. And it turns out that it was normal. It made me realise I've felt things like you felt myself. It's okay – not nice, but okay. We can still love each other. Also, I hate that you've been having a rough time, but I think it sort of primed things for happening between us.'

Ben, having spoken from his own experience – 'I missed you'; having apologised – 'I'm sorry'; and having used invitational language – 'I wanted to understand' – made it more likely that, despite her resistance, Sarah would listen, and herself be curious about him and his response to her behaviour: 'Like what? Like what do you mean, normal?' or 'You felt things like that, too?'

And then Ben went on to say the things he'd rehearsed with me, that he thought it was healthy they'd faced this part of being siblings and hoped she saw it that way. The evening had ended in a reunion, as well as in increased sympathy for and wisdom about each other. This could, they hoped, make each of them more sensitive and careful about how they behave together in the future, rather than be split by this unhappy incident.

Marriage

Loyalty characterises good sibling relations, through childhood and beyond. If your brother is bullied in the playground you want to defend him, even if you and he were fighting like cats and dogs the day before at home. Loyalty is about the 'allies' part of the relationship trumping the 'envy'.

In adulthood such loyalty is normally tested when there are new entries to the family: in-laws. The name captures it: new partners make 'in'-roads into your family and do so, as it were, almost with the force of 'law'. There's a dictum in family therapy that the task of becoming a family means creating a boundary around it, so the family can be defined – who's in it and who's not. That tells you, partly, where to place your loyalty – first and foremost to the people within that boundary. But when you join with a new partner, there are new boundaries and new loyalties. Like the sibling trauma conundrum, if it's resolved it leads to loving within ambivalence. You live with two separate feelings in tension with each other. When you settle down with a partner and become a new family together you encounter that tension between loyalty to your family of origin, including your siblings, and loyalty to the new one you are creating. Partners – incomers – necessarily induce changes in you. The positive pole of sibling relationships includes identification – you're like me, you came from what I came from, you share my practices, beliefs and values – but when we partner up with someone, at least some of those will change and identification will be challenged.

An in-law, or incomer to a family, introduces different family scripts: how to behave and what to expect around particular events. For instance, does your sibling's behaviour confound you, because how she now marks achievements in her family looks like she's thrown away your own family's traditions, and even values? Does it seem like she's gone over to the other – the partner's family's – side? You might feel, for example, that you are excluded from things you'd expected to be part of or are surprised by the amount of fuss made over other things you'd expected your sister not to exalt.

Or, when you get together, do you assume, from how you've been brought up in your own family, that your sibling's new one will be having conversations at meals? But, instead, when you sit at the table are his family reading? Or watching TV? Are they on their tablets or smart phones? These differences pose the question of how to interpret this behaviour: is it rude? Does it mean you, your family, are rejected? Your sibling's new practices can feel an affront, but they will have been the result of working out how to blend their family scripts to live together. But when these new ways of behaving are put in front of you, the sibling, a representative from the former family, no matter how comfortable or not they may be to your sibling, they are not always comfortable or understandable to you.

And that can threaten the sibling tie of loyalty. Who is this person, my sibling, whom I thought was so like me, who believed, as I do, in a 'right' way to behave, now doing something very different? On the other hand, in being curious about the difference and allowing it, you can get to know your sibling as he develops in adulthood, as Ben and Sarah were beginning to do when they faced their different responses to Ben's graduation. To wonder about and accept means increasing your empathy and tolerating – or, mentalising again, if not exactly endorsing – differences to maintain good sibling relationships.

But when tension between two loyalties arises – loyalty, that is, to either the in-law or to you, the sibling – the connection and identification side of your sibling bond is threatened, and resentment and hostility emerge. The potential for such tension occurs particularly at transitions, and, yet, transitions, because they are meaningful, are exactly the times when you expect your siblings to know and validate what the meaning is for you.

How well does your sibling's new partner blend into your family? At births of children, how inclusive are the celebrations, for instance? At parental illness and death, does your sibling's partner share your family's norms of care and how to mourn? The potential for anger and hostility to resurface at your sibling exists at each of these points, because, due to split loyalties, they don't prioritise validation and understanding of you. These are events that test where siblings' respective loyalties lie – with their partner and family or with you? These events can bring to the surface differences between siblings, differences in what you'd assumed you and your sibling would share, given your joint upbringing. That makes them potentially explosive times for siblings. Events and episodes that reveal differences with such a painful impact force you to recalibrate your expectations and understandings of your sibling. That can lead either to new understanding, as for Ben and Sarah, or to emotional distance.

I am always struck when I hear people in my therapy room say they haven't seen or spoken to a brother or sister in years. If you dig, you'll often find the cut-off connected to an event, or series of events, that severed the relationship, often connected to changed behaviour since the entrance of the new partner. 'Can you believe he acted that way?' or 'I learned something about my sister that I never really understood before and I just can't forgive her' are often codas to the tales of events that led to cut-off, which often cast the in-law in the role of true villain. Fair or not, the mythologised possessive sister-in-law, the monstrous brother-in-law, each denote an essential, if not so simplistically expressed truth: in-laws, incomers to a family, always mean your siblings will change.

Especially at transitions and milestones high emotion will be around and conflict, distance or hurt feelings may result. Remember in such moments to emotionally regulate in your dealings with your sibling. And then, as Ben realised in his tentative encounter with Sarah, mentalise and think what you can say, from your heart, if you want to reach your sibling's.

Theresa, Ian and David's father had died unexpectedly two years before their morbidly ill mother. In something of a state of shock the siblings had buried him smoothly, playing to each other's strengths, glued by their shared grief and appreciating the specific types of support each could bring to the situation. Theresa, the eldest, who lived with her two young children and husband in a neighbouring town, had overseen funeral arrangements; Ian, a newly qualified solicitor, just entering a relationship that would become an engagement, scrutinised legal concerns, given their mother's terminal state, safeguarding the three of them under the terms of their parents' will; David, still single and unattached, moved home, overseeing their mother's nursing care. However, when their mother died less than two years later the siblings' relationship came asunder, with Ian's partner, Beth, cast as villain and Ian in a loyalty contest with his siblings.

Their mother's death occurred just two months before Ian's wedding, so Theresa and David naively assumed Ian would want to reschedule it, but Beth stood firm: the wedding would proceed. 'Life trumps death'. A wedding celebrated their impending shared life, she maintained, and Ian sided with her. Moreover, they contended, Ian's mother had been terminally ill and had known she might be dead by the proposed date, so she had tacitly sanctioned it by not suggesting they moved it.

Tempers flared, positions hardened; Theresa and David planned to boycott; Ian and Beth wouldn't yield. 'Grief can go on too long and be indulgent; celebrating something our mother also celebrated doesn't deny our grief about her death,' Ian pleaded, while his siblings' implacable position became, 'Grief has a long timetable. To celebrate too early is immoral. We don't feel it would be right to come.'

This emotionally fraught situation, with an imminent wedding like a gun to their heads, made the loyalty divide seem unbridgeable. If David and Theresa had not attended, for Beth and Ian the wedding would forever mark the moment relations had been broken, and for Theresa and David it would symbolise the moment Ian had failed to honour their family by sharing in their mourning. A bridge can start to be built with understanding and sympathising: with mentalising the other's reality. What are the reasons behind the rationale for each side? What are the vulnerable, softer feelings behind those hardened positions? But each side was too fraught with hard feelings to do that.

Enter their uncle, their mother's brother. Close to Theresa and David, sharing the strength of their grief, nevertheless he brought the perspective of an outsider to things, to be able to wonder why and what Beth was battling for and against. Why was she corralling Ian into such a loyalty test? What, indeed, were the soft feelings she was hiding? What was behind Ian and Beth's behaviour? Less disturbed than they, he was more able to mentalise. What this story also suggests is that when there's deep emotion creating an impasse, sometimes an outside brain – one that can enter both worlds – can help.

Indeed, a wedding represents a loyalty test, he pointed out. It signifies a move away from one family and into a new one. That new one takes prime position. Yet here was grief claiming Ian back, away from Beth, who *was* the new one. Grief – the tender and soft feeling – binds profoundly. It bound the siblings together, pulling Theresa and David strongly towards Ian, and Ian would, himself, be pulled towards them. Grief would be a strong adversary in any loyalty test. Beth probably felt she had to fight tooth and nail against its pull within the siblings. Beth played on their mother's joy about the wedding and it was true, their uncle said, they'd chosen the date with her full knowledge she was terminal. But it was also true that it could still feel like they'd be dancing on a grave. That was a very powerful argument, so Beth probably felt she had to stake her claim, one *for* her and Ian and *against* his sibling bond.

David and Theresa felt their closed minds slowly open. Their uncle validated how they felt, helped explain themselves. The moment the shield of Beth's angry recalcitrance fell to show insecurity and worry, the fight ended; it wasn't a fighting matter. They began to think about Ian, now with a new person to love and honour, different loyalties to theirs.

The uncle told them, 'Your mother once said to me, when she saw Beth was a strong personality with different ideas from hers, that she hoped I could say to you, if she were gone, "Don't fight him. He married her. Please let him be." He did choose her, just as you, Theresa, chose your husband and as you might someday, David, your partner. And you do have to *choose* them in many cases over your brothers and sisters in order to stay with them. Ian's choice is just a bit more stark and painful than usual. Try to understand his dilemma and cut him this slack.'

Their uncle mentalised for them. His own calm wisdom and sympathy calmed them, in turn, and they agreed that they needed to preserve their sibling relationship above all. They would attend. Not to do so would cause a perhaps unamendable breach. Their uncle's intervention enabled their approach to Ian. It's important to point out that what they did and said in no way was a surrender. Yes, there had been friction, yes, they had vastly different positions. They were not saying that Ian's was more 'correct' than theirs had been, so it's important to see how they phrased their approach to Ian.

They acknowledged how hurtful their stand had been to him. That was a repair. They also spoke from their own hearts, clearly stating that they thought he probably understood why they felt the way they did, but that he also had other feelings, other loyalties and priorities to consider. They acknowledged they did not. That was collaborative: we feel this and probably that's shared, but we offer an olive branch to say we understand why you also feel something else. Finally, and this was the seal of a collaborative move, they affirmed that for them the most important thing was to honour the relationship of siblings and they hoped they could build a good one with Beth as part of that. They would attend Ian and Beth's wedding.

At first it had felt like swallowing bitter medicine to cure an illness. Even as they went to the wedding, Ian's position still rankled: the wish that their brother hadn't complicated their relationship by marrying someone who had put this wrench into it was irrational, but understandable, and it persisted. But they also saw this as the next step in their sibling relationship: they grasped, with empathy, Ian's bind as their mother had so adeptly described it. It was on them to try to accept Ian's choice of Beth, who would of course in some way, as now, and maybe again at critical points, pull him away from them.

It was on them to be cautious about and try to understand and predict Beth's insecurity. It was on them to hold in mind the maxim that partners – incomers – shape who you become. And that, in turn, must shape your sibling relationship. As psychologist John Gottman's studies of successful couples over the past few decades has shown: you don't have to agree all the time. But you do have to listen, to try to understand and respect difference.

Birth

Births of siblings' children can also evoke the polarities of sibship. Births can mean both great joy and connection, as you witness some of your genes being reproduced, as you identify with your siblings' feelings of parenthood. But your siblings' children can also provoke rivalries. Whose child has more of the qualities most valued by your family? Whose child garners more grandparental attention and love? And when progeny resemble your siblings in manner, qualities and looks from childhood, both positive and negative, they might arouse your childhood feelings once again. Nothing can produce fierce loyalty as much as your children or your siblings' children – the way they behave, how they are being brought up, especially if it's in defiance of or in ways that vary to the way your own family was reared. These can become the areas between siblings of the tenderest sensitivity, rendering skilful relating crucial. An out-of-control child, for instance, can lead to sibling separation and even 'divorce'.

Jimmy, Nancy's brother, was delighted when Nancy, after many failed pregnancies, had Evie. But from the start she was a difficult baby, crying inconsolably, hardly sleeping and slow to smile. As she grew her behaviour worsened. Angry, aggressive, impulsive, Jimmy's son once had to go to hospital after she hit him on the head with a baseball bat. Gradually Jimmy's concern became mixed with resentful judgementalism: Evie's parents, his sister and her partner, were themselves out of control, not setting limits. Visits in which he silently witnessed her wildness were trials, as he sat tacitly condoning what he felt were tragic parental mistakes, his uncomfortable silence stemming from a fear that he'd irreparably hurt his sister if he spoke out.

His sister's parental mismanagement was also damaging his own family relationships. After his son's injury they refused to see Evie. Arguments flared between Jimmy and his wife. What he called 'tact', his wife called 'cowardice'.

Soon after his son's injury and, seemingly unrelated, Nancy approached him, providing the opening he needed by (he felt) cluelessly asking what sort of nursery school did he advise her to look for? Montessori-type or maybe more structured? He interpreted her question to him, 'wise older brother', as beginning to address the bigger issue: what's the best way to manage this child? 'I'm wondering if Evie might find school a bit much at this point? Might not really be ready?' he began tentatively. He saw Nancy go rigid. Maybe not 'wise older brother'. Maybe 'arrogant, judgemental brother'. 'What do you mean she might not be ready?' she retorted, warily.

He quickly understood he'd better start again, so he paused, calming himself down and, mentalising, he put himself in Nancy's position and realised what a trial living with Evie must be. Evie had injured his son, but then Nancy's feelings for Evie were as fierce as his were for his son and this was the danger point. Nancy's love for Evie would always exceed hers for him. If he trespassed on that, their relationship might disintegrate completely.

So, he conjured up the Nancy he did somewhere still love. Maybe they could start with some shared and honest feelings. Perhaps if she felt he wasn't judging her she could, as she did in childhood, take advice from him? Or if not, maybe it was up to him to figure out how to live with being Nancy's brother at a distance, to tolerate her and her life as best he could. They were at the precipice: distance or support?

Luckily for them, Jimmy is a lawyer-mediator and that's why he could turn to the skills we know are the essential ones. He'd become professionally masterful at controlling difficult interpersonal situations. In our next therapy session, he reported that he found himself drawing on professional skills in this tricky moment with his sister.

What he said to her was, 'Like you, I want this to be what's right for Evie, but also for you. I might be imagining it, but perhaps you feel worse about Evie just because I am there and seeing it. You might think I'm judging you, thinking I'd manage her differently. And, yes, I would, but I accept I'm not you. I'm really sorry if I said things in a way that hurt you, but I feel good you've asked me about schools for her. I want to help and I'm really asking about you when I say how do you think Evie would be at school now – whether your assessment of her is that she could manage it? I don't know her like you do, she might feel overwhelmed, but I'm no expert and you're perfectly within your rights to think I am way off beam.'

Skills are skills, wherever you learned to deploy them, and Jimmy put his professional ones to good use in his private life. Talking about his own experience, asking what hers was, admitting he might be wrong and overtly apologising made Nancy listen. There was no conclusion, no resolution, but Jimmy's empathic offer of his own feelings and impressions unlocked communication. If they carry on in that kind and cooperative way, at the very least it preserves the special sibling togetherness. His use of language was unsurprisingly skilful: as a lawyer-mediator he'd had training in using 'I statements' and his communication was replete with them; and he offered things for Nancy to think about, rather than pronouncing, which had been his first instinct.

Illness and death

Siblings' children can create difficulty, not to mention rewards, but it's the illness and deaths of parents that can induce the keenest re-emergence of rivalries and hostility, although also the most intense moments of shared love and identification.

For the greater part of people's lives help goes in one direction: from adults to children, even when they are grown. While gift-giving goes both ways, for the most part adult parents contribute more in the way of financial aid, either directly or by giving large gifts to adult children; older parents give services such as childcare to grandchildren. And then, at some point, this reverses, as older parents' infirmities require sometimes physical and sometimes financial help. As discussed in the previous chapter, it is when this reversal occurs that sibling relations can become rocky or be mutually supportive – or a combination of both.

Studies of ageing validate what most of us intuitively expect or have ourselves experienced. Until older parents are incapacitated, this inversion is normally gradual and incomplete. A visit to a clinic that one sibling facilitates early on; medical information another digs out; a day another sibling spends time helping a surviving parent deal with financial paperwork. So it goes until, in many cases, the gradual help needed by an older parent becomes total. These are instances when sibling cooperation and loyalty, underscored by similar feelings about parental ties, can come into their own – as can resentment for siblings feeling the other ones aren't pulling their weight.

Gender has tended to operate within sibling relationships at this time, as well. All things being equal, such as physical proximity, ability and ease of making adaptations to accommodate parental needs, sisters, so research tells us, have tended to be the organisers, the coordinators of necessary help. Once help is needed siblings face either competition or cooperation. Questions arise over the following: fairness of effort made – is each sibling doing an equal amount of helping – as measured by what each can provide, within their respective constraints?

Loyalty – is each sibling showing family loyalty by pulling his or her weight within those constraints? And, finally, the bottom, primitive line in the putative scale that measures parents' regard and appreciation for their children's individual contributions – is one sibling being favoured and another disfavoured? Each of these can elicit sibling rivalry and hostility or evince appreciation, identification and connection.

When a parent dies the primal conditions of sibship – connection, support and appreciation against envy and anger – are tested anew, sometimes bitterly. Who gets what when a parent dies can too easily stand in for how that parent felt about you. But, as silent symbols which cannot declare exactly what they mean, things, bequests, can be grossly misread. 'Johnny got my favourite lamp and I got the measly rug,' can confirm a lifelong feeling that the Johnny-come-lately younger brother was, in fact, preferred. However, the terms of the bequest might only have meant that the parent mistakenly thought Johnny liked the lamp better, while you preferred the rug.

Pam and Anna grew up in the shadow of tragedy: their mother died when Pam was six and Anna was two. Their father, too busy running a dry goods shop in the small town in which they grew up, patched in childcare with his sister and mother, who lived reasonably nearby, and then married the sister of his childhood friend within two years of their mother's death. Their stepmother immediately took steps to ensure she was their father's priority. First, she succeeded in arguing that the girls should share a bedroom, so she could take over Pam's larger one for 'sewing'. Then she pronounced that they should eat separately and, so they could 'wind down', be shut in their bedroom, while she and their father ate later, on their own. A spilled bowl or 'funny' look might send her into a rage and the girls, most especially the livelier Anna, were sent to their bedroom with the door locked firmly behind them. Their mostly absent father took his wife's side, pleading for the girls to 'behave' and appreciate the efforts their stepmother was making, given she'd so nobly taken them on. Their half-brother, Andy, was born soon after and with him she was soft and permissive.

'Now you're in charge of your baby sister; you look after her,' six-year-old Pam had been instructed by her father, her grandmother and aunt when their mother had died. And so that was what she did, a dictum she particularly followed in the face of their stepmother's treatment of Anna. Pam was the caretaker sibling, a quality spotted early by the stepmother, so she also helped in the care of the baby, Andy, ensuring Anna was now in competition with him for Pam's attention. Andy and Anna grew up rivalrous; Pam grew up their mediator. The girls' story of their father was not their brother's. His was uncomplicated; theirs tried to be forgiving, but in theirs their father always fell short: he was a less than loyal and loving parent.

The obedient, capable and caring Pam rather predictably became a child psychiatrist, married and had two children. And perhaps equally predictably Anna roamed from low-paying arts jobs, flitting from one unstable partnership to another, always depending on Pam for both handouts and guidance. Andy, sturdy and self-absorbed, became a still single businessman, remote geographically and emotionally to them both. Loyal Pam, as ever, cemented the sibling trio, staging reunions around holidays, inviting her siblings to her own children's birthdays and celebrations of milestones. Things remained like this until their father died after a brief illness that had been kept secret by his wife, which split them into the factions that had simmered throughout their lives, the two sisters outraged at their recurrent exclusion, Andy springing to his mother's defence.

Simmering became roiling boil at the reading of the father's will, which unbalanced Pam's and Anna's relationship as well. All property, most goods and money were left to their father's wife during her lifetime. At her death, property and any money and remaining goods were to be divided between Anna and Andy. Pam's gifts were: a family album of her mother's photos, a print that had hung on her bedroom wall given to her on her birth by her mother's family, and a necklace that her mother had owned. Anna's similar bequest was offset by the will's final terms, as were Andy's more substantial gifts – their father's personal tools and remaining stock from the dry goods store sold a decade earlier.

Pam felt the terms of their father's will were his ultimate act of rejection and contempt. To his end, Pam's father had relied on her goodness: because of her competence, she, in his estimation, had needed least. And that's what she got. He'd relied on her obedience: he'd assumed she'd accept. Meanwhile, Anna was rewarded for ineptness and so she got more. Andy was rewarded both for shirking sibling loyalty and being blessed with maternal love, and so he got most. Out of character, stunning her siblings, Pam let loose. This was unfair. Was she really, despite being such a good daughter, really that unloved? Were her siblings, already divided from each other, not going to join in outrage on her behalf? Were they just going to accept their gifts, quietly, uncomplainingly? For months the siblings didn't speak. Anna's desperate pleas for contact went unanswered. Pam deleted Andy's abrupt, to her, self-serving, texts.

On Pam's daughter's 13th birthday Anna phoned the landline and Pam answered. Her heart melted at Anna's tentative voice, apologising for calling their landline. Anna didn't have Pam's daughter's number, she explained (Typical Anna, Pam fleetingly thought). Pam was touched that, whatever, Anna wasn't going to let her devotion to her niece become a casualty of their own separation. Hearing her voice, she realised she'd missed her sister, rather than the anger she imagined she'd feel. She summoned her daughter to the phone.

'Anna wants to talk,' her daughter said, her own conversation over, holding out the phone. Pam, despite her trepidation, took it from her. 'I've thought about what happened,' Anna started and Pam felt her stomach tighten. But Anna paused, gathered herself, then carried on. 'I know you might not want to talk about it, but can I just say something before you hang up?' She waited. Pam found herself open to listening. She was being invited to listen, but her position, her hesitancy, was being acknowledged: she might not want to talk about it. 'You're right,' Anna continued. Pam relaxed, was curious. She really was being thought about. 'What he did was inexcusable. He made you feel worthless, exploited or at least that's what I think you must have felt.' She was understood! Anna continued, 'I was so absorbed in my own gratitude I couldn't see it from your point of view. I needed that money. It helped me feel free for the first time ever. I think Andy must have been the same, but let's not go there – I just know that we, you and I, both needed so much from him, the only one we could get anything from, and I was so blindsided by his gift. We were wrong and I'm sorry.' Pam felt tears of gratitude.

'But here's the other thing – and by the way, I can guess Andy also feels this, even if he doesn't admit it . . .' Anna now seemed to be changing tack. Pam grew alert: would she be taking back her apology, her validation? But Anna's voice was gentle, conveying compassion for Pam, 'You were always the angel for Dad, the good one. That seemed to us great, but maybe you didn't feel it that way. And you are the most successful. You don't need the material gifts like we do, even Andy, look at him, he can't stay in a relationship, he's tied to that mother, he hates his job. I think we only saw the will in that way, the way Dad did, which was wrong. He should have talked to you. To us. He should have let us decide how to help each other, or not, with what he gave us. The way he did it was awful for you. It would have felt terrible for me if I were you, which I am certainly not, of course. You with all your talent and goodness – you have probably felt we just assume you don't need anything, like he did, and that's all a will's about. It's clear that it's not. He and we got it wrong. I'm only guessing how you feel. I'm telling you why I was selfish. Bottom line: I am sorry.'

Pam's snuffled, 'This has meant so much to me . . . I have missed you,' was heartfelt. Anna's sensitively and wisely phrased action reversed things for them. That action induced a positive response from Pam, which then induced one in return from Anna, and so on. The conversation became easy, warm enough for each sister to catch the other up, to pick up the old ties that had bound them with the promise of carrying them forward. Pam reflected afterwards that the way Anna had so skilfully managed to repair the breach between them had been a revelation. It portended a relief, she realised, from the grip of their rigid childhood roles.

On reflection, what was really striking, Pam realised, was that Anna was so much more relationally skilled than Pam had thought. She wouldn't have described it this way, but Anna's behaviour ticked all the right boxes and, most of all, she'd repaired. She used communication that was direct from her heart, her own experience. She was clear about what she, Anna, had felt and she didn't impute things to Pam. She showed mentalising: she was compassionate yet respectful of Pam's different position to her and Andy, and surprisingly on the mark about it. The effect benefitted them both: Pam was up for rebuilding a relationship with her.

6

Couples: Love and war

'How do I know if she's the one? My girlfriend is pressuring me to move in. I love her, but I'm not sure.' So begins a question to a forum on relationships for young people.

A couple comes into therapy with me. 'We argue all the time. The magic has gone and I just don't know if I've got the will to keep going,' says the 45-year-old accountant, mother of two, her journalist husband sunk unhappily on the sofa beside her.

Finally, Sadie, turning 60, ruefully sends me an email: 'I look down the years left with John and I'm already worried he won't look after me if I'm ill or even if I want to look after him. Now the children have left home, we seem to have little left. I don't know if we can still be bothered to care for each other.'

Each one of these examples shows the dilemmas you'll encounter at each period of love. Depending on your age and stage of life you probably already have, or will in the future, face one of those dilemmas. In the first stage of love you'll be asking, do you commit? If you're in the next one, after you've committed and have moved, together, into lives full of demands, your dilemma becomes, how do we keep interest, care, attraction alive amidst everything else? And if you have made it, or you're waiting to move to love's late period, your question becomes how can love feel renewed in the space and time that opens up? How can we find again the depth of care, appreciation and focus we'll need as we grow more dependent on each other?

But why is it so urgent to have love? To make it last through those stages? What does that word we toss around so loosely – love – mean anyway? It seems to be so important to keep it, but why? This chapter will discuss why and then show how. Once again we'll be using the core skills of emotional management, mentalising, collaborative communication and repairs to manage the disturbances that will arise within love, but for love to be robust it will mean keeping in mind the key challenges that are part of each period of love. With skills and that awareness I will help you to maintain the right balance of positive interactions that can, in fact, preserve love. That is, of course, once you've found it and decided not to let it go.

First, we need to answer that basic question upon which all answers to the questions above turn: what is this thing called love? After that we'll turn to what the dilemmas are underlying the disturbances rumbling between you and your partner within each period. As you learn about the dilemmas, you'll see why they are so emotionally 'hot', why they can be so disturbing and therefore why skilful interactions are so crucial.

Spotlight on falling in love

With respect to Newley and Bricusse, it does not fall from stars above. There's 'falling' and then there's 'love'. Let's start with falling. When you fall in love it's like a switch being flicked, catching your lover in bright neon light; a switch which, in turn, activates your every erogenous zone. It feels like a forcefield draws you together. Your lover in a crowd seems to have a halo. In *The Godfather* this 'lightbulb moment' is called the 'thunderbolt', which is a great description for the physical feeling, the electricity, the magnetism, the shake-up that happens between two people. This moment is so powerful it's like you're stuck together, as if that 'electricity' or 'magnetism' has fused you. Let's think of it as the initial *glue*, then, which is, perhaps, a gentler but still true image.

'The light bulb moment' is how a couple put it whom I interviewed for a study I conducted that looked at enduring love. The light bulb was on for him the minute they met through mutual friends. She had the glossy black hair, clear blue eyes and engaging smile he had always been drawn to; her rich, deep voice gave him tingles; he found himself enchanted by the way her mouth moved when she laughed and her offhand gesture of tucking strands of hair behind her ear; was tickled by her penetrating observations. He told me, 'I knew I wanted to marry her by the end of that first evening we met.' But the lightbulb wasn't a shared moment. She found him interesting, loved to hike in nearby hills with him and enjoyed hanging out together, but he was a 'pal' and not her physical type. Then one day they went on a hike and he taught her rock climbing. In our interview he said he knew the exact minute the lightbulb went on for her – a look she gave him as he drove them home. She agreed. While she couldn't explain it, from that moment she was attracted.

So that's how romantic love starts: a witchy moment that escapes words. We need metaphors, like lightbulb, magnet and thunderbolt. It eludes scientific specificity: we cannot capture why or who, nor the precise characteristics of either the moment or circumstances to predict when or that it will happen for a particular pair of people.

This is falling. It's the start of *potential* love: more than simple lust, the lightbulb moment is *lust* with the *promise* of love. As the interviewee said, 'I knew I wanted to marry her.' His partner felt the same once she'd experienced lust for him. Until then she'd felt affectionately comfortable, but no more. However, the lightbulb moment doesn't always turn into love, which is why it's just the *promise*. The surge of oxytocin – the pleasure hormone – that this glue represents is very strong – lust is a powerful component to initiate love – but lust is a flimsy glue. It can fade, be the plaything of life's vicissitudes. Nevertheless, it pulls you towards a specific person, so it feels very like love itself, which also pulls you towards someone specific. It starts off the falling, but the lightbulb moment, jet-fuelled by lust, isn't yet love. It moves into love when it becomes – you'll see in a moment – an 'attachment', after the falling.

People are drawn to others initially through similarities, but difference is part of the pull, too. People tend to meet up in the first place because of similarities: for instance, they come from similar places, have overlapping social circles. They recognise themselves in the other person: shared experiences, ideas, understandings. Remember the earlier mention of mirroring? Specific neurons called mirroring neurons that are fired off when you feel the same as someone else? They'll bond you. They'll make you feel as if you're actually the same person, because you'll be feeling the same things in your own separate bodies, as if what they're telling is actually happening to you. Similarity keeps you safe and secure.

Similarity, breeding a sense of security, fuses with a curiosity about your lover, a curiosity that's stimulated because of difference. Differences keep you interested. Curiosity is innate. It comes from an impulse to explore, which is another aspect of development that Bowlby noted when he formulated his Attachment Theory and, as I've already hinted, attachments are the basis of love. Similarity and difference foster the joy of love, its bonding and pleasure. You get the backbone of security plus the excitement of discovery. You do have to feel secure to explore your differences with someone you've fallen in love with, but therein lies the built-in difficulty of loving. Differences – in understandings, in aims, for instance – are the basis of conflict, friction, misunderstandings. Love, to develop, to be sustained, needs your relational skills.

But let's go back to the idea that love, even when you're a grown-up, is really about a good attachment. For it to grow from lust love needs safety and trust, just like the first love you read about in chapter 3: your first 'attachment relationship' with your parent. This begins, from the falling, the process of love.

Like that first attachment in babyhood you're putting yourself into that person's hands and they into yours. You begin to reveal things, so you begin to be vulnerable. But think about how you are when you're part of a couple. Now, as grown-ups, that disclosure and vulnerability will go both ways. So, this time as a grown-up you're mutually attached and mutually vulnerable. Love grows only as you trust you're understood and accepted. In that way it's like when love grew when you were a child: you flourished because your parent(s) gave you security; you felt safe. The attachment, the love you're feeling, now as an adult, gets tested as you get to know each other, disclosing, sharing more and more, as you try out just how much you can trust, how much you do mesh in understandings and values, for example. As you increase your exposure to each other, more and more of each of you becomes witnessed and revealed. It's as if you're continually undressing. Doing this back and forth, you each become vulnerably attached, loved and loving. The result is you can equally be hurt and you can equally delight.

We're wired to love. The urge to be attached is innate, but unlike at birth this time you are both the protected and the protector. You flip back and forth, tuning in to your partner, feeling sympathy and helping. A balance, over time, is struck that you each depend upon. It can, of course, become unbalanced at specific times – one needier than the other. There is a concept in systemic therapy, 'emotional hero', to describe this. For example, if your partner has ever lost their job or been ill or depressed for a while, you probably picked up the slack. That is being the emotional hero. However, whether consciously or not, you probably expected some sort of payback. Couples do expect an exchange of heroism between them and you'll see that particularly in the middle phase of love, when people are besieged by so many life demands. Creating this sense of balance of care and attention to each other is critical and describes the dilemma for that period of our lives.

The urge to be attached is accompanied by the need to trust, to feel safe with the other person; that you are, when you're an adult in love, each other's singular ally in the world – the one you can depend on to try to understand your needs and to have you most in mind, as your caregiver was for you when you were a child. Attachments are formed within episodes of high emotion – when you need to trust, to feel secure – and this exposure of yourselves that happens as you come to love exists in high emotion. Sex with someone you're revealing important other things to is part of that. Sex can in itself involve high emotion, especially with someone you're falling in love with. It definitely has high exposure: you're literally and figuratively naked.

Falling, then attachment, equals love. And then you have to 'do' love: enact the things that keep that trust, focus on, mutual interest in and protection of each other alive. That's where using the core skills to skilfully navigate the crux elements that will create problems in each of the three periods (early love, the middle period, mature love) come in and are fundamental. So, what will these be and why?

What's love got to do with it?

So, most of us are basically wired to make us want to be in a love relationship. You sort of can't help it. You're going to want it so there's a reason so many songs and poets and novels and plays and films seem to revolve around its loss and its gain. There's also scientific evidence that if you're in one, it's good for you:

you're healthier, wealthier, wiser. You get a lot of advantages in life from being in a good romantic partnership and the evidence shows that it's particularly good for you if you can sustain it over time. You're really lucky then, not just in love, but in life. It's the most protective relationship you can have, bringing you both health and economic advantages, and being in such a partnership can double the breadth of your social network. That will obviously increase your range of support and it's particularly beneficial for men, because their social networks are usually smaller than women's. Men really gain advantages from being in a solid romantic partnership – and when their relationships break up, they enter new ones faster than women do, which stands to reason, because for them it's a lot healthier.

So all in all it's good to be able to sustain a good romantic partnership, to be what psychologist John Gottman would call a 'master' of such a relationship. And so it makes sense to try to maintain love as it changes over time. Research shows hearts and flowers tend to flag in frequency over time; don't look for it in grand gestures. However, love does not have to tire. I've studied couples who've long been in love. It can last, but it looks, feels and requires different perspectives and expectations as it moves through time. So now we're going to turn to what those dilemmas that form within each of love's periods are and how you can navigate skilfully through them so you've got a good shot at keeping love alive.

Crux dilemmas for each period of love

In the first period, the beginning, after you've fallen, it's all about commitment: should you stay or go? Are you ready to make that choice? If you stay, you begin love's often drawn-out middle period. Most, but not all, of you will recognise how much it's defined by having children. Again, for most of you, that will be while you're working. And most of you in that part of couple life will recognise the problem of protecting time and attention, specifically for your partner and they for you. It's the busiest stage of life for most couples, even those without kids. Because of this, it's about keeping love alive amidst the increased demands of life. Finally, in its third, or last, period, those of you in it, or those who will enter it, will see that it benefits from a recommitment, specifically to caring for and appreciating the best points of your partner. This becomes particularly apparent if you've been a couple with children, as those children move out and leave you on your own together. In this stage, as you start to relinquish or diminish work, space opens up for you and your partner for time with and attention to each other, but it becomes most poignantly apparent as ageing takes its toll and you come to rely on each other for mutual care. At this last stage in love's life the crux dilemma for you is how to grow what's positive between you again.

All these dilemmas are hot ones. They boil down to how loved and secure, how primary you are for each other. It's about how you deal with the mounting frustrations, resentments and disappointments that build and threaten love, so you can keep its tenderness between you fresh amidst the too often feelings or cries of, 'You don't pay attention to me! . . . Why do you always focus on the bad and not see my good? . . . Are you going to choose to be with me or not?'

Your core skills will be key in keeping your love sturdy and rewarding. According to John Gottman's research, it's how expertly you can manage difference and difficulties between you that will make or break your relationship, so you need skilful interacting. Love is possibly the most tricky kind of relating to keep going: it takes almost continual monitoring of your interactions and it's the relationship in which you probably interact the most as you live together side by side. There will be plenty of scope for the use of repairs, and all through the lifespan of love, any of the following dilemmas could prove fatal to it.

Commitment

Love relationships that happen early in young adulthood, even when relatively long term, do not necessarily develop into the committed relationships onto which futures can be built. That is in large part because such a decision takes wisdom, the wisdom of secure self-knowledge: who you are, your tastes, values, talents, aims in life. To get to a point of relative firmness about your 'self' in that way is about completing a necessary developmental stage in life. Who you are is no longer your preoccupation – if you're out of that phase you'll probably remember how much it was part of your thinking and decisions. Instead, you know you're out of it because you feel pretty settled, confident of your direction and values. You've committed to a future, whether that's a work direction or a relationship that can fit into the shape of the life direction you've begun to shape more firmly.

The American psychologist who was a key theorist of development over the life cycle, Erik Eriksen, would describe Gemma's phase of life in the example that follows as preoccupation with who she is. Falling in love can in fact help you to figure that out; it can be part of the process of how you complete that developmental task. As you share and get to know someone else intimately you find out what you like and what you don't like about yourself, adopt new ideas and tastes, and discard some in the process. How much do you really want security? How much do you need to stay the same to feel safe? Are you just living out a script you've been handed? You can fall in love with someone, but realise after a bit you don't really fit so well. It's a time of life in which making a commitment to stay might not make sense, if you feel too vague about who, in some essential way, you are.

115

Gemma was a young woman of 20, living with the boyfriend she met working on a farm. She arrived, in despair, at the clinic I worked in. She'd had a boyfriend in school, but though she'd briefly felt 'in love' with him, they'd broken up fairly amicably when he went off to college. She drifted into farm work, not really sure what she wanted to do after school, and she quickly got into a relationship with a co-worker, a few years older, then drifted into living with him. While she didn't feel truly in love, she liked the familiarity of their life, so when he proposed she agreed.

Then, one evening out at a pub, she'd met someone travelling through, a man who – exotically – worked in a circus. The 'lightbulb' had gone on for her – still evident in her liveliness describing him – and she'd slept with him that night. Then he'd flitted away as quickly as he'd entered her life, leaving Gemma guilty, tortured and consumed by fantasies both of him and the broader life his had suggested. Should she ditch security? Was it moral to renege on her promise or immoral to marry while wishing to break free? Through her therapy sessions over a few unhappy months Gemma came to understand both her ambivalence about marrying and her susceptibility to the lightbulb moment as 'messages'; she wasn't ready to settle. She left therapy and, eschewing security, fled to her sister's in the city to try living differently.

The next stage of development is where commitment to a relationship takes place. It's about making a choice to be with someone who consolidates who you are. So, commitment has to feel commensurate with that. It's why the critical question for the users of a website I once contributed to for young adults was 'Should I stay or should I go?' A study of gender differences in commitment confirmed the perceived notion we seem to have that young men can be labelled 'commitment-phobes' and that, at this point in our culture, as a rule they take longer than women to commit. The findings suggest that men tend to think women want them fully formed, sure of what they can bring to the table. As a result, many men do seem to balk at what feels a tall order – to commit – when they're still unsure they're the full package. This seems to me to indicate the persistence of an outdated expectation about the man's role, probably still attached to the idea of the 'male breadwinner', that is understandably making young men falter.

The dilemma in this stage is informed by the question of who you feel you are and the same goes for your partner. How formed do you each feel in your respective identities? Are you at different points in how secure you feel about who you are and want to be, and where you're going in life in general? Does one or both of you feel insecure about commitment and is that causing problematic interactions? Or if it's not about how formed your identity is, because you're older and you know yourself pretty well, perhaps it's more about how well you fit together and, if you don't, how do you say 'no'? Either way, in this, the beginning phase, your interaction skills will be needed.

The story of Phoebe and Nick shows how when one is at a different phase of development, yet there are still feelings of love, the question of commitment becomes the sticking point. How they resolved it also shows that, while painful, endings can be done with dignity if they are done using skills and being attentive to the dilemma underlying your relating. It's about staying mindful that commitment is about security; that being good at how you are as you relate, even in breaking up, can help ease the pain.

Phoebe and Nick got together in year 12 of the sixth form. Theirs was an easy-going relationship, born first in a friendship that had begun when they'd done an English language project together. For Nick, finding a like-minded soul, interested in books, films and ideas, was a revelation. Nick had always wanted to be a teacher – something that seemed to embarrass his 'macho', military family. He'd felt a misfit there – his parents' wish for his future, since he showed no interest in the armed forces, was that he join the garage his father had bought on early retirement from the Air Force. Then his parents separated messily the summer before he began sixth form. With his older brother already in the Air Force, stationed in Germany, Nick felt more drawn to Phoebe's stable family. He folded into Phoebe's life, essentially moving in with her.

If their need for each other felt in that way imbalanced, the relationship for Phoebe was crucial in a different way. Recovering from an angry break-up with the overly demanding Tom, her first boyfriend, Phoebe was cautious. Nick's gentleness, their growth from friendship to love, gave her faith and stilled the remaining shame she experienced at how shabbily she'd broken up with Tom. 'Don't touch me!' she'd found herself impulsively hissing at him, months of rage at his possessiveness erupting. 'We're over!' Phoebe valued kindness and knew she'd been cruel, no matter how badly treated she'd felt.

The process of university applications was Phoebe's first hint that she felt less committed to their future than Nick. He imagined them at the same university, or at least in the same city. Phoebe's fantasies roamed around images of pubs, lectures, walking in quads, and she faced – without admitting it to him – the truth that Nick did not feature in them. Phoebe was guiltily relieved when Nick didn't get into the same university as she and would be going to one in a city a long way away.

But here was the dilemma that faces so many at this juncture in a long relationship: she loved Nick. He loved her. How – and why, really? – should she end it? Nick started working for his father to afford the car he was determined to buy so he could visit Phoebe. He even talked about 'their children', something that would horrify her. Maybe she wouldn't even have children – the life of a war correspondent, for that was one fantasy, would surely make that impossible? The pressure grew the more the difference in future plans for their relationship became clear. She loved him, but she'd have to end it, for him as much as for her. She'd form her message as, 'We need a break,' so it wouldn't be a break-up, but a growth opportunity for them both.

Breaking up is hard to do, so the song goes, and getting support for your decision, for maintaining the decision through inevitable wobbles, like any other difficult moment can be helped by having a chorus that champions you, so she confided in a friend, Sarah, who'd had experience of having broken up herself the year before.

Phoebe asked Nick to go for a walk to the river to a spot they'd gone to earlier in their relationship. Having rehearsed with Sarah, she'd predicted she'd feel sick. Sarah had warned her to emotionally regulate – not be impulsive as she'd been with Tom, otherwise she wouldn't say what she wanted to say. She might even back down. She'd thought about how and what to say to Nick: how he'd feel – his neediness for her, his aims, so different from hers, in life. Phoebe had done the mentalising. Sarah's wisdom, based on her own experience, had warned her that to get Nick to understand why she was breaking them up couldn't be her objective. Making clear as compassionately as possible her own reasons had to be the aim.

This is a key point: it's almost never the case that a couple is evenly matched in timing for when a break-up occurs, even when a relationship has clearly hit the rocks. To get your 'stories' of a relationship to match so the other person goes, 'Yeah, of course you're right,' can't be your objective. Your hope, instead, can be that if you're as clear as you can be in a way that will be heard – you say things sensitively and compassionately – your partner will eventually, when the hurt has healed, think back to your words and get them. So, Phoebe would say that she loved him and she had always felt loved by him, because that was true, and she felt broken, too, to be breaking them up. He probably wouldn't get that, but it would be worse if they let things get bad, when they would surely resent each other, and then she'd explain her reasons for breaking up. And this is what she did, calmly and with gentleness, and – she thought – thoughtfulness about how he might be feeling as she delivered a decision he wouldn't want to hear. She'd made herself calm; she tried to stay mindful of her objective and his feelings even as he got scarily angry; as he cried. She cried, too, but kept in her head the idea that she needed to do this and he had to hear it, even through pain: he wouldn't be helped if she backed down. She'd resent him.

Although Phoebe had been skilful, when it comes to a decision in love that isn't a shared one, there will be inevitable resistance. So, Nick hadn't understood and the issue – stay or go – was raised again and again in tearful meetings until they each left for university, Phoebe wavering. She needed a background chorus of Sarah reminding her of the reality: that she wasn't ready to make the commitment Nick wanted. A final angry encounter severed contact with Nick and at least they went off to their different universities with clarity: their relationship was over.

When you do break up, healing depends on changing your habits and customs. Starting at different universities clearly helped them both. Their roles in each other's lives faded – helped by making sure they did not check each other's Instagram and other social media. Each glance could reignite their meaning to each other. It does in any breakup.

In their case Phoebe's gracious, skilful breakup had the desired effect. After two years had passed Nick contacted her to let her know he was engaged to a fellow student on his course and that now he understood how different their aims in life were. Because Phoebe had broken up with Nick with dignity, compassion and clarity, she had felt sadness and pain, but critically had felt free of remorse. She knew she'd done something necessary.

Maintaining focus

The next stage is a long and testing one for most of you. It is about how much you focus on your partner and how much on other things. It starts with that choice: how much or how little you blend your respective families and friends, your work and home. There will be demands on you from all corners to spend time, to think about them, to make choices that favour others. How much do you include each other in those choices? Those same earlier demands now combine with the most demanding thing of all – children, if you have them.

If you've got children, you might recognise how they can both bind and divide. They bind because you each feel uniquely passionate about them. But you might divide over how to raise them: if you're not united, children will create splits between you. Perhaps you feel, in common with many in this period, that your partner no longer cares especially about you as that very particular individual they fell for: 'I'm taken for granted.' That's a feeling that can build when the 'couple' gets lost raising a family. The children literally get in the way as you do 'family things' instead of 'couple things' and so the vital connection, that singular focus, the curiosity and interest in each other that brought you together, fades. Without time, energy and focus, this is the stage in which the lightbulb can dim most strikingly around the very lust, pleasure and emotional connection it once

121

brought on. Resentment and disengagement tend to burgeon in the face of the feeling that you're no longer singularly chosen.

John Gottman's research lab came up with a 'five to one' magic balance: if your interacting is roughly, on average, positive five times more than your negative, you're okay. You can use your skills to turn things around, but always watch that balance. If you do, you work at making the balance better. A relationship can take negative encounters and relating; it just needs more – five times more – positive than negative kinds. You need to say out loud the positive things – the expressions of appreciation and gratitude. You need to be proactive in repairing hurt feelings or misunderstandings, showing that you care about your partner's feelings and that you're thinking about them. You need to find enjoyable moments in which you share pleasure and note it. You need to show in how you manage differences, difficulties and crossed wires that you are respectful of your partner's position – in other words, mentalise about them and show that in how you phrase what you say. A punch in the emotional stomach carries a lot of weight. It needs a lot of good interacting to offset it. If that good balance is consistently out of whack, you find yourself building a negative narrative: 'Look at what they just did, just like always: they are so *thoughtless.*' This is the period, the demanding middle one, in which committed couples most frequently break up, but equally you can turn that around and make the ratio into a good one, using your skills.

Inevitably this stage is about divvying up your personal resources – time, energy and attention – so you don't lose focus on your partner. Without focus on each other during this stage, the connections wither; disappointment and disengagement grow as you don't feel 'chosen' and instead feel rejected. Maybe that's when you too often choose free nights with friends instead of your partner, or maybe the 'not choosing' is more implicit: you lose mutual understandings – that lovely mirroring that started you off. You keep getting crossed wires. You feel dismissed and you tune out your partner. You experience sullen silences. You are always finding fault. Your areas of vulnerability are provoked as your partner forgets and is absolutely not as protective as they had been. They might even be cruel and actually use your frailties against you. And when and if they do, you fight back. You might be, or they think you are, just as cruel. Whatever – there's a build-up of vicious interactional cycles. Gottman's magic five to one balance has gone the other way.

Love needs focus, lust needs stoking – use it or lose it. It can, in fact, even if it feels dead, be resurrected. For instance, contrary to instinct, that means having the will rather than the impulse to initiate sex, as clinician Suzanne Iasenza argues, and plotting time for it, as therapist Esther Perel recommends. Sex research has suggested that, especially for women, unlike in the beginning of long-term relationships, lust can often be summoned *after* slow, sensual arousal. This is probably because, as interviews for a study of married people who'd had affairs that I conducted indicated, women continue thinking about daily demands for longer – the proverbial 'doing the shopping list' during sex – and are more conscious of their other roles, primarily maternal and work ones. These demands and roles intrude on sensuality, but slow foreplay, gradually coaxing towards responsiveness, does create time and space for those preoccupations to fade.

In fact, infidelity is one of the most common reasons couples come into therapy and unsurprisingly, given what I've just been saying about this middle period, anecdotally this is the time of life in which therapists are most likely to see couples. That research I did on affairs suggested that while they can occur at any point in the life cycle, the possibility for them to occur increases in this period. Added to opportunity – this is a period in which both men and women are out and about, and meeting each other, sometimes through work, for instance – there's the fact that, again unsurprisingly, surveys on satisfaction show that couple satisfaction plummets in this period. Loss of focus and rising dissatisfaction combine with opportunity, and other attachments can form.

However, my clinical research suggests that it's also the case that an affair – a new attachment – can mask the fact that you're still attached to your partner, even if you feel disengaged, and that there can be repair and resurgence of love after infidelity. It does not inevitably lead to the breakdown of a relationship. Even with infidelity you can turn things around, focusing, reconnecting, devoting time and attention again, re-finding the pleasure and emotional bonding that united you at first. And do keep in mind, before you conclude that this period is all *sturm und drang*, if couples stay together without lost focus on each other, studies show that happiness rises again, primarily after children leave. Focus can increase and satisfaction can rise. You re-engage. You find your mutual pleasure again. Below we'll meet a couple who needed to do just that.

A couple in their early thirties took what I call the 'teacher slot' in my practice: the slot that starts around 4:30 pm, between the ending of the school day and the start of dinner preparation. Indeed, one of them, Rosie, was a teacher. Dressed in a sweet dress, Rosie was the slighter, apparently softer of the two. Her partner, Carol, bigger boned, immaculately groomed, wore an expensive suit. They sat close together but not touching on the sofa.

They'd been together ten years as partners, having been friends in school but not lovers until meeting again after their university years. They'd had eight easy, happy years in which Carol had soared in PR and Rosie had taught in a primary school, finding pleasure together hiking, sketching, exploring museums and films, and enjoying a close circle of friends, occasionally punctuated by Carol's glamorous work functions. Two years previously they'd married and soon celebrated the birth of their daughter, Carly, carried by Rosie. Rosie had taken two years' leave; Carol, the main earner, had taken only a few weeks.

And like so many couples, they – reluctantly – identified the change between them as starting with Carly's much wished-for arrival. The baby had messed up sleep and sex, and had driven a stake through time spent and activities done together. 'It wasn't that I expected it to be equal,' Rosie began, turning to the heart of things, this change that had produced in its wake such an unexpected frost between them. 'I knew I'd be the more traditional mother and I'd be doing most of the feeding and the bathing. Carol was clearly a bit afraid she'd break her or drown her or something and really hadn't thought much about what it would be like to have a baby. I understood that. I didn't mind in the early days doing most of it. She was working, earning money, a lot of it, for us. We'd agreed, but, for instance, Carly was colicky for a few weeks. I was a wreck. I needed Carol just to take over, totally, not just to give her a bottle in the middle of the night. She did that and I was grateful, but she had really important meetings, couldn't take time off work, all of that. So, I didn't ask. But she didn't offer.'

Rosie went on, while Carol listened, fidgeting, looking sheepish. 'I could tell she was pissed off with me. I mean the house was a wreck. And I didn't want to go anywhere. I am still nervous leaving Carly with anyone other than my mum. I'm sure I was really boring. I mean she was lovely with Carly when she was around, but she wasn't enough. A work party for a client here and there, and coming home late after a crucial meeting, hanging out with her friends – I mean, I know they're work friends, but . . .' Rosie turned to Carol and almost smiled. Carol warily seemed to relax.

Rosie went on. 'She's around more now and she clearly is more comfortable with Carly being that bit older, now that Carly's talking . . . But, well, I have been just so angry a lot of the time. I mean, couldn't she see? And the thing is, I wanted her to be happy just to be with me and Carly, but she wasn't. I didn't want to be with her at all, because of that. I'm sure she felt the same.' The anger Rosie described apparently came out as sullenness, resentment and withdrawal. They snarked and withdrew. They were certainly reporting a poor five to one ratio.

Carol sat up, enlivened now that it was her turn. 'Yeah, that's about right,' she confirmed when Rosie had finished. 'But you've left out that I was working a lot because you finally got pregnant, you actually had the baby, just at the time the firm was making people partners. To benefit us, not me, but us, I needed to make partner. We'd discussed that. I had to be at work. I had to go out with clients. I couldn't just be with you and Carly. You knew that. We agreed.' Carol bristled. Rosie sank sullenly into the sofa, and looked away.

That was the scene they set for me. It didn't take much to point out the gaping hole that was left between them, filled up by other people and activities for Carol, the baby and other mothers for Rosie. It didn't take long for each to agree that they'd each made choices, each choice justifiable, but each one cumulatively creating the hole. It was a hole they didn't want, but as it got larger it became harder to bridge. They agreed that they wanted help in learning how to do that. So, after learning about interactional cycles and the skills needed to change them, we took a 'typical episode' and began work. This allowed them to look at what was 'wrong' in the interactional cycle and to try to think of new, 'right' ways to interact. If it's a 'typical' interaction you can apply what you've learned when something similar comes up and, over time, the habits of vicious cycle interactions can change into habits of virtuous ones.

One evening the week before, Carol had again come home late. She hadn't phoned, leaving Rosie to feed, bathe and put Carly to bed on her own. She'd sat and sullenly chewed her pasta alone, dwelling on Carol's selfishness and her own inescapable banality. At which point Carol's key had turned in the lock. From the entryway Rosie heard Carol rifle through the day's post. From the corridor came a truculent, 'I know you're pissed off. I couldn't contact you. I had a meeting. There was no way.'

Rosie took her plate, clattered it into the sink, slammed Carol's uneaten pasta into the microwave and withdrew upstairs. Carol shouted: 'Well, someone works hard around here! Someone makes sure we can afford our child! Someone is out there, being valued, getting promoted, in the world of the living!' and then went on to sleep on the sofa. In the morning – and they described this as typical – as a peace offering, Carol brought Rosie a cup of tea, enacting a fragile recovery that left them both feeling vulnerable to another eruption.

When it came to mentalising, it hadn't been hard when they were laying out the story to be generous in their speculations about each other, to resurrect the more tender feelings they'd had for each other in their earlier period of love. They hadn't forgotten how they used to feel about each other or their considerable knowledge of who they were. In this way they had the elements of mentalising which they could apply if and when a contentious moment arose.

So, mentalising would take in such questions as: why might Rosie be resentful? In her family she is usually described as a 'carer' and readily takes on that role. Could that be contributing to it? And why might Carol overwork? Could it be that the fear of the poverty and chaos in which she grew up was driving her to be overly financially 'responsible'? Why might she have avoided early care of Carly? Could her own chaotic and abusive childhood have made her fearful about caring for a fragile being? What had having a child brought into their mix at the same time as heavy work demands? What might that mean for adaptations within their relationship at this point? Carol had fallen for a generous, tender-hearted and hard-working Rosie, whose normality Carol had craved, and Rosie had fallen for a strong-minded, independent, driven Carol, who had brought colour into Rosie's 'normality,' or, as she feared sometimes, her 'dullness'. How could these differences work for them now, in a different phase of their lives, so they were positive rather than divisive?

As Carol remembered she got tearful: 'I'm sorry! You must have felt abandoned. I miss that Rosie, who's my "rock". Maybe you missed me?' Rosie's nod and smile said 'yes'. Rosie sighed, 'I don't want you to be bored and I don't want to be boring . . . I do miss you and your spark. But, look, it wasn't how I'd thought having a baby was going to be. I admit, I don't think I realised how it wouldn't have felt like that for you. I'm sorry, too.'

We began the episode replay with Rosie stewing in the kitchen and Carol arriving on the defensive. She had expected trouble. As she turned the key in the lock she was tense, but she emotionally regulated, then closed her eyes, silently mentalising, but then saying out loud rather than what she'd normally do in her head, for the purposes of the exercise, all of what we'd enumerated earlier: who the Rosie she knew was and why might she be upset. Rosie, listening, nodded and Carol knew her mentalising was accurate. Then came the action: the collaborative, invitational communicating, which included a repair: 'Hi, honey! Hope you're okay? I'm sorry!' she called out. 'I should have called or texted! That was really bad!' and she mimed going towards Rosie and then leaned in to give her a kiss. 'And' – she turned to me – 'once I'm in the kitchen with her, I'd tell her why I was late.' She turned to Rosie, 'I'm hoping you'll forgive me when you hear why: can we talk?

'Look, sweetie, it was unforgivable for me not to phone, and to be so late. If it were me, I'd have been worried and I imagine you were. Or maybe you just felt abandoned. I would have felt that.' She looked into Rosie's eyes. Rosie closed hers and nodded for her to go on. 'I just want you to understand I would have phoned, but I got taken aside by Alan. He wanted to tell me I'd got that bonus. And then he offered me a drink to toast me for bringing in the most revenue in the quarter. I should have asked him to wait a minute and just taken a second even to text. And then I felt guilty and got angry at you, which was crazy, for making me feel guilty. That was wrong, and I was thoughtless.'

We see here clear, collaborative communication and a repair. Carol said what she imagined Rosie might feel, what she felt, and was clear in her explanation.

Rosie took Carol's hand. 'I'm glad you understand how upset I was. Thank you for that. It means a lot to me that you said you miss us. I know getting that bonus was a great thing for you. You're great enough for me without it, but I know it means a lot to you. I hope you know I am so proud of you.' Rosie also used repairs and clear collaborative language: her thank you, her acknowledgement of Carol's meaning to her, acknowledgements from each that had become increasingly rare since Carly's birth.

Over the weeks of therapy the couple practised their skills in sessions and at home, reminding and reassuring each other to accept the inevitable onset of irritability and exhaustion that arise when a small child makes unstinting demands on energy and time. When they felt irritability, or encountered it in the other one, they turned feedback loops that threatened to go negative to a positive direction. And so they remained allies and as allies they wanted to spend more time with each other, with Carly and without. The positive loops increased. Rosie even donned a cocktail dress for a party with a new client of Carol's. They learned to 'monitor': to be careful not to choose others too much over each other because that would mean love could drift again.

Empty-nesting

So you've got this far. Your work and other interests, your routines and your social worlds have become stable. Your children, should you have them, have been launched, although the timing of that varies, of course. It may be painful to wave your child goodbye, but some couples long for it. If you don't, though, try thinking that this is the time for you two to experience a resurgence of good feelings. The research on satisfaction backs up that this is possible.

So, there will be a time when you become just a couple again. Attention can more easily return to each other. This is a period when you can choose to build back on the best you bring to each other. It's a period that can begin with new-found attention to pleasure in each other, as you have the time to focus on it, and with that investment, when you need more care in the face of ailments, illness and losses, you can rely on the nurturing that the special attachment of love promises.

Psychologist Erik Eriksen called this phase, if you get it right, one of 'ego integrity' – consolidating what works for you. As you age you increasingly live, more or less consciously, in a 'years left to live' frame. It's a stage with encroaching limits around physical conditions and losses of positions, jobs and people, including the loss of your children in your home. Individual losses, yes, but they, in turn, rebound on the couple, circumscribing a changing, different life together.

But loss opens spaces and brings new choices. Should you fill them with each other? If so, how and how much? Your partnership becomes part of the appraisal of how you live within new limits and openings. If Eriksen is right, can you build on what's been good? Can you minimise or overlook difficulties? Because, given how difficult the middle phase has been these will have mounted. Can you forgive hurt that could have grown if you haven't managed these well? Instead, drawing on that ego integrity – maybe it's best thought of as sharpened wisdom – can you now, together, identify what to foster in your relationship? It's a period of recommitment. Those couples who have not lost focus on each other find new, or resurrect old, pleasures within the space created by things now diminishing or gone. We know that in the prior raising-a-family stage satisfaction is likely to have dipped. It's normal to face reappraisal. The early years of this stage are traditionally a time when divorces again spike, almost as high as in the previous stage. Habitually vicious interactional cycles can have conspired during the middle stage to make people forget what once worked and couples get divorced because they can't imagine it's possible again. Life with a partner is life sprinkled with caretaking. Faced with this stark realisation some sacrifice a partnership in which they feel caring has dried up.

So, when Chris, a fisherman in his mid-60s, was given a diagnosis of slow-growing prostate cancer, things came into sharp focus for him. Susie, his wife, would caretake grudgingly, resentment and disengagement having become their habit after Chris's affair 20 years earlier. Walking back to his car in the hospital car park he recognised he couldn't entrust his declining, final years to Susie and the marriage ended. Recommitment in this 'years left to live' phase means fostering survival and health.

But then there is the couple in their 70s I interviewed as part of a study on enduring happy couples. They had raised six children alongside dual careers, clearly thriving, despite bad hips and a weak heart between them. This couple – while also alluding to each other's still annoying habits – reported recently evolved sweet rituals: waking up and reading the paper to each other in bed; making up songs together; on long drives singing scores to Broadway shows. They'd begun this period already comparatively robust, because they'd programmed in focus on each other during the packed childrearing years. Throughout those they'd held their Wednesday and Saturday nights alone as sacrosanct, twice a week, sitting at a table in their local restaurant, remembering the point of being together.

Another couple reported that, after their first child's birth, appalled by the initial effect on their sex lives, they'd agreed to set an alarm a few times a week at 6 a.m. for sex. In their 60s they were still consciously making time for it, if slightly less frequently. I'd met them in the retirement phase of their lives happily renovating a small house together.

Barbara, a university administrator in her early 60s, had just asked her employer for a three-month sabbatical to drive across the US in a camper van with her ten-years-older husband, Bill, before they came to see me. Their only child had recently taken a job in California, with his wife and small child. They would end their adventure at his new house on the west coast. Barbara phoned for therapy: this could make or break them and they needed help to make it the former. Although Barbara made the approach to me, it was Bill's despair about their relationship that had shaken things up. He'd proposed the trip that had roused Barbara's alarm.

This was a couple, their first session made starkly clear, who had lost the memory of happiness together. Bill, older, was in a winding down phase Barbara had not yet reached. He felt the onset of the dependence they'd have on each other if they survived the years ahead. Perhaps, like on the TV series he'd seen as a youth, *Route 66*, where two mates adventured together across the country, away from the distraction of others, he and Barbara might recapture what they'd had in the beginning: eyes once again for each other.

He wasn't off base in his solution. If they were ever to reset their relationship they did need to revert their attention back to each other. But his radical solution, with no plan about how they'd behave towards each other, terrified the more earthbound Barbara, who imagined the other possibility: they'd feel trapped and step up their mutual antagonism.

Over the years they'd both lost the habit of intimate interaction. They'd become like ships in the night, except on weekends when they'd routinely visit their golf club and end up at dinner there with friends. And at the end of that night they'd routinely have sex. Their disengagement was clear in our early sessions. Bill seemed rather clueless when asked if he knew what Barbara, a university administrator, actually did at her job. Though she'd worked at the same university for over 25 years he had rarely met her workmates. For her part, Barbara said that after years of frustration she'd stopped asking Bill what went on at his law office. 'It was like when we used to ask our son at dinner "What happened at school today?" and he'd answer, "Nothing." So you just stop asking,' she ruefully reported.

'But we got on pretty well, didn't we, even so? Life got filled up, didn't it – we seemed to be very busy, weren't we?' she said, turning to Bill, in our first session. Bill looked sadly at her and nodded. When I asked what 'well' meant to him, Bill answered – after some probing – 'We didn't argue. We had our routines. We had fun with friends, did nice things together like our weekends at the club. You know. Mostly it was even, calm.' Barbara had sighed, a sigh I guessed of resignation, and agreed. What had filled their time, if not conversation or much activity between them I wondered? 'We had our work,' Barbara, the couple's more voluble spokesperson answered. 'I had my friends, I did yoga and Pilates and played tennis . . . Bill had his golf, his TV.' She glanced warily at Bill, who looked sheepish and they each went on to elaborate the details of the slow decline of engagement with each other that had turned into a polite and emotionally distant relationship, tolerated until Bill's retirement. Barbara's irritation was evident as she described Bill as 'just hanging out' – she glanced sadly at Bill, took a breath and admitted: 'I really feel guilty saying that, but even more guilty about what I felt when I'd see him "just pottering" – leaving projects unfinished. He'd put up shelves – they're still unpainted. He tore up his study carpet – there's still an exposed ugly wooden floor. I can't bear to look at it: it looks like an untreated wound. I felt guilty leaving him alone, but I had things to do. I was still working! I still had my life!' Bill pursed his lips. 'I was so glad when I'd come home and see that he'd been out, at the golf course, I can't tell you!'

The discomfort in the room was palpable and it was mostly emanating from Bill. He wasn't the passive depressive Barbara was describing, but a man with anger simmering just below his outwardly collected surface.

I asked Barbara, since Bill had retired, was there any shift in Bill that she had felt was positive or promising? There's a phrase sometimes used in therapy called 'problem saturation' – you get so preoccupied by seeing the problems that you're blinded to any positives. It was vital for them at this stage to find positives. Bill looked angry but also dampened, put down by Barbara. He also looked stranded – a portent of what each might in the years to come need: an ally so illness and ageing do not ambush them. What might turn this couple's narrative of disengagement around to make re-engagement towards kindness and care occur?

Barbara was stopped going down the well-worn track of what was wrong by the question of what, if anything, was right. 'It was very nice,' she began, some relief in her voice, 'to see that he started doing some routine tasks around the house. He was being helpful doing things he used to do, but, really, he had stopped doing pretty much after our kids were born. He took over the laundry. He did a lot of the shopping. He was good at tidying up. You know, this reminds me: we really had been more of a team when we were first together. Like we used to alternate cooking. That stopped years ago. He sometimes cooks meals now and I am so pleased when he does. Yeah, there's certainly more of things like that.'

She'd remembered they could be a team. They'd once been one and now they were beginning to be one again, but it hadn't been noticed. What else could be resurrected? Could they imagine relating again to each other as they'd once done when teamwork characterised them more? Barbara offered that she saw it on the Saturdays when they met up, after their separate golf games, with friends. There were glimmers then of the Bill she'd fallen for. Bill raised his eyebrow sardonically: 'You're not the only one.'

Bill's story was of feeling shocked and useless after retirement, and dismissed and rejected by Barbara, whose attention to her ongoing job and others reinforced his sense of uselessness. He'd thought she was kind, but was beginning to revise his notion: she was unkind to him, not trying, he said, to understand the wrench in his life retirement meant, being critical of his efforts, leaving him on his own. 'I didn't want to be alone.' Those words were said not angrily, but plangently. They were clear and heartfelt, and they contained an invitation to Barbara to be with him. This was the turning point in that session for the couple to emotionally connect. Barbara turned to him, eyes tearing, and with tenderness. Bill spoke gently. He'd stilled his anger, so he was in emotional control, and he'd used collaborative communication.

'That was why I came up with this idea: take you out of your job, hope you can see that would be a good thing, and then you'd spend time with me! I hope we can talk about how we could do that.' He was showing some signs of having mentalised: Barbara would need to think leaving her job would be good for her; he went on to invite her to think about how it could work for both of them, together. Now freed of her resentment towards him, Barbara heard things differently. It wasn't the 'mad' idea she'd originally thought. Now she was struck by the imagination and enterprise Bill's road trip proposal showed. To sign up to it they needed to learn how to interact safely together again. That was something they signed up to equally. Now they were beginning to add in wisdom about the crux dilemma in this period of their love: the importance of looking at each other positively and finding things they wanted to do together again, building the positive loops between them in that way.

To look at a typical episode, Bill described a recent Saturday, beginning with Barbara rising and doing yoga while he – annoyed, resentful – tried to sleep on. Barbara then had made the 'clipped' enquiry, 'Are you getting up? I'm making eggs,' and, without waiting for his answer, left the room.

Barbara described what happened next: 'Yes, I made the eggs as usual. We sat at the table and read the paper. He wasn't dressed or shaved. I had a tennis date, cleared the dishes and I left.'

Bill took over: 'And didn't say anything. We didn't talk. Silent breakfast. I asked where you were going–' Barbara interrupted, 'No, you didn't ask. You said: I guess you have a tennis thing. As you kept reading the paper. Didn't look up.' She turned to me, 'So I just left.' The day wore on in a similar fashion. When Barbara returned there was no greeting; the only cursory conversation was about arrangements for going to the club.

They drove in silence. But then there was a change of mood at dinner with the friends. When they came home, they had been laughing together and they ended up having sex.

So, when asked to describe each other, the Bill and the Barbara they remembered from before parenthood, they described kind, interesting, fun people who had shared a love of watching sport, of dancing, of films, of going out to restaurants, of visiting new places for weekends away. Barbara used to like hearing about Bill's office politics; Bill was once interested in what she did at the university. I asked if they missed that talk and time together. Of course, after putting themselves back into that time, reminiscing, they did.

Again, as with Rosie and Carol, behind each of the interactions that in Bill and Barbara's case had shown irritation and curtness on Barbara's part, and withdrawal and disinterest on Bill's, lay the fact that they missed each other, the people they'd once been. Put dramatically, they'd felt abandoned by the partner they'd bet on having. They now expressed their soft feelings. Their hard, defensive behaviours that had masked them had disappeared. Consequently, they heard each other, and the loops between them became positive and productive. 'I wish she'd greet me' and 'I wish he'd get up and join me, feel glad about having breakfast together' are collaborative ways of speaking. The session when these feelings were expressed made the lights come on in their eyes and as they turned to face each other their bodies softened, as their voices had done.

When we replayed these interactions, Bill started off. On seeing Barbara when he awoke, he stopped and thought about his feelings and his thoughts, ones that had made him resentful – 'she's up and abandoning me already!' However, in the replay, because he'd been taught and asked to do the steps of emotional regulation, that thought vanished with his anger. Then he was free to think other things – to begin to mentalise and to do so with compassion. He'd just reminded himself in therapy that he missed the Barbara who had energy, enjoyment and zest, and there she was, having already done yoga. 'Look at her,' was his new thought. 'It's admirable: up on a Saturday, already exercising!' In doing that he was also replacing the negative attribution of her yoga practice with a positive.

Replacing the rebuff – turning over in bed – was a new bid for a different interaction, one that was collaborative, inviting: 'You're amazing, up and out, and lively already! That's great.' He mimed painfully rolling over to rise, '. . . and now I will do what every bone and muscle in my body is saying to me "don't" – I am going to rouse myself so we can have breakfast together, if that's okay with you. Can you wait for me?' Bill used invitation, humour – self-deprecation about his being in bed. He'd softened things. The request – 'Can you wait for me?' – wasn't a demand, but an invitation to think about whether she could.

Miming being stopped in her yoga tracks, Barbara smiled brightly at Bill. 'Of course, I'll wait. That would be lovely!' She then leaned over and gave Bill a peck on his cheek. 'I have a tennis date afterwards, so I'll have to leave by 10. I worry about you being on your own and I don't want to make it worse – is that going to be okay?' Barbara has made a repair: 'I don't want to make it worse.' She's also showing she is open to his thoughts on how she might go on repairing: 'Is that okay?' In the therapy they began a virtuous cycle, replacing old, negative ones.

After meeting weekly with me for a few months they left on their trip with great optimism, with Spotify playlists and a list of films they wanted to watch on the trip together, to sustain them, for a wonderful adventure in this new phase of their shared life.

Mary, in my study of enduring happy couples, aged 90, wrote to me a year after her husband of 65 years had died: 'I miss him every day. After the menopause, with no fear of pregnancy, I enjoyed sex for the first time ever. I'd been afraid of pregnancy; I hadn't known about sex; I'd grown up in the 1920s and we married when I was 19 and he went off to war. I hardly knew him and I didn't know what to expect. Sex was scary and then a duty until the menopause. What a revelation! We raised daughters and things were okay, but we were so busy. But when he retired, we joined the bowls club and for the first time together we made great friends, all now sadly dead. I miss them too. Who knew that the years from 50 on would be the best of my life? But they were. We really got to know each other then.'

That last stage can be surprisingly loving and gratifying. In both of these accounts the couples did 'get to know each other', as Barbara and Bill did again, and Mary and her husband did for the first time. And for both, in doing so, they saw what was really good, positive and affirming about each other and about being together, and kept concentrating and building on that.

Friendship: Shifting loyalties

When I was seven my five-year-old-brother and I attended a summer day camp. We lived in a leafy suburb of New York in a neighbourhood filled with families like ours, replete with children our ages, but we were being sent to a camp where we knew no one and we'd be in different groups. It was scary. How I wished Patty, my next-door neighbour, or Ellen, my friend across the road, were attending with me. Alas, each were enrolled in different summer programmes. Happily, after a few tearful, recalcitrant days, my protests and fear abated. For I, like my brother and most of the other children, had by then found allies in my camp group. We had made friends.

At lunch all the groups sat communally under a large oak tree where we unpacked our lunch boxes and ate our sandwiches. But every day one single boy, the same boy, sat alone. He had large, golden-flecked eyes. I haven't forgotten those eyes because they pierced my seven-year-old heart. I saw in them sadness. Each day I felt helplessly compelled to focus on them, paralysed by wishing, but not knowing how, to help, hoping for a smile to relieve me and, I thought, him. He never smiled. And he always sat alone. Our ritual reports to our parents in answer to the daily 'what happened today at day camp?' question began to contain updates on Albert, updates that never varied. My mother's attempts to soothe never did: 'Maybe he has other friends . . . Maybe he's sad about something else . . . Maybe he isn't really sad at all.' He was alone. And was always alone. Albert became a concern, a puzzle to me about how he could go on, coming each day to camp, and yet remain friendless, because not to have friends, especially in the obvious company of everyone else having them, felt to me such a profoundly distressing state.

A seven-year-old does not have sophisticated tools for understanding her social world, so perhaps Albert was not in fact lonely. I might have been observing something else entirely. He might well have had a whole busload of friends outside day camp. He may have disdained us and have chosen to sit alone. But the point is that, whether or not I was accurate in my perception, my distress was underscoring the importance, the value of friendship. Even small children sense how negative friendlessness can be.

When James Taylor sang about having a friend, we all knew what he meant, didn't we? A friend is someone who knows you, who is there for you, as the sitcom theme tune has it. A friend is someone who has your back, especially in times of woe. But is that all? Is giving support, being there all that defines a friend? Most of you will have friends on Facebook: do you all support each other? A one-off encounter with someone might be 'friendly', but are you friends? Or doesn't friendship imply development, interactions over time, so much so that you might hang on to a friendship because of a shared history?

This chapter is going to look at the elements you should be mindful about within friendships, the elements that can make or break them: shared levels of commitment to time, attention, closeness and depth; the ability to flex the commitment if life changes make that necessary; managing envy and competition; and maintaining trust. We will focus on identifying those crucially potentially disruptive elements and then we'll see how, keeping them in mind, you can use your skills to turn things as positively as possible, or end relationships with clarity and dignity for both of you. But first we probably need to define friendship, which is a multi-layered thing, and, as we do, remind ourselves of the significance to our wellbeing of having friends, and why it's valuable to try to maintain those friendships that can sustain us and to keep them positive.

Defining friendship

Most people say good friendships are marked by good will and include kindness, supportiveness, respect and admiration; also equal commitment to each other's welfare, time, attention and focus on each other; and, finally and most importantly, honesty and trust. In fact studies show that honesty and trust are the ones men and women say are the most important. More than that, 'close friends' have further qualities. They support positive feelings; give guidance and advice, and emotional, physical and practical support; are the ones with whom you have open and sometimes challenging conversations, share confidences, activities and visits; and from whom you expect validation and acceptance. So, Ross, Rachel and company have got it right – friendships are about being there for you – and they are deeply important, and felt. As a recent article on the importance of making and keeping friends in the *Atlantic* magazine said in its title: 'It's Your Friends Who Break Your Heart'.

Friendships are also, it seems, marked by pleasure in each other's company. They're associated with happiness, feeling understood and knowing that you are liked – those are things that are part of what comprises life satisfaction. That's probably why a large US study found that both having friends that make you happy and having a large range of 'happy friends' who bring pleasure and good feelings about yourself is a predictor of your own happiness in the future. You're less likely to become depressed. The study suggested it can even help prevent you becoming obese. Good friendships are really powerful.

So, think of friendships as part of your health kit. For your wellbeing you need good, close friendships. We've already seen that loneliness is bad for our health. Well, having a strong social network is even more important for preventing certain killer diseases – in particular, strokes and heart attacks. It's more important than anything other than not smoking. The study that found that if you are in friendships that make you happy, you, yourself, are more likely to be happy suggests so much about the 'good life'. Think about having a friend who always brings you down: you probably do end up beginning to shy away from them or resent that friend wanting your time and attention. In fact, a study found that people's blood pressure went up when they were in the presence of friends who generated conflicted feelings in them, even when the conversations weren't conflictual. Then think about a friend who mostly makes you smile, or after you've spent time with them you've come away feeling somehow satisfied. Life filled with friends who enrich and enliven you is a life in which you feel replenished by your relationships.

Having a wide friendship network can even help your career: a wider network of people on whom you can call for support and who know, like and respect you means you are more likely to be able to call on that network both to help you in your work and to develop within it. Friends can even literally keep you alive. The more expansive your friendship network the more resilient you'll be under crisis; widows and widowers, for example, adjust to life after death much more easily and quickly, and even tend not to die so fast, if they have a network of friends on whom to depend. When I was a postgraduate student, I was part of a team working on how self-help groups help people adjust to life crises. Widowhood was one of these, death of a child another, and the third was the stressful transition to parenthood. Forming friendship links with others who'd undergone what you had was crucial to being able to move forward with your life in the first two examples, and adjust well in the third. In a society in which people are increasingly becoming or choosing to be single for much of their lives, and in which a good proportion do not have children, a network of friends forms the pool of people who can sustain you, especially in times of need, in the way family members were once expected to.

And there's more: the ability to make friends is a good sign. It seems that being able to make friends is a key indicator of relational capability – the whole focus of this book – that is, being skilful in interactions. Relational capability, you'll recall, is that ability that has been found to be the single most important factor in success in life. Think of Albert, the boy who opened this chapter. I was worried he couldn't make friends. If you're a parent you might be comforted when you see your child making friends and that's because the advantages of relational capability start early. Children who have friends are likely to be able to form nurturing relationships outside their families, something particularly important for those born into dysfunctional ones. Children who make friends are less likely to be bullied, and bullying can have lasting effects. Being able to make friends indicates you're able to get people to help, be on your side, and it signals that you're reliable and trustworthy in return. Being able to maintain friends protects you through life's vicissitudes. It brings you resources – friends are avenues for your own development. You can see it in your own children if you have them: they take on some of their interests and new skills through playing with their friends. If you know how to make and maintain friendships, it's because you have the ability through them to develop and to understand difference; friendships draw on skills needed for getting through tensions and differences. And if you have a good network of friends, you are more likely to surmount crises because you can call on them to help.

Friendships also have to navigate differences and that's an important plus. Think of your own friendships: it's likely that they began in similarities, but you became intrigued by their differences. Friendships bring children into worlds outside of their families and these are the first places where you experiment with being different. The first steps to mentalising begin in childhood, because friends are where a small child first encounters real differences in people. In friendship a child has to work out how to move through those differences they note when they begin to make friends and this is the necessary platform to the eventual mature ability to mentalise.

Problematic friendships

But having friends is not always simple. Friendships will vary in levels of depth and what they're for: are they for practical support, shared hobbies or intimate disclosures? Commitment to levels of depth, time and attention, and to shifts in those as life stages shift, are elements that can explode or certainly disturb a friendship.

What happens when expectations of each other as friends aren't shared? Different expectations can lead to real pain. You have a friend who makes you feel guilty because you don't have as much time for them as they seem to want you to give them. Friendship is clearly also about how much and what you commit to a particular person. Or you've got a friend who keeps letting you down. You make future plans to do something and they tell you casually that they're not going to be available after all. You feel crushed, but the friend seems to think your reaction is out of order. At the very least it's awkward when there isn't a good match, but even when there is, for many friendships these matches are likely to change as each of your life circumstances change. Have you ever had someone you thought was a close friend move and then hardly ever hear from them again? Or a friend has a child when you haven't and your circles of friends shift and you no longer do so much together? If the respective circumstances between you and a friend don't match, that can often lead to pain and disappointment.

Have you felt that maybe you should explicitly state or change the terms of a friendship so it's clear what you've committed to? If friendships are about relying on each other, for support – whether it's levels of disclosure or practical help – or availability for shared hobbies or times together, and then one of you changes, or doesn't share those expectations, that can feel like a bitter blow as well.

Yet another potentially disruptive element is envy and competition, which can rumble away, ready to disrupt even close friendships. You'll no doubt recognise from your own friendship history that your close friendships usually form over similarities – like love relationships, you'll have tended to meet people like you and you bond when you find things that are shared. But they can and do form across even radically different life circumstances. That's particularly so if the most important part of your identity is not about where you come from or what makes you like people who are from a background similar to yours, but about something unusual. Take, for instance, the Beth Harmon character in the Netflix TV series, *The Queen's Gambit*, whose core identity was 'I'm a champion chess player.' Her best friends cut across ages, nationalities, genders and most other sorts of experiences and qualities that more typically join friends together. But that identification can itself be the site of envy. Envy arises even in identical twins, as a recent account in another journal, *The Yale Review*, related, 'I can be a very generous sister . . .as long as I am winning.' The observation applies as well to the identification that happens in close friendships. It can also be set off by differences in friendships – why don't I have what that friend has? That indicates the other side of friendship: you'll be attracted, again, like love, to differences in people. So, whatever characterises your pool of friends you're going to have to manage differences once they emerge, most particularly when they emerge over expectations of the friendship or envy and competition.

And those expectations of support, understanding and pleasure in each other can also be undermined by the envy and competition that can spring from similarity. You can feel envy if your friend 'wins' or gets something you covet: why not you? If you are different, and that friend achieves something you wish you'd achieved, you can feel jealous. If you're similar you may compete. If you're such good friends, why does your friend need someone else – why are they choosing someone else to do something you'd particularly like to do with them? Or tell them something you thought should be meant only for your ears?

So, what does happen when the similarity that starts a friendship off turns sour? Trust is at the bottom of the mirroring phenomenon that's an essential part of bonding, that frisson of likeness that starts a friendship off, that a friend who is like me will understand what can hurt me. And vice-versa. When you do cultivate a friendship, trusting each other because you feel so understood – and the more you feel that the more likely the friendship can go more deeply – what happens when that very friend betrays your trust? Or feels you have betrayed theirs? When you feel really similar, you're more likely to trust in a friendship. You're more likely to deepen it. If trust is the singular marker of a friendship, the thing upon which you rely, then if it's broken, friendship's tender heart is also broken. Broken trust is a broken friendship.

If trust isn't maintained it will rock a friendship. The potentially most destructive element within friendships is deception, suspected deception, or actions that appear to undermine trust. If you don't have trust you can't feel secure or believe in all those things that studies have shown people nominate as identifiers of friendship. If you feel your trust in a friend is shaky, you might not take the risk of continuing that friendship, so being tuned in to establishing trust, and then perhaps knowing how to sever a friendship that no longer feels trusting, is another element of managing friendship. The use of good interactional skills will be critical here, because, as you've seen, it's good to have friendships, but they should have those critical qualities of trust, supportiveness and levels of commitment that make them good for you. Employing your skills will help you be aware of the signs of them faltering and then managing that. We're going to look at some examples of people in friendships in fact trying to manage these elements as they arise, using their skills, so you can get a picture of how you might do so yourself.

Commitment to adapt

What is a close friendship? Robin Dunbar, who is one of the world's chief researchers on friendship, defines closeness as trusting enough to disclose, have challenging conversations, be honest in their responses, and someone you trust to give the support you need when you most need it. They are 'reliable allies'. Dunbar also identified that you're likely to have 'circles' of friends, with as many as around 150 people in the outer ones, who aren't close but are still 'friends'. As you move in towards the centre, you'll have only a few, maybe even only one, whom you'd nominate as your 'closest'. If you have a domestic partner, they're likely to be one of those 'closest', and if you're a man that's more likely to be your only nominated one. If you're a woman you're more likely to have two or even more, but if you change jobs and neighbourhoods, if you start having children, have new partnerships or move to new places many of those nominated close friends are likely to change. And you'll realise that it's more likely that friendships drift and fade as your life circumstances change: that's how most friendships do end, not necessarily by choice but circumstance. However, even if ended that way there can be deep sorrow at their loss. That's where many potential tensions lie: how do you move through changes in commitment within friendship and in particular to its levels of closeness? You can feel especially upset as things change when the friendship is very treasured. Or you can prepare for it, negotiate ways through it with the friend, through making use of skills in having conversations about what the acceptable changes would be.

In my early 20s my best friend from university and I lived two streets away from each other, each in our own tiny bedsits, in lower Manhattan. Every day we'd phone each other to catch up. She was the person I'd want either to moan to about my then-boyfriend's latest stupid exploit, or to enthuse about the all-shiny, potentially flawless person perhaps replacing him, or to crow about a new work project, or to help me think through a problem, and to hear from her the same. A few times a week we'd cook for one another, essentially learning together in those first apartments how, and trying out new recipes – she was much more adept than I; mostly we ended up eating at hers. When I got into graduate school in Chicago, almost a thousand miles away, her mother, knowing how deep our friendship went, greeted the news with, first, 'Uh-oh', and then congratulations. Would our friendship continue with such depth? Clearly, we couldn't continue to share meals or the daily minutiae of our lives in a time when the internet did not exist and we lived within limited means, which precluded frequent long-distance phoning or meeting up.

We instead committed to other ways of preserving our intimate connection: our levels of disclosure remained the same. This wasn't something we had to say explicitly, but what happened more or less explicitly was when and how we would make time to connect with each other: when we would commit to visiting each other; when we would next phone each other; eventually how quickly we would reply to emails; and, presently, when we will do FaceTime. It is also true that as we have faced disappointments – trips cancelled, phone contact too sparse – we have each been very careful to consider the other's life circumstances and phrase our overtures about the difficult subject delicately: we've mentalised. We've communicated collaboratively. We've been honest and straightforward, and in the main have tried to be clear when we've felt disappointed, although I do remember her asking me a few times, 'Are you mad at me?' And then I would have to be clearer about how I felt: no, not 'mad', because I understood the complexity for her of trying to make contact, but, yes, I was disappointed. Over the years, we have established a more or less comfortable regime of contact within the changing geographical, economic and ultimately familial demands that have formed the constraints of our lives, making use of at first letters and phone, eventually the internet, and visits to both maintain and also reassure each other of the bonds we value. It has taken continued commitment to continuing contact, but we have made the adaptations our changing life circumstances have demanded. We speak, text, WhatsApp more now that we don't have children at home or the intense demands of high-pressure working lives. Each time over these years that we have related in whatever modality we have renewed our feelings of closeness, securing and reassuring each other: 'I'm there for you.'

Changing circumstances

Ed's story shows that sometimes, when life demands changes, you can't retain friendships, particularly if you don't have the skills to hold on to a friendship, even a valued one. I briefly saw Ed for therapy when he was depressed after he left university. It became clear to me that his difficulty lay in part with sharing with his close friends how he felt about their commitment to the depth of their friendships – how close they were, how much time they spent together, what they actually did together – and it stemmed from his refusal to amend what that could mean as their circumstances changed. Ed was having a rough time adjusting to life in London away from his university friends. He related to me a still bitter experience he'd had with his best friend from home when they'd left for university. Ed had not got the grades he wanted for his first-choice university and, reluctantly, he'd started at a different university, but he'd resisted making new friendships there because he'd resisted committing to staying. At first, he and friends from home had messaged each other frequently, posting photos on Instagram, apparently all rejoicing in their new lives. Ed knew his own posts looked and sounded false, but assumed – and that was the operative word, as he didn't really know – that anyone who was his real friend would have seen through his smokescreen and realised that 'Things were crap.' His best friend, Tim, messaged him daily for a few weeks and then only intermittently, while Ed doggedly messaged at least weekly, hurt at getting no replies until in anger and desolation he stopped.

So, when at Christmas the old group got together as if nothing had changed, and no one made reference to Ed's silence, Ed's rage at his friends, especially Tim, burgeoned. As people began to straggle out, a concerned Tim put his arm around Ed, enquiring, 'Hey, mate, what's wrong? You've been, like, mute all night? Is everything okay?' They were outside now, beginning their old, familiar walk to their respective houses and Ed, furious, turned on Tim. 'What's wrong!' he exclaimed in disbelief. 'What's wrong is you, as a friend. I message you, you don't reply. I have only the stuff you put out there for everyone to see: your great new life at uni. Nothing that's about us, about you and me. What kind of friend do you call yourself, anyway?'

Ed reported Tim's, probably baffling to him, reply: 'Well! I guess I call myself as good a friend as I ever was. I mean, we went off to uni, to different places. You're at yours and it looked okay. Anyway, if I don't message it means I'm busy. Aren't you? I'm at uni. You're at uni. We've got things to do. We've got classes. We've got studying. We've got uni friends. I mean, what's the deal here? What kind of friend do you think *you* are?' Ed stalked off angrily. He'd persisted in his view of friendship, one that did not allow for their different notions of how it might evolve – or not.

You can see in this description of how they were interacting that Ed employed none of the interactional skills he would have needed to try to preserve something with Tim, or even to try to understand what was behind the gap between them. He hadn't emotionally managed himself when he'd confronted Tim. He'd failed to mentalise. Tim, he believed, should have felt and behaved just as Ed had felt and would have acted. He'd been confrontational rather than collaborative. There was no question that he'd been consumed by misery and that had blotted out any attempt to imagine Tim's life as different to his; he was only seeing Tim's actions as a comment on how little Tim must have valued his friendship. When you're in extremis, as Ed had been, the skills can be a bridge too far. But if that happens, when something like a valuable friendship in conflict might be injured by your failure to be skilful, the skill of 'repairing' afterwards can be the way to save things.

153

Unfortunately, Ed wasn't very interested in preserving friendships, at least not enough to stay in therapy and work at how he might have tried and might do things differently in the future, so repairs did not take place. In fact had he been able to use the skill of emotional regulation to put himself into a calm and thoughtful state instead of a distressed one each time he thought of Tim, he might then have been able to reflect on things not just from his own miserable perspective, but also from Tim's, which would have been – after the fact, but still valuable – mentalising. Then he might have felt compassion for Tim and been able to offer an olive branch: 'I realise now how you must have felt that night after the pub. I really lit into you and I'm sorry for that. That was out of order. I wasn't in a good place and I was mixed up, though that's no excuse for behaving the way I did, of course. Up to you, but if you wanted to I'd like to meet up; Am home for Easter if you are . . .' That's a repair which is an apology both for the manner ('no excuse for behaving'; 'I really lit into you and I'm sorry for that') and also for the content ('I was mixed up'). It used invitational language: 'Up to you, but if you wanted to . . .') and lots of speaking from his heart, owning his wishes without assuming anything about Tim ('Up to you . . . I'd like to meet up').

As life stages shift

Friendships end more usually through drift, as changes in life circumstances create situations too difficult to bridge. But sometimes it is possible to manoeuvre a friendship skilfully through life's changes, as my university friend and I did, to compassionately appreciate differences and manage them, as the story of Rebecca and Carolyn shows. It's a story of how Rebecca was able to step into Carolyn's despair over their difference, and reassure her, so the friendship could carry on.

154

Rebecca was an interviewee in the study I carried out on enduring happy couples. She talked about how over the course of her marriage she found time opening and closing for friendships, and that being married and having kids had over the years shaped for her the kinds of friends she'd made. Her closest friends during the period her children were around had been women with children. Both before having kids and after they'd left she'd made many more friends with women who'd never had kids. One of her closest friends at the time of the interview was Carolyn, who had chosen not to become a mother.

They'd met as new hires at their company. They'd recognised in each other a shared sense of style, humour and alienation from the mainstream of their department's tastes. When they'd first become friendly Rebecca's two children, teenagers, were still living at home. Rebecca then remembers tiptoeing around details that involved her children, tailoring their friendship around their difference, meeting outside work sparsely. However, as Rebecca's children's lives became more distant and separate the friendship expanded, and the strain of keeping things apart disappeared. Ten years into their friendship, Rebecca, like several other of Carolyn's friends, had her first grandchild and the unwelcome difference re-emerged like a pesky sore.

One day, meeting up at a cafe on the banks of a river, watching toddlers play nearby, Carolyn picked at the sore. She'd been darting glances at the children running and laughing, shrieking; theirs, and equally their mothers', cries of delight impossible to ignore. 'You have joy in your grandchildren . . .' She looked away from the children and at Rebecca. 'I feel like I felt when all my friends were having children. I'm left out again . . . But I find myself caring more now than I did then. Then I was sure I didn't want kids. Now . . .?' She shook her head ruefully. 'Now I find myself thinking: should I have been so sure?'

Carolyn slumped, Rebecca thought, by sadness, and went on. 'You know, it used to be difficult to be in a group when friends talked about their children and I was the one who didn't have any.' Her tone grew firm as she became the Carolyn of old. 'But because I knew that I didn't want them, I felt clear. So, I would mostly be cross they were insensitive about my lack of interest and being the outsider when they went on and on . . . I wasn't on the defensive. It was just annoying.'

She seemed to hear the small children again. 'But now I am in the midst of people talking about their grandchildren and their grown-up kids, I find I don't feel the same way. Now I ask myself if I made the right choice.' She sighed. 'I am sad as I look at what lies ahead and what I ended up not having.'

As Carolyn spoke Rebecca felt, at first, sadness, compassion – loss and regret were easy to feel for anyone, but a finger of irritation began to show itself. Were they back in the realm of Rebecca stifling stories of grandchildren just as she had with stories of her children? How was that fair? Why shouldn't Carolyn be the bigger person here? One of the reasons Carolyn had decided not to have children was because her own mother had not been a good parent, but Rebecca thought that was a stupid reason. Couldn't she see she'd end up regretting it? These were the sorts of feelings she'd never express to Carolyn, but the sorts of things other mothers would whisper among themselves about friends without kids: 'Why didn't they think more clearly?. . . Couldn't they see what they'd be missing?' The old familiar 'us' versus 'them' divide that had been so toxic for friendships when all of them were starting out with families – or not. Did it have to come up again, making her feel bad and judgemental and 'different' from her friend again?

The point here in her story is that it is sometimes difficult to summon up the necessary compassion for a valued friend – but not impossible. Rebecca tried. She stopped herself –labelled what was going on for her. In doing that she was inadvertently calmer rather than irritated. She was emotionally regulating. She realised that her irritation was a knee-jerk reflex from a long time ago. Carolyn had her reasons and they were strongly felt. That's the point: feel for her, not for how you would feel or have felt back then. Carolyn now was feeling a real regret for the prospect of being alone, but it did not mean – as it would have done for Rebecca – that she'd regretted her choice, but rather its unfortunate and sad repercussion. That was mentalising.

So, she was able to show Carolyn not just empathy but understanding of what it would mean to her. She was ready to offer her thoughts in a collaborative way, invitingly, from her own perspective, not second-guessing, but conveying fellow feeling, making what she said safe to hear. 'I can begin to imagine . . .' she murmured, then added, ' For what that's worth,' to convey that she knew she was speaking from the privileged position of having children who might ease loneliness towards the end of life, hoping Carolyn would understand the addition of 'for what it's worth' was the best she could come up with, across the bitter motherhood/sisterhood divide, to say, 'I don't judge you. I feel for you.'

Then she reassured her: 'I can try to feel what you're feeling. Of course, I can only begin to imagine, but our friendship is very important to me and what I want to say is that if you can put up with the times I will have to be with my grandchildren, I will be there for you. Yes, there's now an incursion into my time that wasn't there before they were born. Yes, I might be away on weekends when before we would have gone out together. But, believe me, it's not like when I had kids – I'm sure you get that. I adore them but they aren't filling my life. Even if I wanted them to, my kids and their partners don't want that! At this point in my life, as in yours, friendships are even more important. We need each other.'

Carolyn took Rebecca's hand, squeezing it in gratitude. The difference had been managed and the friendship had been healed, as it had been in the past, when their levels of closeness had fluctuated and they had adapted.

Commitment to closeness

Friends do not always share an equal desire for closeness. Navigating a comfortable level for both can be tricky; it also can lead to the friendship's ending. In Ruth's case, as in Ed's, the friendship ended, but at least it did so with more dignity and it gave Maryam, even if it was at a later point, the chance to understand what the difficulty in carrying it on had been. That was because Ruth used her skills, showing that she had tried to understand Maryam's perspective; had controlled her own seething feelings of irritation; and had invited Maryam to understand her perspective. She had avoided apportioning blame and had shown compassion towards Maryam.

Ruth is a psychiatrist I saw when she was going through fertility treatment and in consequence suffering depression. Although that was the main issue, a recurring drama for a few sessions was her friendship with a younger colleague, Maryam, who was from a different culture. Ruth was Jewish British, married and trying for a baby. Maryam was British-born Somali and Muslim, and, from what Ruth had gleaned, had turned down numerous arranged marriage propositions and was anomalous in her family: the only unmarried sibling and the only highly trained professional. The gap in their respective life situations that had led to what Ruth felt was a disturbing imbalance in expectations about their relationship had not been a problem while their friendship had been confined to work. There they'd resonated with the way each had worked with the therapy group they had co-run at an outpatient clinic for a largely immigrant Somali community. They'd established a shared set of values; respect for each other's compassion and insights. They'd found shared humour; they'd come to depend on each other to unburden clinical and administrative frustrations, and to rely on each other to share clinical burdens. It had been an engaging, supportive, stimulating – and friendly – clinical partnership.

Over lunch they'd offer bits of personal information, anecdotes. Ruth remembers feeling at that point that she'd begun to hold back, as soon she realised how different their situations were. It hadn't really seemed to resonate with Maryam when Ruth would offer stories about her husband, and she'd definitely shut down, changing the subject, on the one occasion Ruth had mentioned having fertility treatment. 'It's not a relationship I should carry on outside work,' she'd concluded, a bit sorrowfully. But Maryam obviously thought otherwise. Soon, invitations to go out to dinner began, but they were always last minute, when surely it was obvious that Ruth couldn't go as she was married and her husband was expecting her at home? Isn't that something Maryam should have assumed? Or had Ruth just not understood Maryam?

Ruth's polite refusals didn't stem the tide of Maryam's social invitations, so finally, Ruth did agree to something. In retrospect, she felt she'd chosen exactly the wrong event, a family party, but as it was on a weekend when in fact she was free, she would have felt ungracious if she had turned it down. Maryam's family were warm and engaging, but she was truly alarmed by the fact that they'd all heard about her: she was, they seemed to think, one of Maryam's most intimate friends and Ruth had seemed to confirm it, she realised, by being there, at Maryam's niece's

159

birthday. She wanted to kick herself, but she was also supremely irritated at Maryam. What was the matter with her that she couldn't see that Ruth did not, could not, share Maryam's expectation of closeness? Yes, they were in very different life circumstances. Was there also a cultural contribution to their different expectations? For instance, was the fact that Ruth was married not a factor in Maryam's expectation of a friendship between two women? She was tired now of darting and diving and she needed to face Maryam to try to explain why she couldn't commit to their friendship. So she worked out what she would say, and how she would be when she said it, and this is what she said happened.

She took a breath to calm herself, something, in fact, she'd already learned in cultivating a productive 'bedside manner' with recalcitrant patients. 'I'm really sorry,' she began firmly this time, without the pleading tone she'd formerly always used in an attempt to blunt any sense of rejection Maryam might have had. This time her task was to explain, clearly, in a way she hoped Maryam would be able to hear. She'd chosen her words to be respectful and as kind as she could be, but also to be clear. She thought she had an understanding of Maryam, that she was lonely, had misinterpreted the work comradery as friendship, had maybe a different idea of what being married meant for availability. In any case, she felt she had put herself into Maryam's shoes with empathy: she'd mentalised. She believed that mentalisation had led to her forming her overture to Maryam in a truly collaborative way, so Maryam would hear her and come to understand. She spoke with warmth, especially looking at Maryam's innocently expectant face.

'I want to be clear with you, Maryam, so you'll understand. I think – correct me if I'm wrong – you might have felt bad because I keep refusing time outside work with you, and I don't want you to feel bad about that, though I can surely understand if you have felt that way. You see, of course, we're really in different stages in life. Our situations mean we have different needs and different demands on us. I think if you do ever have a partner maybe you'll see – I don't know. But for me, I have a husband. That means, for me, anyway, I can't just take off to be with a friend. We have certain routines, like being home to eat together. I have the feeling that maybe it's different for you, but it means that every time I say I can't go out, I feel like I'm letting you down, and then I feel irritated. I don't need our friendship to be the way you do, to spend that time together, for instance. I'm not at a point in my life when I am just, I don't know, available. I don't need that. Or anyway, that's what it feels like to me. Maybe that's not right, but the bottom line is I don't think I can be the kind of friend you seem to need.'

Ruth's mentalising had assumed, perhaps inaccurately, that Maryam's experience of, or at least observation of, women like Ruth, married professionals, would mean she should have been able to understand what Ruth was trying to convey about the constraints of being married. Her explanation to Maryam was based on that assumption. She felt that she was being clear and also compassionate, acknowledging that Maryam might have felt hurt and allowed that she, Ruth, might be wrong in her assumptions. Her language was tentative and by saying she wanted to be clear so Maryam would understand she invited Maryam to try thinking about it from her perspective. In all those ways she'd been collaborative.

However, Maryam's response – 'I wonder what your *other* friends think of your need to be with your husband all the time?' – suggested that Ruth was wrong about her. Ruth wondered if maybe the issue was Ruth's own ignorance about their cultural differences: maybe Maryam, indeed, did have very different ideas about marriage and friendship, and how they intersect, and if so, Ruth would have really missed the point. Either way, she found

Maryam's response upsetting. Ruth was left feeling both that she'd hurt Maryam and also that she'd probably misunderstood Maryam fundamentally. But as she talked about it with me, she was comforted in establishing that what was important was that she'd done it in the way she had – with clarity and charity and she hoped that Maryam could at least sense that. She couldn't know if she'd done it perfectly clearly, she didn't know enough about Maryam, but she'd tried her best, and perhaps because of the way she'd done it, one day Maryam would be able to reflect and understand.

Commitment to balance

Sometimes clear differences in expectations mean those differences do have to become explicit, so you can know whether you share the same meanings about your friendship. Either new terms are mutually, if sometimes uneasily, agreed upon or the friendship ends. Both parties need to commit to how much and what each one gives to a friendship, so there is a sense of appropriate reciprocity or balance. Otherwise, it feels burdensome on one side or on the other, which is humiliating and erodes the trust, pleasure and goodwill essential to healthy friendship. The question is what is comfortably reciprocal for each person, although valued contributions may be hidden and observers might only be able to see the outward ones in any given friendship.

Steven and Ross's friendship appeared very unequal. Steven, a vibrant, high-octane businessman I'd met and become friendly with when he'd engaged me to do some coaching at his company, had periodically hauled Ross and his family out of financial holes and persistently brought them into his large circle of high-powered friends, who had found little in common with the uncommunicative and charmless Ross. They'd wondered what Ross brought to Steven's table, beyond history

– they'd been university mates – and Steven's loyalty. When Ross died prematurely Steven articulated through his grief what Ross's deep contribution to his life had been: acceptance, peace, kindness and tranquillity. Rather than expectations from Ross, Steven's financial gifts to Ross had been tokens of his love. Ross had given Steven what the psychologist Carl Rogers would call 'unconditional positive regard': appreciation with no strings attached. That was hidden, but deep, and had made their friendship feel balanced to them both. Mike's story, on the other hand, shows how Mike used skills to manage very unequal expectations that emerged within a relationship.

In for him a consciously charitable role, Mike, a former star rugby player, engaged in an online friendship with a young fan who came from a deprived background and who had followed him on social media. After a number of exchanges, Mike thought he could be helpful to this young man by introducing him to a charity Mike sponsored. The fan began volunteer work there and they met in person when Mike gave a talk to the staff, with the fan going out with Mike and a group for a drink afterwards. He must at that point have followed him home, because he began slipping notes through the door, including one addressed to Mike's wife, with offers to help around the house. At that point Mike felt the line had definitely been crossed and he wanted to end the relationship. This was a relationship that, because there had not been clarity from the start, had become totally unbalanced. The fan had thought it was a friendship in which Mike would be his hero and he'd be elevated into Mike's intimate life. Mike had thought he was helping someone, lifting him into doing 'good works', which is why he'd introduced him to the charity. For him it had been a mentoring relationship, but clearly the fan thought it was more than that. Mike was in a quandary: how could he retreat without damaging an already fragile person? This was how he presented his dilemma to me, for I'd been seeing Mike and his wife in therapy, and we had a session to figure out what he could do.

Mike wanted to reassure himself of two things: that he would make clear that the fan would not think Mike was his emotional supporter, but also that the fan did have sources of support that were more appropriate for him. Mike's goal was to sever the relationship compassionately. To do this he had to mentalise as best he could into the fan's life: how might the fan feel when Mike withdrew? We discussed what he knew about him. Mike knew he was fragile. He knew from conversations he'd had with him that the fan attended a regular support group for people with a history of addiction. He also knew that the fan had an older brother whom he'd turned to for help in the past. That is, there were other people, Mike could be reassured, who were more appropriate supports for the young fan. The fan would be hurt, but he could, in theory, use the supports to help him manage it.

Then we thought about what Mike could say to sever things. We thought about Mike talking directly to the fan, but there was no way, Mike felt, that this young man would understand that they weren't really 'friends', and this wasn't helped by the fact that Mike had not been clear about how he saw the relationship and had not set boundaries. Mike had invited him to the charity, invited him along for drinks, blurring the lines for a vulnerable, unsophisticated young person. To say, directly, 'This is not a friendship. I was only trying to introduce you to something that might be helpful to you,' would only have been hurtful and unproductive. However, sometimes actions can be clearer and kinder, and we felt they might be a compassionate way get Mike's position across to the young man. So in this case, after the mentalising, which only came about because in therapy Mike had brought in his distress, had labelled it in session, and used the therapy session to calm himself so he could think his way to mentalising, came collaborative communication that didn't involve words but compassion and clarity of actions. Clarity in this case came from consistency: Mike did not waver. He stayed off social media and avoided visiting his charity for as long as it took to be sure his message had been clear.

Most of their relationship had been conducted online, through Mike's social media presence, so Mike took himself off social media for a while. The younger man had developed a daily habit of turning to Mike's posts. Without them the relationship could slowly fade. Mike gambled, correctly as it happened, that the fan would then stop coming to his house, which was both a relief and a possible sign that he was getting the message. Contact that Mike could control diminished, until it vanished completely. Mike stayed away from visiting his charity for months in case he met the fan when he turned up. In simple learning theory terms – that is, how do people learn things? – this is called 'extinction'. You stop doing something, over and over, consistently, in response to someone, and the person gradually learns not to expect it. His own behaviour changes in accordance. Soon the fan's posts diminished and finally stopped, as did his turning up at the charity, a fact that saddened Mike. He'd done what he described as 'gentle cold-shouldering'. Sad, but relieved, Mike felt wiser about the power of celebrity and the choices he makes that result from it.

When life situations mismatch too greatly, needs and expectations of closeness, of what can be shared – investment of time, energy, interest in each other – may fail to mesh. Imbalances often occur when one friend has more time and space for conducting the friendship than the other who, for instance, doesn't have children, or a demanding job, or doesn't have other close friends or family claiming time and loyalty, or is lonelier because they're not living with someone while the other friend has a partner. An issue close to the one of balance of expectations in friendships is being clear and establishing the boundaries of the friendship: what can be expected of you in terms of your time, energy and interest? If you try to set a boundary, such as 'I can't go out on weeknights and every Saturday is sacrosanct for my partner,' but your friend is starving for your company, boundary-setting is problematic, because the balance is so off. Being clear about what you are prepared to, and can, give, especially when life circumstances are different, would change the balance, maintaining the friendship if that friend understands, adapts and finds other friends who match better.

Competition and envy

The fault lines that come from competition and envy are deep. You stop sharing the understandings that underly, support and give life to the friendship. Competition means assumptions about shared support are up for question: are we friends most of all or is winning the thing? Envy can even come from the pleasures of similarity, because if one friend confidently takes ownership of a particular shared quality the other friend may resent it – they may share the quality but not an understanding of what it means to each of them. The deepest cut to friendship is when there is deceit, because trust is friendship's topmost quality.

Competition and envy in friendships are often the currency of drama. Fiction loves to depict envy, usually between women friends (think about films like *All About Eve* or *Single White Female*), while movies about male friendship are often driven by competition (for example *Chariots of Fire*). Envy tends to be portrayed as corrupting, but competition can be healthy, although work competition can destroy a work friendship. Each state causes discomfort at the very least, throwing up problems over just how honest or truthful friends can be with each other. But, as Susie Orbach and Luise Eichenbaum point out in their book celebrating their own friendship, *Bittersweet*, it doesn't have to lead to destruction but can, in theory, be acknowledged and managed. That's because, they maintain, it's a product of similarity and admiration, both of which are healthy parts of friendship.

The story of Alison's management of Peggy's envy shows how sensitive handling of it, through using the key interactional skills, can maintain a relationship that was difficult. Sometimes friendships need to be maintained rather than ditched for a host of reasons. In Alison's case it was about maintaining wider family relations. The frictions created by sometimes inevitable envy or competition might then have to be managed, but, as Alison shows in the following account, it is possible.

I saw Alison for therapy after the death of her sister, but during the course of therapy she kept bringing up painful episodes with an old friend, Peggy. They built to a story of recurring envy – Peggy's of Alison – with Alison recurringly blindsided by it. She would have ended the friendship, she maintained, but now there was no choice: their children had recently married each other. Alison was so distressed after one family gathering that we turned our focus away from her grief over her sister and towards how to respond to Peggy to minimise hurt to them both, hers from Peggy's barbs and Peggy's from envy.

They met as flatmates in a large flatshare while in their first serious jobs – a relatively carefree time in which there were parties, a shared friendship group, and experiences for both of love and heartbreak. Alison married first and moved away;

167

Peggy had an unfortunate love affair with a married man who moved with his family to the US, leaving her pregnant. Peggy never married. Alison had two sons, divorced after 20 years and has been in a happy 'living-apart-together' partnership for the past five years. She's had two long-lived relationships, while Peggy has never had another romantic relationship. Moreover, the baleful comparison in which Peggy feels inferior extends to work. While she once held a significant position in local government, Peggy resigned in high dudgeon over differences with colleagues. She now works from home, alone, running an online business, and her embattled relationship with her doggedly loyal daughter is her main social tie. Meanwhile Alison became, and remains, a head teacher, happy in her work and respected by her colleagues, many of whom are friends. Peggy knows this and knows that Alison appears to have loyal, enduring and mostly conflict-free friendships, while Peggy has a history of broken ones. Alison is now careful not to bring friends around when Peggy visits: she's endured too many rude and awkward episodes. When Peggy visits Alison's partner stays away. Alison has come to dread being with Peggy.

However, a family event was coming up, so we used that as a test case for Alison to rehearse how she could use mentalisation about Peggy, mentalisation from what she thought she knew about Peggy. The root of Peggy's sense of deprivation was probably her lonely and unhappy childhood in which sibling rivalry was rife. Alison knew Peggy's sniping and ungenerous behaviour was provoked when she saw others' happiness and that Alison's life of plenty provoked those feelings. She also realised that Peggy's own lack of relating skills disabled her – she couldn't even identify envy in herself, let alone manage it. Thinking of Peggy in this way could help shape her responses, so she would be more likely to get better responses from Peggy, and it might also shield her from Peggy. It was clear that at the very least Peggy aroused Alison's irritation, rising to rage at its worst. To a degree Alison had already been emotionally regulating in their encounters and when she had managed not to utter angry words, so often on the tip of her tongue with Peggy, they'd avoided flare-ups and not disturbed their children. She knew she could do it, but it would take a lot of heavy lifting on her part.

Through role plays, Alison rehearsed emotional regulation, plugging in her more compassionate thoughts about Peggy in mentalising, and trying out phrases that would avoid retaliation. We worked to find the points of shared objectives, such as being joint family members, or other shared interests. Peggy would surely snipe at decorations in the house. She'd almost definitely make snide insinuations about Alison's partner. We played out a few scenes with me flinging gentle insults at Alison to prepare her. Alison did recognise that she felt sorry for Peggy and thinking of her as 'disabled' relationally helped Alison step up to the role of greater expert, the position of 'conductor' to ensure the relating went in a positive direction.

Alison came back for a session with me following the family lunch, held in her reportedly glorious garden. Although the weather had been perfect and their children in good spirits, Alison noticed Peggy had continually undermined her throughout the day, sometimes subtly, from the food served – 'Oh, Alison, what a palaver! It's just family. I don't know why you go to all this bother!' – to the way she drove, on collecting Peggy from the station – 'Oh, Alison, you always were a terrible driver! We used to joke about how it's like taking your life in your hands when you get in a car with Alison. You might end up anywhere, because she has absolutely no sense of direction!' Then, after lunch, as they and the children strolled around Alison's prized garden, Peggy's digs became more overt. Amidst coos of approval from the others, Peggy commented, sourly, 'Dear, oh dear! Who does the weeding!' like a pinprick through Alison's beaming pride. Disturbed, she recognised she was about to fire back, bit her tongue, relaxed her body, did her calming breaths and regarded Peggy's small form. Pathetic, she looked, with the emphasis on 'pathos', not meriting the energy of anger, because she was too sad a figure for that. 'You know I learned something: you can actually feel compassionate for someone without liking them,' Alison reported. She had emotionally regulated. She was in a position to think of Peggy in that way.

Contemplating the pathetic woman before her, in Alison's glorious garden, Alison herself radiant from the admiration of her children, the image of Peggy returning to a dingy, lonely home in just a short while, shifted everything. Peggy's barb, hanging in the air, seemed ridiculous. Peggy was a gardener, tending with love and interest her own small garden. Sharing gardening tips had, over the years, even been one of their few safe topics. She'd mentalised and was able to form her response into a collaborative one.

'You are of course an expert gardener,' Alison began. This was the language of collaboration – 'we are both gardeners' – and generosity – 'I recognise your specialness.' She described turning to Peggy and their children, conveying an openness to them all, metaphorically making a family embrace, then laughing in self-deprecation as she said, 'Because, hmm, weeds, you really can't get on top of them, but it sure doesn't help if you try with these on!' She removed her very scratched spectacles and gazed at them comically. Humour brings people together, and self-deprecation – Alison's mocking of herself, her scratched glasses – was her humorous attempt to equalise power and status. Her approach worked and the day proceeded without further incident. Alison felt relieved and equipped for their next encounter.

When trust is broken

However, outright duplicity usually means trust, that quality people rate most highly for friendship, has been broken, as the story of Jamie shows us. Sometimes harmful friendships need to end. Friendship always risks the cruelty of outright rejection. 'I don't want to be your friend anymore,' said in one way or another, explicitly or implicitly, inflicts a tender and bruising cut. It's the playground taunt, a sharp stab that remains ever painful. Many of the stories in *Dumped*, a collection of accounts of women whose friendships ended, boil down to primitive cries of 'Why?!' It's different if you're given a reason for the breakup, which you can agree with or not, but not knowing why a friendship has ended can cause intense anxiety about yourself. Ghosting is, indeed, cruel, but some friendships do need to end. Duplicity, breaking faith and trust litter the stories of broken friendships in *Dumped*. Once trust is gone friendship's central spoke needs repairing or the proverbial wheels won't ever work again, but often it's beyond saving when a friend breaks the most tender bonds of trust within a friendship.

That was the case for Jamie. Her friend was the proverbial 'other woman' in her husband's infidelity. Friendships are more dispensable than a couple relationship when infidelity is the case. Research shows that infidelity itself does not automatically lead to a couple's break-up, although it may begin a decline that ends in that. That's because, unlike in a friendship, there are so many mutual investments and concerns a couple shares that ending the relationship is much more complex than ending a friendship.

I saw Jamie when I was coaching her at her workplace a few years after she and her husband, Bob, had repaired their own relationship after his infidelity. Jamie showed how you can choose to end a friendship, but do so skilfully, with clarity of communication, a modicum of compassionate mentalising, and certainly cool emotional regulation. Her story came out in the

171

course of our work, repairing a breakdown in trust between her and a female colleague. What did not get repaired after her husband's affair was her friendship with the woman with whom he'd been unfaithful. That woman was someone who had apparently so identified with her that she had envied and wanted most what Jamie had: Jamie's stable and happy relationship – with Jamie's husband.

Soon after Jamie's college roommate, Sue, who had lived in a different part of the country, got divorced, she came to stay with Jamie and Bob for a long weekend. Sue had once been Jamie's most treasured friend, the friend she'd met at university with whom she'd felt most comfortable, whose opinions had most resonated with hers. As roommates they'd swapped clothes and books, and had comfortably shared the small bedroom their university dormitory had allotted them. That was how things had gone until after one long vacation Sue got together with the boy from home she'd eventually married. From then on she was gone most weekends and by their third year had moved off campus to live with him. Jamie simply couldn't stand him and the two friends, still affectionate, had drifted apart. Still, they'd remained in touch enough for Sue to contact Jamie to let her know about her divorce and to ask to see her again.

They took long walks during the day in which Sue poured out her heart and then, in the evenings, with Bob, they enjoyed warm, drunken meals. Bob had never much liked Sue before, but this time everyone got along. Sue was looser and more fun: she was the old Sue, Jamie's wonderful friend, now that she wasn't with the husband no one had liked. Jamie and Bob owned a boat, and in her divorce settlement Sue had aquired a cottage on the coast not very far from where they'd occasionally sail. So, during one of their drunken meals they made vague plans to take the boat up the coast and meet up at Sue's cottage. They never did.

Bob had frequently sailed on his own, so Jamie didn't think much of the fact that he was sailing a lot more that summer than ever before. But later in the season, rummaging around down below deck on their boat, Jamie found a flowery bright scarf under a pile of waterproofs. She immediately recognised it. Sue had worn that scarf on the weekend she'd spent with them, so that was how Jamie discovered that Sue and Bob had been having an affair all summer, ever since Sue's visit. In that moment it dawned on her that Sue had envied what she'd seen Jamie had; that she must have felt on some level, even if not consciously, that she could just take what Jamie had. Meanwhile, Jamie imagined that Bob might have fallen for Sue for some of the same reasons he'd fallen for Jamie, but in Sue he had seen their shared qualities afresh. By Sue taking Jamie's place in Bob's bed, it chillingly seemed to suggest they were interchangeable. Sue had moved in on Jamie's life out of envy, as a competitor.

So ended their friendship. For Jamie there was no turning back. Sue had crossed an uncrossable friendship line. Jamie, mentalising adeptly, was clear about her own feelings and the rationale for them. She didn't have the full flow of empathy she'd once had for Sue, but nevertheless stepped into her world, the world of a desperate, even pitiable, woman. When in the grip of desperation friendships were meaning*less* to Sue, but they were meaning*ful*, important and required loyalty for Jamie. Eventually when her rage had gone cold, she had done her emotional regulation, but her anger and contempt remained. The reflection that Jamie was able to do once she had calmed her rage was cool and rational. That rationality in turn, led to her being able to communicate constructively – collaboratively also, in the sense that she could say what she needed to say clearly and briefly in a way that Sue could understand and hear precisely. At that point Jamie thought that to communicate dispassionately would be constructive, much more so than showing hot emotion, so Sue could hear her message and not mistake her meaning. So Jamie communicated to Sue both concisely and with crystal clarity.

She wrote a curt, crisp letter to her: 'I am sorry you must have felt either desperate, or maybe entitled, or something I do not yet understand, but cannot in any case excuse, to have come into my life again and then to take what was not yours – my husband – from it. Your actions with my husband – not your husband, mine, I seek to remind you – mean the end of our friendship. Bob and I will work out what our marriage can mean. It's our marriage and you will not be, and never should have been, part of it. Sadly, I am driven to conclude that I must tell you not to contact me ever again. You will certainly never again be part of my life. Bob will himself, he tells me, make plain to you not to contact him either, but that is for him to do. I'm sure you understand that you and I are through.' Her marriage and its repair was not Sue's story to hear. This was, Jamie made clear, about their friendship, and it was over.

Repairs needed

Friendships that falter can be reset. Friendships that are broken at one point don't have to end completely but can be repaired, even if something as delicate as trust seems to have been broken. Chrissie and Sid's friendship is a story about that.

They met when Chrissie, an economist, advised Sid, a business consultant, on a project Sid's firm was developing. They ended up publishing a paper together and Chrissie became a permanent consultant to Sid's team. Their work partnership was seamless and stimulating; going out for drinks after long workdays they found they had interests in common, a shared sense of humour, and a similar upbringing and take on family life. They became friends outside work, their partners getting on, the foursome now a group. 'Do you fancy writing a book together?' Sid suggested to Chrissie one day. She jumped at the chance: she'd never imagined she could get an agent and put out a book – she was too junior to even contemplate such a thing! But Sid was already a pundit, a recognised expert, with an agent and three books already out there in the business market. This book would be different, for a wider audience: the general public.

Sid's agent sold their 'very exciting' proposal easily and the co-authors, with equal advances for a book with initially equally authored chapters, were off. But at that very point Sid took on a bigger project: changing jobs, running a bigger company. He just wasn't available. Chrissie, teaching part-time at a university and researching on soft government contracts, got on with her chapters. As Sid missed more and more deadlines Chrissie offered to take on the chapters he'd planned to write. Sid apologised but let her do it. In the end he wrote three of the 13 chapters and Chrissie had to edit those hastily written three. Nevertheless, despite whatever inconvenience his unavailability had caused, Chrissie was sanguine. She'd loved writing. The book felt under her control. Sid's contribution was fine and she remained grateful to him for getting her a contract at all.

The book was a popular success. Fronting much of the press, Chrissie became its known author. Increasingly, she felt not just control, but ownership of it and, with that, increasing resentment about their equal royalty checks. Publicising the book had taken up much of her time, along with doing her normal work and looking after her young family, and she and Sid had hardly spoken during that period. Maybe Sid was feeling guilty, because her interviews were splashed all over the media? Maybe he saw how unequal their contributions had been to this book?

The silence, the gap in getting together, grew and Chrissie became more and more convinced that, of course, Sid wasn't in touch with her because he felt guilty. Great a guy as he'd been, maybe she just hadn't seen this side of him. Maybe he just

175

took what he could and that was why he was so successful. She
didn't send him a Christmas card that year. The following year
he didn't send her one either.

Then, after a few years, they met by chance, Chrissie surprised
by the warmth she felt at catching sight of his familiar form. By
then, with a new book contract, steady consultancies and a high
work profile, resentment felt beside the point. Sid had been the
key to opening those doors and she remembered his friendship,
the ease they'd had, the pleasures they'd shared. Her negative
narrative about him – his selfishness, what she saw as him being
self-serving – had faded, because where was her real evidence
for it, anyway? They embraced and went for a coffee.

Chrissie's opener to him was an invitation, coming from a
sense of openness towards him. It was collaborative, driven by
her fond feelings, but sitting there came the wash of the other
side of things. Just how could he square that circle, the fact
that unequal work deserved equal recompense? A pit formed
in her stomach, which she dispelled by what we'd recognise as
emotional regulation. Deliberately relaxing when she knew she
wanted to have a benevolent conversation, the pit dissolved.

'It's great to see you. We've missed you two,' she began
and, of course, Sid felt reassured and it felt safe then for her
to take the plunge: she'd done the first rule of collaborative
communication, made things safe. 'I might be wrong, but the
book ended up coming between us, or for me it did. I know you
to have been a sensitive friend, so even if you didn't know why
or didn't feel it too, you probably sensed that. I just couldn't
understand. It isn't that we both didn't agree at the end that I
did most of the writing, but then I didn't get most of the money.
That just felt really unfair. Maybe you saw it differently, but I
just don't get how you could. Look, I should have tried to talk
to you. I didn't say anything and that is entirely wrong of me.
Seeing you today reminds me you can't be the guy I've built you

up to be in my head.' In all of this she showed good mentalising – she'd thought about Sid and who she'd remembered him mostly to be, about what he'd need to hear, including how much she'd missed him and that she valued his friendship. And she used good, clear collaborative communication – 'I statements', for instance, abound – 'I should have tried to talk . . . I didn't say anything and that was entirely wrong' – and she packed it full of repairs.

Sid took a moment, thanked her, then adeptly explained his perspective. In doing so he repaired, too; showed understanding and feeling for Chrissie – that is, mentalising; and he used collaborative language. 'I didn't know you felt like that. I guessed you were resentful. I was upset. I waited for you to tell me. Probably I should have approached you. Your question is fair and we saw things differently. For me, the publishers were paying for the ideas and structure of the book: what we proposed came from both of us equally. Without you saying otherwise it seemed you shared my understanding and liked doing the promotion and the writing. We both got it wrong. I just made assumptions. I'm sorry.' Each repaired, through entering the other's world empathically. The friendship had been broken, but by the use of their skills it was reset.

8

Work relationships:
Setting boundaries

When work goes well you feel good: it's a big source of your self-esteem and your wellbeing. You know by now that so is getting on well with people, including people at work. So, what's involved in making those relationships go well? What do you have to bear in mind about working with others that can help you use your interactional skills as well as possible? This chapter will identify the main issues that get in the way of having good working relations and show how you can skilfully negotiate them.

First, let's set your work scene. Where are you working? How are you doing it? Since the pandemic, work has changed and might, still, for you be changing. While most of us ultimately *have* to work, whether we want to or not, if we can have some domain over how, where and when it's done, and how well we work with others, it makes a difference to how satisfying work can be. If you're an overworked care worker or a delivery person you've got little of what's called 'locus of control' and the more you have of it, the more likely you are to be satisfied at work. 'Locus of control' is about the degree to which you feel you can determine the conditions of your work situation—the way you work; how you work; why and when you work. But even when there's little control there's some left in your hands to create good relationships with whomever you encounter at work. It's also true that if your workplace is one that cultivates conditions to help relationships thrive, you've got a head start, but with the help of this book you can try to use your skills to manage tricky relational situations whenever and wherever they arise. The skills in this book are about giving you that 'locus of control' over the quality of your work relationships.

You'll recognise it if you're in a place that values relating well. It will be a place which fosters collaborative work practices over competition. It will be a workplace where managers see employees' welfare and development needs as unique and to be nurtured and which highlights creating trust; which values showing empathy for people. It will be a workplace which welcomes open communication channels, especially between managers and employees and which assures, at the same time, safe boundaries around personal issues and disclosures It will also be one which fosters supportiveness, not just from managers, but also from co-workers. If you work somewhere like this, you're lucky. If not, you still can make your working life with others better.

But even in the most supportive workplaces you'll recognise that time-honoured work issues crop up to – potentially – undermine relationships. This chapter is going to boil them down to a manageable dominant few so when they do crop up you'll be in a position to use your skills to manoeuvre around them. These basic work issues are: establishing trust; knowing boundaries; managing competition; and navigating 'difficult personalities'.

Let's start with defining what it is that makes work 'work' – why, like love, it is such a central theme in life. Why does it need to be satisfying? How does interacting well with others make a difference to that? Then we'll look at the thorny issues that keep getting in the way of your satisfaction and examine how using your skills might help you negotiate through them.

What is work?

When you carry out 'work' you are producing something. How others interact with you can help or impede that production. When we work, even if we're doing it solo, whether paid or unpaid, work is a nexus of social connection. For most of us it's a part of our lives in which we grow, find our pride and a large part of our identity, and it's always a social phenomenon. That's seen in what's reflected back to us by others with whom we work; by people affected by our work – clients, colleagues, managers; by how our friends and families see us as 'workers'. When we lose work identities our self-esteem can get lost or dented, as people who lose their jobs, or those who struggle after retirement attest. When feedback says your work isn't any good; when you are left floundering without trusting there is someone on your side; when you feel your effort is unappreciated, or blocked by competition, or difficult behaviour from a co-worker, boss or client, your work tends to suffer and so does your wellbeing.

If you've got children, picture how they play. A child at play shows work's primitive form and that it is implicitly embedded in a social world. That child is serious. She's making something or she's making sense of something. She's discovering her world and how to manipulate things within it, how to create things that result from thoughts and notions she develops. Through play she realises what she can do. For example, she watches a snail, prods it, then pushes it along as if in a race and watches it 'win'. She takes a lump of clay, feels its texture, pounds it, then squeezes it to create a snake. And how she's related to as she 'works' – praised, encouraged, appreciated, curiosity fostered or blocked – can help or impede how she feels about her work and herself.

That child gets feedback from the snail's progress or the satisfying shapes of the clay, but also from her parents' grins of pleasure at her discoveries. In the grown-up world of work other people – clients, colleagues and managers – provide feedback, the bottom line of work as a social phenomenon. Feedback is your manager's praise for your completed report. It is your teammate's stimulation from your idea as you co-create a new product. Your progress and effectiveness are measured against that of your peers, which is another kind of feedback. Appraisers who show they wish to promote your potential rather than to criticise, and who tailor it so it's specific to you and helps you improve, are working with you collaboratively, the shared aim being your better performance.

If it 'works' as it should, a grown-up's work can look and feel the same as child's play. If, like that child with her parents' delight, you're nurtured by people's support, your productivity and sense of self-satisfaction flourish. If you're lucky enough to be in a job matched to your talents, then with that sort of support you'll soar. The psychologist, Mihaly Csikszentmihalyi, came up with a concept called 'flow', when you feel like everything comes together, when work just 'fits' – your talents match what the job needs, and they're promoted and nurtured by your work situation. Support helps that. Because interactions, we know by this point in the book, are two-way streets, there's much you can do to create that support through trying to turn interactions at work to be positive as much of the time as possible. Let's turn now to those things that can get in your way.

Trust is the bottom line

Let's go back to that child at play, where she's in 'flow', her parents watching, encouraging and appreciating. Children at serious play feel safe, secure and trusting. In general, children who thrive, their natural curiosity encouraged, are children who exist within a secure family environment, securely attached to a parent. When they play they are showing their freedom to get lost in the task, the 'work' at hand. A former student of mine carried out a study on attachment relationships at work, interviewing a group of consultant NHS doctors and their junior doctors, who clearly had attachment-like relationships, and your managers at work can take on the qualities of 'attachment figures' for you.

Think about the person who manages you or the people you manage: how do you feel about them? Have you felt, like those junior doctors did, the unusual sort of power that vibrates between you? One of my PhD supervisors churlishly once complained, 'Why is it that students always expect so much from you as a supervisor?' I was taken aback. Of course, we expect so much from you! You wield unusual power over us. You can make us feel like dirt or shining stars!

To be in flow, relationships need to feel secure; that is, to be built on the sort of trust that the child at play shows. To work at your best, you need to have clarity about expectations from each other and those expectations need to be reasonable for you. The freedom to discover that the child at play displays is guided by her trust in the adults' care: she knows she's safe and can trust them. When a parent moves a baby away from an electric socket as he crawls towards it, the baby's security in further exploration is actually increased. He's free from harm; he can trust himself to explore. That comes in part from the limits his parents have set for him, because they build basic security.

To thrive at work grown-ups need relationships to nurture the same states and feelings that fostered the security of the child at play. Research resoundingly endorses this: both for the individual and for the organisation, supportive, positive working relationships which create a sense of trust, humane connection and understanding seem to promote effective, productive working. A study on trust at work showed that trust felt real only if it was tested in reality – slogans and mission statements are useless in themselves. Your manager needs to give you leeway to make decisions tailored to your talents and needs, and that leads to reciprocal trust. Trust also needs clarity. What are you being trusted to do? Has the person investing trust in you judged your capabilities sensibly? Trust is a contract.

Establishing what the limits are

Knowing the boundaries helps you at work, as it did the baby steered away from the socket. At work that means, first of all, knowing the scope of your job, for example by having a job description. Boundaries around who does what and when make clear not just what's expected, but the limits of your work in relation to others.

In any organisation, boundaries can also clarify and support its hierarchical functions. They're efficient – people don't have to reinvent the wheel each day – because they tell you what you're each meant to do and why. Your manager sets the agenda; you carry out assigned tasks. Role clarity over the duties of each team member helps each understand both the scope and the limits within the group.

Boundaries that are flexible enough, but that create safety – yes, the baby can roam the room, but he can't go near the electrical sockets – support trust. But research indicates boundaries shouldn't be too strict: people want fluidity of communication between themselves and their supervisors. In fact, most work assessments include 360-degree appraisals: it's normal now to appraise upwards as well as downwards. If you're permitted to critique your manager, what effect does that have? It's better, says one study that showed not just that people wanted to provide feedback to their manager, but that managers who took it got increased buy-in and productivity from their staff. More fluid lines, even given power differentials, in both directions, can help people work better; boundaries, yes, but not too tight. Many years ago, I saw a couple who had worked for one of the big four accountancy firms. They'd fallen in love. One of them

184

had had to resign, because at that time having relationships with co-workers was forbidden. The one who remained, full of resentment and chafing at a rule he didn't support, soon quit. Setting too-strict boundaries can antagonise rather than enable.

Managing competition

Competition inevitably enters the world of work; you measure your performance against others in similar roles. It arrives through public nods of praise, from scoring points in discussion to selection for plum jobs or projects. Comparisons are natural and valuable: they lay out standards. Collaboration values an individual's contribution to cooperative projects, but if competition is valued over collaboration then it can stifle creativity and productivity. Have you seen a parent unreasonably obstruct their young child at play, perhaps denigrating their efforts, or discourage an older child with seemingly reasonable ambitions? That's primitive competition with the parent's fragile ego stopping the child from flourishing.

Competition that occludes your productivity and satisfaction can feel deeply undermining. When someone else's ego is in the way, blocking you, trying either to usurp or undermine your effort and achievement, your pleasure in work will be stymied. That's the sort of competition that blocks, not the sort that sets helpful standards. Competition that does not promote exploration and development stands in the way of progress – and that leads us straight into the next problem area for some of us at work.

Really difficult people are what many see as the biggest work stumbling block. Let's think about that competitive parent. They and their fragile ego are the prototypes of work's 'difficult personality'. Their insecurity about themselves means your efforts and achievements might be a potential threat to them;

to their own sense of adequacy; to the way they feel they look or feel successful. That's why they might block you, compete with you. As with the threatened parent, 'difficult personalities' are threatened people, who feel challenged by others who might outstrip them, expose their ineptitude, or usurp their power, territory or authority. They are people out of their depth even when outwardly superior.

So, these four things – a lack of trust, inadequate boundaries, unmanaged competition and difficult personalities – can subvert your work relationships, impeding productivity, satisfaction and wellbeing. Let's turn now to see each in play and look at how you might be able to use your skills to manage them.

No basis for trust

The following example shows us what not to do to establish trust, but we'll then imagine what should have happened in order to get it.

The importance of establishing trust came strikingly home to me when I had one of my first jobs, a summer one at a residential camp, two hours from New York City, for children with emotional difficulties. I was a teenager with absolutely no training in the field. I was hired to be an assistant counsellor, with a vague job description. I had only worked with a group of autistic pre-pubescent girls, assisting an experienced older woman, until one day I was summoned by the camp's director and given the task of escorting a teenage boy, only a year younger than I was, home from the camp by public transport. I was invested with 'trust' to undertake this task, but with scant knowledge of me, the camp director had no reason to trust I could do it. Did I know how to negotiate the journey? Had I had ever done anything of the sort before? Had I worked with teenage boys, let alone teenage boys with known behavioural problems? Had I ever been put in charge of a single child for any length of time? None of that was established and to each the answer would have been 'no'. I didn't feel trusted. I was being exploited. I was the youngest, at the end of the food chain. I was unlikely to refuse and I didn't.

I wasn't told why the boy was being sent home suddenly, just that he'd crossed some line. I didn't know if his parents would be home, if I was to check in with anyone. I knew the boy was polite and personable, but also that he'd spent time in the equivalent of a juvenile detention centre, and I had no information about how he might be reacting or feeling. I was given money and an address, and instructed to take the boy, larger than I was, home to what was likely to be a rough neighbourhood in Brooklyn, where I'd never been (till then I'd lived a ridiculously protected life). The boy, Chris, and I set off.

I got lucky. Chris was much savvier than I was and turned out to be immensely kind, at once spotting my naivete. We had a pleasant, chatty ride. He guided us to the right subway, on to Brooklyn and finally home – and an empty apartment. Although at first nonplussed, he reassured me that he knew where his parents were and led me to the corner tavern, where his blasé mother, on a barstool, casually greeted him. After polite introductions, he guided me back to the subway. Soon afterwards, having lost all trust in working at that camp, I resigned.

What could I have done differently? Inexperience was a problem, certainly, but even more it was the power differential between me and the director. I should have established at the outset whether this was a trustworthy enterprise or not. I'd have had to be tactful, because I needed the director to want to be cooperative, but fear of losing my job silenced me. When the person you're dealing with is your superior, being afraid of censure, punishment or job loss inhibits you, but at the same time loss of trust will undermine your work. Unions exist precisely because they create power blocs; making alliances with colleagues over issues of concern to your work safety and security follows that model of creating a power coalition against managerial power. It helps if there's a mechanism to correct the power imbalance. I didn't try to find one, but I might have enlisted my senior counsellor to support me against the director.

So now we come to the skills required. That very insecurity, that very fear, indicate that trust and the first of your skills – emotional management – is what you need: get hold of the feeling and manage it. That's undeniably hard. Arming yourself in advance will help. For instance, I could have, first, imagined losing my job: What was I afraid of? Might there be pluses in its loss? Was there anything I could offer to the director – correct information about myself – to start with? In other cases, if your fear is losing your job, imagine alternatives, for instance a change in position, in departments? What other jobs might be possible? And, most importantly, in both the long and short term what might be okay or even better if you lost that job?

In other words, face down the things that frighten you. Then, calmed, move to mentalising. What's the other person's position? At the very least, they're trying to solve their own problem. Even crediting that can be a start, blunting confrontation, suggesting cooperation. I was a bad solution for my camp director's problem, but he did need one. If you can, you might mentalise further – maybe for my director it was a simple problem of misguidance: maybe he thought I was older and wiser than I was.

Here's how it could have played out differently. I would have faced down the ultimate fear that I'd be fired, which, in truth, wouldn't have been dire for me – I'd have emotionally regulated. Then I would have moved to mentalising, putting myself in my director's position and working out why he might have chosen me. That would have been difficult, but if pushed I could imagine he might have been misinformed about me.

Phrasing these thoughts and that I recognised his need for a solution in a respectful way – collaboratively communicating – would be next. In that cooperative spirit I'd clarify why I was the incorrect solution, not giving him an alternative, but at least helping him discard his first really bad one.

I could have said something like: 'I appreciate your predicament. It's your job to figure out how to get Chris home. It's flattering you thought I was up to it, but maybe you thought I was older and more experienced than I am?'

And then I could have gone on to let him know the facts, so he was properly in the picture: 'I should clarify, I am in no way suitable. I'm only a year older than Chris. I've never done such a trip before on my own, I've never been to Brooklyn and I would feel lost. I don't feel safe or knowledgeable to be in authority over a boy my age, to keep him safe, particularly as I have no understanding of the situation.'

If the camp director had responded with some reasonable explanation for his mistaken choice and that he now saw the light, I could have reinvested trust and maybe not have quit.

Comfort zones

The other lesson I took from that episode was the need for clarity, both around what was expected in my role and that of others with whom I interacted: their boundaries or how their job roles were defined. When I was working just as an assistant counsellor, things went smoothly. It was when I was randomly taken into a different role I was out of my depth. My senior counsellor, an experienced older woman, made me feel secure.

She was clear that my level of ability in dealing with children with severe emotional difficulties was very low and so I assisted her. She instructed me and I was to follow her suggestions. When I was out of my comfort zone, which I frequently was, I should ask for help. Increasingly she gave me tasks she'd judged I was becoming slowly more capable of doing. That made for trust, bolstered by clarity over what my job comprised.

One episode stands out as showing how this operated, how her behaviour clarified for me that my role was to assist her and learn how to make our campers safe and secure. One of the autistic girls, one with no language, was in my charge that day. She had been bitten by a tick and became very agitated, her agitation rising at the prospect of its removal. I was at a loss as how to communicate anything soothing to her. My efforts to remove the tick were increasing her distress and I called for my senior, even though she, herself, was caring for a distressed girl at that moment. Mine was the greater emergency and she motioned for me to monitor the other girl, to distract her with a game, which I did, and then to watch my senior manage the now hysterical other one. She sang to the girl. She knew, but I didn't, this girl would be soothed by certain songs. She held her, singing to her, and I was then able to remove the tick.

For smooth functioning there's usually some degree of hierarchy in organisations or groups, as there was for me as an assistant counsellor, with ensuing clarity over who's in charge of what. When I was a trainee in family therapy, I had a steep learning curve when I worked with a chaotic family and assumed, incorrectly, some demarcation of power and responsibilities. They were three wild teenage girls and a mother who'd been very young when she'd given birth. The family seemed like a collection of orphaned sisters. Trying to get a handle on how this family functioned, in our first session I'd innocently asked who cooks dinner? They'd stared at me blankly: in that family it was every girl for herself. Installing the mother into the position of authority she craved, but had no idea how to achieve, was the first order of treatment for the family to start to function better. Defining what was acceptable and permissible for 'daughters' versus a 'mother' was essential. One thing a 'mother' could do, they all agreed, was to see there was food and to ensure it was cooked, even to be the primary cook. And as 'daughters' they would be expected both to be there when she cooked for them, and to help her prepare and clean up afterwards.

Being clear about the boundaries, the definers, of a job description functions in the same efficient, protective way. During the pandemic a GP practice had to recruit more people to help input data as they vaccinated their patients. A few of those recruited were now retired GPs, including Sarah, who had formerly worked at a practice nearby. A former patient, just exiting from an appointment for a diabetes assessment, recognised her, sitting behind a computer at the far end of the reception office.

'Dr Harris!' she exclaimed, sidling up to her, 'It's so lucky to see you here. I've just been told I have to start taking Metformin and I'm not happy about it. I want to know what you think about it. Can you advise me whether it does bad things to your digestive system or not?'

Sarah could see the receptionists listening, with some anxiety, ears pricked for her response. She had to be calm – emotionally regulate – and she had to be mindful – be in a position to mentalise, both of the anxious ex-patient and also of the receptionists' sense of propriety. She considered her response, to make it as clear but respectful as possible – be collaborative in how she communicated, lest the ex-patient feel rebuffed or the receptionists feel she was overstepping her present role.

As gently and politely as she could, Sarah explained to her former patient that she was, in this practice, at this point, not acting as a doctor, but simply helping to input the information about who was vaccinated, with what and when, and, besides, was formally retired. That meant she couldn't act as a doctor for her. That was the role of her doctor, in this practice. The receptionists, in their role, turned back to their desks, with evident relief. Sarah was giving both her former patient and the receptionists a clear message: 'My role here is not to dispense medical advice. It's to input data.'

The importance of clarity about a job description is illustrated by the story of Charlene, a trainee counsellor at a charitable trust for children with developmental problems. Her training included, and it was part of the job description, weekly check-ins with her course supervisor. Charlene was encouraged to unburden herself in these, but the purpose of the check-ins was unclear. She'd created her own understanding, deciding that they were to clear her mind so she'd be free to concentrate on the children, with the disclosures confidential to her and her supervisor. But one day, in the office kitchen, the head of the charity had gently enquired, 'Is there's anything you need from us, Charlene, in your difficult time?' In a recent check-in, Charlene, trusting confidentiality, had talked about a romantic break-up and had wept. She was stunned and felt betrayed.

Upset, and on the brink of resigning, Charlene marched into her supervisor's office. Lucky for her the slot on the door read 'Do not disturb', giving her cooling-off time so she could emotionally regulate. She took deep breaths, put herself into the requisite relaxed 'thinking' state. She mused about resigning, which would set her back months in training, but how could she stay without trust? Why would the supervisor share Charlene's secrets? That thought stopped her: the missing piece, the 'why' of the other person. By asking that question she was already beginning to mentalise: why would her supervisor have allowed disclosure to the charity head? Perhaps Charlene did not, herself, understand the purpose of check-ins. She needed to think about what her supervisor might have been thinking about and why.

She opened the meeting with: 'I want to understand the purpose of check-ins. I've just had a shock that indicates I might not get it. Can you help me understand?' The supervisor was surprised, but happy to help. By asking for help in understanding, Charlene had set their conversation up as a collaboration – she'd used the collaborative approach of inviting her supervisor to help her. The supervisor explained that the charity needed to know about major life upheavals, but it was a collaborative conversation, because Charlene had set it up that way, and a common understanding was achieved.

When I think back to my assistant counsellor job at that camp for children with emotional problems, I see that my senior counsellor modelled great collaboration. While making things clear about how to do the job, she was instructing me in ways that helped us, together, to foster a safe environment. One of the reasons that collaborative practices at work are better for productivity is that they promote belief in yourself. I believed I could work with those difficult girls because my senior counsellor believed I could. And in no way was my incipient expertise threatening to her. She wasn't competitive, even when one or two of the girls preferred my company to hers.

Work friendships inevitably develop, but friendship's norm of mutual support can be threatened by competition to get ahead with its need to focus on self-interest. Can you stifle envy? Or jealousy that your friend performs better? Or insecurity aroused by their knowledge of your foibles and your mistakes? Might these be used against you in competitive situations?

Here boundaries around what you can and can't disclose, what comes first for each of you, friendship or work, when you are explicitly or potentially explicitly in competition – help. Is your own development at work blocked by the effects of competition?

A lectureship in their field was coming up and both Laura and Jake were considering it. Laura, whose best friend was Jake's partner, didn't like the thought that if one or other of them got it that might generate envy and the friendship might have to end. The job had drawbacks and she told her friends she wouldn't apply. Then, when she heard that Jake was in fact applying, she reconsidered. She would be better for that job, she judged, and without telling anyone, gambling that Jake wouldn't even make the short list, she applied. If she got the job, they'd probably all realise she was a natural for it and, since Jake wouldn't have stood a chance, they'd adapt. The short list was announced. Both were on it. Jake got the job, the couple never forgave Laura for what they considered deceit propelled by ambition, and the friendship ended. If she'd been honest, Jake said, they'd have known that, when in competition, self-interest for Laura trumped things. Fair enough – maybe it would have also for him.

If your priority is your own progress over the friendship, when competition presents itself, as it did for Laura, then there is clarity about the friendship's limits. However, under the cosh of competition it may be possible to adjust friendships at work. You may, for instance, be able to say something to your colleague, as my friend, Rachel, had to do when she and her work friend, Amanda, each heading a team within a company that could reasonably be awarded a particular project, were competing for a glamorous contract: 'Let's put an embargo on talking about which team wins the Gucci contract and what we're doing up to then.'

Competition is rife at work, where you are continually assessed, either implicitly or explicitly. It will rear its head whenever rewards or privileges are at stake, whether they be raises, praises or even respect. A boss can feel competitive in the face of an underling if they feel territory is being appropriated. Stefan's supervisor, as you will see, became competitive in response to his well-intentioned yet fumbled attempt to be helpful.

Stefan works shifts in a factory that makes glasses. He and his colleagues have traditionally worked collaboratively, under a long-time supervisor who cultivated a supportive culture. They have tried to support each other and cooperatively worked out swaps when children were ill, when vacations were up for consideration, when there have been long-term illnesses. Shortly before the pandemic struck their supervisor retired and a new one, from a harsher work culture, replaced him. She kept a strict record of hours. Any changes in routines, including decisions about shifts and swapping, formerly worked out more informally among themselves, had to originate with her. The pandemic intensified her rigidity, while it increased the workers' impulse to be collegial, all aware, as they were, of the new burdens it imposed on those of them, as manual workers who couldn't work at home, with children now compelled to be at home. Among themselves, they worked out a sample work plan that took account of who could work nights and who could not, and who could work in the day and when.

Stefan offered to take their solution to their supervisor. 'I have two children,' his request began. 'I've arranged with Maria and Norbert to swap their night shifts to my day. They have already agreed.'

'I have a tricky operation to run,' his supervisor responded, her body stiffened, her arms crossed against her chest like armour, 'and it's my responsibility to sort it out, not yours.'

She stared down Stefan glacially, until he nodded in defeat and left, despondent.

Clearly the supervisor had felt stressed, probably threatened – her armoured demeanour – rather than helped by Stefan's actions. It occurred to Stefan that, while he'd felt he was helping her by finding solutions, she'd felt he was muscling in on her job, making her look less competent. Competition makes people anxious: you're not on their side. Stefan was making her anxious.

Could Stefan have phrased his approach differently? Approached her so she'd have felt that though he recognised she had the responsibility and power, if he and the others collaborated with her so she could do her job best – make sure the shifts were covered – he'd have reassured rather than worried her? If he went back to his supervisor, he'd now, himself, be worried: the competition between them had surfaced. It would make him nervous of approaching her; it could easily surface again. In a re-do of things he'd have to be as self-possessed, as in control of himself as possible, as calmed and poised as he could be. Emotional regulation was imperative. And he'd have to mentalise better, now knowing clearly that competition – respect for her role – was a hot issue for her.

If Stefan kept in mind the issue of competition, that she'd need to know he wasn't usurping her but cooperating, he could use his skills to message support and respect for her explicitly, bringing her on board, while underscoring, as he used its language, the virtues of collaboration, phrasing things safely for her, making them at the outset safe because of that collaborative. 'This pandemic has been a problem, hasn't it – it keeps meaning changes for us all – you, our families, work.' That starts out with something collaborative: we're all in this. He would show he'd done the mentalising about her and her position – particularly as she was new, trying to establish her authority, and had come from a different, more hierarchical culture.

Then he could note this with acknowledging how changing any schedules obviously posed a problem for her, in her role as supervisor – he'd have established he acknowledged her superior role, making it safe for her. The collaborative part would then be underscored by how it's a problem for him and the others who need to move things, because of the demands imposed by the pandemic. It's now a shared problem, theirs and hers, because they need the schedule change: 'We all want to make this work for you, and us, and the company, since we all have this great big change thrust onto us, especially those of us with children now at home all day and without people to look after them.' But he's also communicating that it's not his role to solve the problem, but hers. He could use the language of invitation: 'So we came up with this, which could work for us, but, of course, we don't know – could you look at it and think about it and see if you think it works?' or 'You might have other ideas – we thought this might be a start.'

Within a work hierarchy, crossing boundaries because of friendship tends to be less of an issue, but it does come up, especially in flat hierarchies or organisations with egalitarian cultures. Research on this by the consultancy Mind Gym has emphasised the need, particularly for managers, to be clear about boundaries: to be open and available, but within clear limits. A manager needs to show appropriate availability and interest in the individual, and flexibility to adapt so that they can guide, but also to indicate that boundaries exist, because they restrict unhelpful self-disclosure and guard against intrusiveness. Cultivating 'friendliness' rather than 'friendship' should be the objective on both sides of the relationship. Boundaries around role definitions, as within that chaotic family I worked with – the mother organises meals and the daughters assist – help guide your behaviour and your expectations of each other. That's true for both sides of the management divide.

Peter runs a small appliance shop. He hired, on a short-term contract, a young assistant, Jesse, straight from a traineeship. The boy was charming, sweet and seemed lost, so Peter invited him home for dinner. Peter's wife took to him, too. Soon Peter was sharing lunch times with him, advising him on his love life. The problem was that Jesse was not very good at the job. With a looming end to the temporary contract Peter was in a bind: he'd befriended the assistant he no longer wanted as an assistant. When he didn't rehire him and gave him a shifty explanation, fudging the issue, Jesse was incandescent: Peter was disloyal!

If instead Peter had tried to imagine himself in Jesse's position – mentalised into who Jesse was – it would have been far better. Jesse was too young and needy not to confuse the job with the friendship. Peter should have been clear when he took him on: 'This is the situation you're being assessed on to see if you stay on: it's a training position. We'll see how you do, at work, in the job I'm training you in. You'll determine whether it suits you and I'll determine if you show promise. Then we'll take stock.' He should not have cluttered things by inviting Jesse into a friendship. Peter had created the messy situation and his discomfort meant he avoided thinking about it when the crunch came, so he didn't prepare for letting Jesse down. His own lack of clarity around what he was trying to do for Jesse, and the way he had mixed business with pleasure, made his thinking about how to fire him fuzzy. What had Jesse meant to him? Was he an employee or a charity case?

Flustered by his own confusion, Jesse's termination was thoughtless and rushed. Peter had been stressed by having to fire someone he liked; he was suffused by guilt. He was in no fit state to think about Jesse as Jesse, nor then how to phrase things so Jesse would at some point perhaps be able to understand. He most certainly hadn't mentalised, and the naïve, needy Jesse justifiably felt let down and misled. It was unlikely that the fact Peter had sometimes pointed out Jesse's errors would have alerted him to the possibility that he would be let go, yet Peter was counting on Jesse to be sophisticated enough to do so. Peter fudged the issue, even being dishonest. He thought he was letting Jesse down lightly if he argued that he no longer needed an assistant. He even fooled himself that he could get along without one, although he'd taken Jesse on because he did need help. In consequence, Jesse wasn't buying it. To Jesse, with the boundaries around friendship and work too blurred, Peter looked two-faced. 'Why would you be so nice to me,' he beseeched him, clearly shocked by his dismissal, 'if you didn't think there'd be a job?'

'Difficult' personalities

You can be working from home, virtually, hybrid or on the road, in a gig set-up, in tight hierarchies or loose structures. You may only in theory be your own boss – as a gig worker you might be defined as self-employed but in reality have little control. Whatever your setting or work practices, when there are others with whom you relate you'll come up against difficult people. You'll encounter them when there's unfair competition, blocked progression and uncivil or unsafe treatment.

In their helpful book on relationships at work, Octavius Black and Sebastian Bailey of Mind Gym run through a cast of typical difficult personalities you're likely to meet at work. They label them playfully, but each make life seriously uncomfortable for you. For instance, the person who shrinks from collaborating and tries to disappear into the background, Mr Don't Mind Me; the person who, sometimes through hysteria, gives you little leeway, the Control Freak; the one who accords little respect to others and who appears impermeable to others' input, the Know-it-all; and the person who shows little emotional variation, empathy or social engagement, the Cyborg. I'd add into that typology a few more: the People-Eater, who is so consumed by ambition that they'll step on any toe they perceive is in their way; the Entitled, the imperious worker who, whether they have the talent or not, expect to be given special treatment and privileges; and the Needy Child, who falls apart and, similar to the Entitled, expects special treatment – in this case that others will both carry them when they're upset and pick up the pieces after them when they make mistakes. Finally, there is the Ice King or Queen – inaccessible, withholding, uncollaborative. Each of these exhibit idiosyncratic, typical patterns of responding. There are probably other presentations of being 'difficult' and you'll no doubt have encountered a few of your own.

Each difficult type might initially look different – hysterics, coldness, arrogance, control – but they are all showing rock-hard, *defensive* behaviours. They're not interested in fostering you at work, or, maybe more to the point, they *can't* foster you; their fears and insecurities are in the way. You threaten them. You've triggered them. That may sound counterintuitive, especially when they are powerful or aggressive characters, but remember the point in Chapter 3 (see page 37) about emotions: the hard ones are defending the soft ones and the soft ones are about vulnerabilities. Given that work is the site of competition, of discovering your self-worth and effectiveness – remember the child exploring and discovering her effectiveness through play – work is a hothouse in which insecurities breed. Reframing 'difficult', obstructive people at work as 'insecure' or 'threatened' will help you because you can mentalise about them that way. And if you do this you are more likely to respond to negative overtures with the sort of positive ones that can, at best, turn things around or will at least discourage more of the negative responses.

Think of it this way: just as you might feel like a small child again, wanting to flee or fight back when faced with things that throw you, frighten you, or put you in situations that make you feel incompetent or flustered, so difficult personalities feel that way, too, disguising their fear and insecurity. They aren't aware for the most part that they're in that state. They aren't in control of their behaviour. They're not thinking about how their behaviour is having an effect on you. They're not thinking interactively as you, the relator with skills, would be. And here's the point about their 'difficult' quality: they are likely to become 'difficult' in their predictably characteristic ways – the Ice Queen, the Needy Child, the Cyborg, the Entitled et al – when under what they perceive to be as stress.

You, having learned the skills, don't have to know the origins of their stress, why they're reacting to things as they are. It's enough to recognise that they're in the state of fight or flight and, once you do, once you understand and validate your own state of distress in response and have calmed it down so you can be in a position to think more clearly, you can actually help tame that person's stress and get a better interaction going, through your compassionate and wise use of skills.

The Ice Queen

To manage difficult personalities can be particularly complicated when it is your boss or manager who feels threatened. It's hard to see why anyone is threatened when they have obvious power over you, but, like Stefan's supervisor, threats can come from below as well as above. In the following story of Alex and his boss, his boss got competitive with Alex. When someone in power gets aggressive it can suggest they're competitive, flexing their muscles. When someone in power blocks you and

is known as 'difficult', you might start thinking, 'Work is a place
in which people can so easily feel vulnerable, so even though
they're my boss, I need to think of them as threatened and
insecure, because in some way whatever I'm doing is making
them feel vulnerable.'

Alex was hired at the Isla Carpenter Creative Consultancy
for the creative industries, by its founder. Young, iconoclastic,
established already as a designer himself, Alex's brief was to
bring in new projects to attract a younger clientele. 'I'm caught
– I love what I do but she takes all the credit – everyone thinks
it's all down to her,' Alex complained in our coaching session.
He was describing his boss, the founder of his agency. He'd
expected collaboration – blending her business acumen with his
innovations. He delivered what she wanted, but, unexpectedly
for Alex, she competed, publicly taking the credit, then studiedly
avoiding him. She was cold, unapproachable; he was truculent
when he was with her; their cycles were decidedly negative.

'She's the boss!' he cried. 'I don't want her job, and I'm
giving her what she wanted! That's for sure, because she likes
it so much she steals my thunder!' Why might anyone in her
position become aloof, proprietorial and withholding? What
could be some good guesses – that's all they could be, as a
hallmark it turned out of Isla's persona was to be very private –
to answer that?

This much he did know: Isla, a star in their design field, who
rose from hardscrabble beginnings to run a fabled consultancy,
apparently had little personal life. Her office was furnished with
awards, etchings and photos of her dog – no mementos suggesting
children, partners or friends. This was a marked contrast to
Alex's, which loudly proclaimed a life of relationships and varied
interests, not to mention awards for the very achievements Isla
had hired him to expand upon. Maybe Isla found someone like
Alex a threat. Changing the frame around her from powerful

boss to lonely figure whose identity rested so firmly on just one thing, her work, changed Alex's feelings and perspective about her. Compassion began to temper his belligerence.

Alex now saw the 'uptight' Isla as less scary and more scared. He knew when she was 'scared' because it showed: her features went flat, hiding her feelings; her neat, stout body hunched; her voice became tight and icy. Uptight Isla bred uptight Alex, who had been scared by her. Then back again, in a dance of antagonism. Alex saw himself as Isla had: tense, grimacing. They mirrored each other. If he didn't show 'scared' she might not show it back.

In a role play Alex tried something different. In it he approached her for input into something he was developing. 'Isla ...' he began, but to me he still seemed anxious, his body stiff, his jaw clenched. We restarted and Alex was encouraged to imagine himself as the Isla who had only her business, who'd see him as living so much more fully than she ever could, yet still being a great designer. 'Picture her office, then yours,' I prodded, and Alex smiled, dropped his shoulders and relaxed – visible signs he was emotionally regulating. He began, and his overture showed he'd mentalised: she was the boss but she needed to feel safe around him, someone with whom she felt competitive. His words reassured: he used collaborative communication. 'Isla, I see you're busy, but is there any time that suits you for a brainstorming session – I'm stuck about our new venture and I know you'll be able to help.' That was respectful. He acknowledged both her greater expertise and her packed schedule – she was the boss – but showed that he was not trying to usurp her position ('*our* new venture') and was inviting ('is there any time that suits you for a brainstorming session?'). Trying out this new way of thinking about Isla and using his skills could equip Alex for future interactions, though it would, of course, require persistence. Eventually, in theory, then their cycles would turn positive.

The Entitled

Neil was an esteemed personal trainer at a high-profile gym, personable, warm, attractive and in demand, who'd risen to become the gym's head of training. He trained the trainers at a gym which promoted collaboration: the sharing of referrals and new techniques. Soraya's arrival on staff shook the culture of sharing. A very gifted young woman whose appetite for improvement seemed insatiable, she gobbled up much of Neil's time. Neil saw her as impassioned and keen; her colleagues, whose company she'd disdained, disagreed. She was, to them, 'entitled', claiming Neil's time and energy. It wasn't until one of the trainers warned that Soraya was being underhand that he changed his view. 'Soraya is suggesting you're leaving. She told that to one of her clients,' the trainer said. 'I didn't think you'd do that to us – tell her, but not us.'

Her vaulting ambition was fraying the collaborative culture of their gym. The staff should never suspect him of disloyalty. Puzzled, he remembered a lunch with Soraya when he'd thought they were simply sharing random thoughts and musings. She'd divulged her ambition: to run her own gym. In what he thought was the same spirit, he'd shared that what he dreamed about was doing the same but in Jamaica, where he'd been born. But that was a pipe dream, not a plan. Had she not understood? Or had she spread a deliberate, lying rumour? In any case, she was stirring things up and she'd betrayed him.

Suddenly he saw how she wasn't part of their team, which strangely both struck him as the key to her and also calmed him and he thought further. Wisdom from martial arts training reminded him there is always vulnerability under the attack. Mentalising, Neil considered how Soraya was protecting something. Something lay under her attack on him and their teamwork. It was important not to arouse whatever it was. He'd invested in her and there might be a chance of salvaging a future for their work together. His hunch was that Soraya was driven by a false notion that there's only one star for any stage: Soraya. He was mentalising as he imagined being with her next.

It was hard to maintain the notion of a fragile Soraya in the face of her cool composure when he summoned her to his office, but a tight jaw and fists, under cover of a brittle smile, suggested defensiveness: she'd sensed something afoot. He relaxed, yoga breaths were second nature to him, hoping his calm would in turn relax her – his calm might prompt her to mirror him. His approach was to be that of mentor, guiding her to the next step, which was working well with colleagues.

In a gesture towards friendliness he turned partway towards her and, keeping his usual gentle tone when teaching, began, making it safe: 'You know how pleased I've been with your training: you're developing into a brilliant technician. You catch on really fast about how to get people motivated to do the body work.' She visibly relaxed. Neil watched a more genuine smile start to form, so he continued. 'I think we need to do the next step – not about how you train bodies. Are you ready for the next bit, do you think?' he invited her, and she nodded, if looking puzzled. Still, they were on common, cooperative ground.

But to do the hard next bit, to keep her on board, he had to show he'd tried to think what that next bit would feel like to her, communicating his compassionate mentalising. 'I know,' he smiled, 'I must sound like I'm talking in riddles. Before I say what I mean I just want to check out something – some thoughts I've had about you and what might be a problem going forward.' She looked bemused, but curious: they were still collaborating. He took his slow breath in and six counts out, to remain relaxed. 'Here's my question,' he began, still inviting her to help him think about his 'problem'. 'Am I right in thinking, Soraya, that you might believe the only way to convince me that you're "good enough" is to push for more and more, get special this and that, work all hours?' He paused, peering at her intently, so she'd see he really needed her help. She sat back in her seat and seemed to consider it. 'I don't know,' she answered, looking blank. 'Maybe.' They'd been collaborating but he'd pushed her out of her safety zone. She'd closed down. He'd left her hanging; she was out of her element, insecure.

He re-started, with a gesture again towards safety – his own experience of being unsure. 'Look, if it were me, I'd want to know when I'd done enough. I think I was probably unclear. I saw you putting so much – too much I think now – into your work and I began to think about you.' She was back, leaning forward, curious to hear that she was so much in his mind. 'I started to wonder what's enough for her? Do you follow me?' She looked puzzled. She shook her head, and showed, in the tightness of her body, that he might be losing her again. 'No. What do you mean?' Neil's voice stayed soothing so she'd again feel safe. But Soraya felt she had got the question wrong and had become uptight again. She couldn't not get the right answer, could she, thought Neil: she has to be the flawless 'star'. He was losing her cooperation.

'Soraya' – he shifted gears, leaning in to her, earnestly inviting her to help him, again – 'I want you to help me to try to understand. You know I think you are such a talented trainer. I want you to thrive in your future. But here's the thing: there's other parts to succeeding in this field – the part beyond just being the best gymnast, getting the most clients. That's about getting along with people you work with. You need people to plug for you, don't you think?' Neil had tried to make a strong bid of showing he was on her side, helping her move to the next training phase, but Soraya reddened, drew herself up and hardened her body. Neil took another yoga breath; he'd listen, not defend, not fight her as she seemed to be gearing up to do with him.

'I know what you're talking about,' she began acidly. 'But let me stop you there. You've been a good mentor, but I think I've outgrown you.' She'd gone defensive, then offensive. Staying calm, listening, Neil was able to stay in his mentalisation mode – feeling more sorry for her than anything, not attacked, her weapon pathetically blunt. He continued softly, fending off offence with geniality. Maybe if he stayed 'safe' for her to the end she might some day remember the wisdom he was trying to impart. 'You may well be right that I've outlived my usefulness to you as your mentor, certainly if you want to stay at this gym. For that you'd need to work on a different set of skills. We're not unique, but here there's a culture of having each other's backs. For that you need trust and you'd need to learn how to earn that. That needs honesty. You weren't honest with me, nor with your client about me, were you?'

She drew herself up, giving him a steely gaze – an attempted 'sticks and stones' defence; he couldn't harm her. He continued, gently, still her 'teacher', and so not just safe but also in a collaborative project with her, that is, to help her develop; maybe he could still enlist her. 'You are great in what you do now, but this is your next frontier: getting on with others, being trustworthy and respectful.'

'Well, first of all, I'm sorry,' she huffed, shifting in her seat. 'I must have misinterpreted what you told me. But' – and she suddenly sat still and straight, as if bigging herself up to equal the larger Neil – 'now that it's come up, I need to say this: I should have already been promoted. I'm better than the others.'

Neil answered firmly, finalising the meeting. His mentalising had been on target, but his skilled efforts had failed. Now he had to be clear and concise to get a message through for her to hear it, 'But you see, your drive to be exceptional overrode the really important thing: working cooperatively. You were dishonest. As your mentor I'll tell you: that will undermine you, here or anywhere. You've undermined me by deceit. Even so, I'll write you an honest reference: I can be truthful. You are gifted in your physical abilities as a trainer, but you lack a basic skill – honesty and regard for others. That makes you a bad bet as a colleague. I'd also say that I hope one day that will change.'

Soraya looked stunned. She rose to leave, spitting as she exited, 'You will be sorry.' Which he was, but only for the loss of what she might have been. He had, despite its ending, acted in this encounter with integrity, fairly and compassionately. Like Phoebe with Nick in chapter 6, Neil hoped someday Soraya would hear his clear, even empathic, words and learn. Sometimes a difficult personality is far too brittle and fearful to tame, but if you can make an effort to try with them it's better than letting their fragile ego dominate.

Difficult clients

When you're on the other side of the counter: when you are the purveyor of a service or a product, the presumption of power often tilts towards the client. Clients can almost always go somewhere else, or they can leave, no matter how great or exclusive your offer is. The business credo 'the customer is always right' says it: the provider bends to the client. Watching the grotesquely demanding clients in the TV series, *The White Lotus*, set in a luxury hotel in Hawaii – the imperious Tanya, a Needy Child, and the obnoxious Shane, an Entitled and Control Freak – is compulsive, because you want to see how far they'll go.

When I was a trainee psychotherapist at a clinic in Chicago, handing over her notes, the intake interviewer warned me, 'I'm sorry, Janet, but I think this next one's going to be difficult. She wanted to see you outside, on a park bench. I had to tell her that that wasn't our policy and she wasn't happy about it at all.'

That was just the beginning. Pacing back and forth, refusing to sit, rejecting the symbolic hierarchy of the 'expert' position of me behind a desk – customary for therapy offices then – I felt my client's power. She was primed to reject me and was already rejecting the conditions of service. I pulled up a chair and gestured for her to sit in another one. So began our scratchy first encounter.

An accountant married to a vicar, she wanted children, but he wanted to delay becoming parents. Her incandescence grew as she expressed her fury at the church, his congregation, at marriage, at the demands of her job and, finally, at the constraints of the therapy she found herself in. I was at sea: what was it she wanted from it, from me? The compelling evidence before me said she was at least in part aggressor rather than just victim of her circumstances, but I bit my tongue and strained to empathise, muttering, unconvincingly, 'That must make you feel terrible.' Incensed, she hissed, 'Of course I feel terrible! What did you think I'd feel?' and began to pace again. Her rage literally danced around me. Straining for calm, I was hyperaware of her as a client, actively rejecting my wares, with my supervisor watching behind a one-way screen. Overwhelmed by insecurity, I was paralysed: nervous, unable to think clearly and certainly not empathic towards that pacing, hissing, enemy shaming and blaming me. I was certainly, for her at that point, a bad therapist.

Standard practice in that clinic meant a break halfway through a session. I left her in the room to meet with my supervisor, who thankfully did the mentalising for me. Underneath her rage, he postulated, 'She is an angry little girl who feels unloved. Somehow you need to convey that her wish to be loved is valid and you feel that it is!' I nodded with a sinking heart. I disliked this woman. Love? Could anyone love her? I was still rattled and wasn't able to feel kindly towards her. My supervisor continued, 'But that's her story, underneath her fury. You've got to feel that and validate it before she'll accept you and let you know more. But you've got to be receptive and right now you're rattled. Manage that: think why, calm down. And then set boundaries. She needs to accept your role is to be the therapist and this is how you do it: she sits across from you, you talk, you ask her things and you help her think her way out of her pain. She's acting like a three-year-old, refusing to accept your terms. That's not "safe": she can't help herself if she carries on. She's having a three-year-old's tantrum. No! You can't meet her outside. Yes! She does have to sit and face you!'

I did calm then. I could label what I was feeling and why. He helped me face down the fear she'd stirred. If she fired me it would be seen as a learning experience. Her client power shrank dramatically. Seeing her as a three-year-old reduced it further. And it worked for my mentalising. I had a three-year-old at the time. Her tantrums looked a lot like his. He was a pain when he had one, but I still loved him. Someone should have still loved her and quite possibly no one had. Going back to the session I felt prepared, skilled up, equipped.

As it happened, the break itself broke the therapy. Her rage had been refuelled as she sat, abandoned, hemmed in once more by a tyrannical clinic. Pacing again like an angry animal, as I opened the door she stopped and hissed, 'You don't get it, do you? This is not what I want! I want you to come outside, sit on a bench, be my friend and love me! If you won't do that right now, I am going to leave. Will you?' My stunned pause was her answer. She stomped out.

She, the client, had rejected me. I didn't get the chance to use skills with her. I'd let her, my client, control me. I never got to do what I then role-played with my supervisor: to calm myself; to offer to her help from my best guesses about what lay underneath her hard rage, the softer yearnings, and a chance to help her understand her rage and despair. Where, after all, did she feel loved? And how could that be changed? Could we see if what therapy could do matched what she thought she might want? That is, I'd have offered, I hope safely, an invitation. It wasn't likely she'd take it up, though. Our clinic wasn't selling the instant love and friendship she wanted. She was the wrong client in the wrong place for us both.

It isn't always clear what the client wants or needs or what you can supply. Sometimes the objectives change as things proceed. Skills always remain key. You'd try to enter each other's minds: for one side, what is wanted and why? For the other, what is being offered and why? Is there a mismatch, a gap in understanding? Because if so, you can repair, wind back and reset: 'Let's go back a step to see where we might not have understood.'

9

Transactions: When there is no relationship

Imagine yourself a visitor to a city. You've got an early start for a business meeting that has you standing in a long rush-hour queue at an underground train station. Even though there's a queue for the automated option, there's an even longer one at an attendant's booth where you can also buy the tokens or pass needed to board the train. You opt to stand there, because you have a transport question that isn't addressed by the various maps and internet sites you've consulted. That underground booth has little light, a thick, protective window and two small slots which cash and cards can slip through, with two microphones for communication, operated by two attendants in cramped tandem.

You're in a rush. So are most of the others in that underground station. People in the queue are palpably harried. By now if you've been practising your skills you're likely to be very observant. You'll notice the non-verbals on display in the interactions around you, particularly in the scene unfolding ahead: body language, manner of speaking, the content and the tone. You'll imagine the guesses the players in the scene – the customer, who is a well-dressed woman with a foreign accent, and the booth's attendant, a man dressed in the metropolitan transport uniform – are probably making in their distinctly limited form of mentalising, based presumably on stereotyping, as they interact. This is the scene you witness:

Customer (her tone of voice is anxious, her body language is nervous and distracted, with her hands going in and out of her pockets as if trying to locate something as she speaks): 'Hello! I am trying to buy a pass to travel or – to buy – what are they called? Tokens? I am not sure. Please forgive me! But what I want to know is . . . I mean, please can you tell me how many rides I get for £10?'

Attendant (he is not looking at her, instead he rolls his eyes at his colleague and then stares down, his tone of voice bored, sharp and clipped): 'You get five tokens for £10. Or a pass for £10 for six.'

Customer (her tone of voice is now worried and she has slumped in what appears to be defeat): 'Oh! But I only have enough then for I think it is four!. . . (her tone now changes to apologetic): 'Oh, I'm sorry, I am confused. I don't live here.'

Attendant (he taps his fingers, rolls his eyes, showing impatience, and his tone is now sharp): 'Look, there's a whole queue behind you. £10 for five. Or £2.50 each. We only take cards for £10. Otherwise, you need cash.'

Customer (her body language is now stiff, she straightens up as if to gain dignity, her tone is formal and icy): 'Well, thank you so much. Please give me three tokens.' (she reaches into her pocket, pulls out a handful of change and aggressively pushes it through the slot).

Attendant (he shoves through the tokens roughly, affecting a contemptuous expression).

Customer (deliberately and slowly she takes the tokens, one by one, avoiding eye contact, her tone is frosty and sarcastic): 'Thank you so very much. Hope you have a *really lovely* day!' (she turns on her heel as she departs).

Parking, for the moment, perhaps your own frustration in your own rush hour journey, you, the observer, will conclude outcomes, as follows:

For the attendant, he successfully got rid of a customer he seemed to wish to get rid of. In that regard his interaction was successful. You might guess at his limited mentalisation: perhaps 'Bloody foreigner' or 'Bloody tourist'. He hardly glanced at her, but presumably he heard her accent. Or 'ignorant!' and 'ignorance' makes for trouble if you're trying to run a rush-hour public transport operation smoothly. Though he did get rid of her in fairly short order, the result for his own wellbeing wouldn't have been a success. He'd have had a sour feeling. It was a disagreeable encounter. That might have gone forward into the following encounter. It might linger, that is, unless and until something more pleasant, a sunnier encounter perhaps, dispelled it. He probably raised his blood pressure and missed the chance for a shot of oxytocin first thing in the morning from a spirit-raising, helpful and friendly encounter.

For the customer, she got her tokens, though it's unclear whether she was any the wiser about payment and what she got for her money. She didn't seem to be bringing much consciousness about the attendant and what sitting in an airless, cramped booth in rush hour might do to his disposition. He was, it seemed, simply a mechanism for her getting what she needed, maybe just 'he's a functionary.' Mentalising score? Pretty low. Her anxiety seemed to be all that mattered in her approach to him. For her, too, the interaction had been sour, with apparent humiliation fuelling passive aggression as she slowly took her tokens, then real aggression in sarcasm. A missed opportunity for her too to add to the sum of her wellbeing.

Neither was attending to the other; each had become stereotyped, objectified, their humanity railroaded by each one's respective emotional states. Too often strictly transactional encounters lend themselves not just to such thoughtlessness, unkindness and often unproductiveness in outcomes, but they also make negative contributions, withdrawals as it were, from the bank of your health and happiness.

———

Moments of transitory, transactional relating are scattered throughout most people's days. We live within webs of services given and received, our lives momentarily touching others we'll never knowingly see again. Or, even if we do, they can remain without individual identities, as we will to them. How many of you know anything about the person who delivers your post every day? During the pandemic transactional relationships billowed. How often did your door ring with a delivery person leaving a package outside your door? You might have thanked them. Or not. They might have given you a friendly wave. Or sullenly dropped your goods at the bottom of your steps.

Purely transactional relationships are about goods and services delivered and received, but they're fleeting, existing simply within the moments in which goods or services are exchanged, unlike, say, with a medical practitioner, who also delivers a service, but one which includes an objective to understand something about you. Their purpose, in contrast, doesn't contain a presumption of, or need for, building knowledge or understanding between you.

Yet when transitory relating goes well it can make you feel good; you've increased the sum of good things between you and another person and you've also avoided decreasing it. If you're the one doing the service and you've been acknowledged for it, you feel good. If you're the receiver and you've got what you wanted, you feel good. If you acknowledge it, show gratitude, you get even more good feelings. If the interaction has gone beyond civil thanks into even further pleasant territory – something shared, like a joke, or compliment – there's an additional sheen cast upon your wellbeing.

In my first year of school, I was bussed to my kindergarten. What in most ways was a simple transactional relationship – the bus driver picking us up at our respective stops and dumping us all at the school – took on the sort of warmth of a more substantial relationship. Yet we did not seek to know more about him beyond how he delivered his service, nor he about us. The point was, though transactional, he delivered his service in a wonderful way, consistently, every day. We knew his name – Teddy – although he never learned ours. He greeted each of us jovially as we climbed the steps and sidled into our seats, and as he started up the bus, he also started up a song. We all joined in. 'John Jacob Jingleheimer Schmidt, that's my name, too!' began one that I can still sing from start to finish decades later, along with 'There was a farmer had a dog and Bingo was his name-oh!' and a host of others. We five- and six-year-olds started our school days with a smile.

On the other hand, after graduating university, when I was working in my first job in New York City, my first interpersonal exchange of the day would be with a surly subway token attendant at the 96th St IRT, as it then was. On those days I would board the train having to calm myself down after some sort of aggressive interaction – either witnessed or directly experienced. Transactional relating, even if fleeting, can trigger a mood. It can even go on to colour a day.

Transactional relating may seem insignificant because it's passing, but even getting the best for yourself briefly, or making someone else feel good for a moment, adds to the sum of your good feeling and benefits your physiological health, mainly because you've avoided an unpleasant or aggressive encounter. Your blood pressure doesn't rise, because adrenaline does not get stimulated. There was a daily train announcer on the New York commuter train I once regularly rode who broke the tired commuters' silences with a loud and chirpy 'Tucky-hoe!' when the train would reach the stop Tuckahoe. Smiles would break out across exhausted faces. If you strive to interact transactionally as pleasantly as possible, or at least as often and as much as possible without aggression, over time that healthy sum increases and so does wellbeing. Moreover, you are putting into practice good relating skills and the more you practise the better you get.

But transactional relating done pleasantly or even bottom-line civilly poses a particular challenge stemming precisely from the fact that you don't build towards the relationship. You've got little skin in the game. Mostly the stakes of getting it wrong aren't high. You'll never see each other again. It, too, shall pass. Things go pear-shaped – so what? You don't feel great. Given the low investment in relating, when you don't get what you think you need, what you expect, if a service seems substandard or the one you've given is rudely received, you may well not behave well. In transactional relating it can seem as if the other person is not a fleshed-out human, like someone you know. You can't bring in shades of grey to offset your rush to judgement. Mentalising is severely limited: you've got only the immediate context of your meeting to work with and stereotypes. All you've got is façade: a human cardboard cut-out.

And yet this book is trying to make the case that all relating adds up to give you better – or worse – wellbeing. Of course, the stakes and rewards in intimate and important ongoing relationships are much higher if you get them either wrong or right. But still, to attempt to override the inhumane and make relating humane, when you can, makes a difference to your mood, even on the level of reducing stressful hormonal release on the one hand and increasing pleasurable hormone release on the other, and so too your wellbeing.

As an example, a few weeks after lockdown in the UK had eased, I found myself eating inside a restaurant. I'd arrived there from a soggy walk on what was probably the 30th consecutive day of cold rain, although the calendar unbelievably claimed it was nearly June. In my long absence from the world of hospitality, a requirement to use the NHS app in public places as part of the Covid track and trace programme had been introduced. I had already downloaded the app for a different purpose, but I couldn't work out how to use it for this purpose and I fumbled, fairly uselessly, until a clutch of students, witnessing my cackhandedness, kindly guided me and I was duly allowed in to find a table. But by then I was rattled, in addition to being waterlogged. I was hungry – and then my friend was late. Disgruntled, rattled, wet, hungry, I seized on the first thing I saw on a menu plonked in front of me. The club sandwich would make it all better, I thought, savouring the memory of the bite of bacon and tomato against the sweetness of turkey and mayonnaise.

So, when a few thin slices of dry, flash-toasted white bread cradling wilted lettuce leaves and a few wan bits of orangey tomato covering meagre offerings of wilted bacon and dry turkey – and absolutely no mayonnaise – arrived, was I gracious about it to the waitress serving us? Not at all. I let my irritation turn her into a cipher. I'd no concern about who she was and how my curtness would have landed on her. Well, that's not entirely true: she'd become part of the machine of the restaurant, which conveniently supported the lack of humanity in my end of the transaction. 'Can I bring you any sauces?' she sang to me and my now arrived friend. 'Yes!' I snapped, looking at the woebegone French fries which I had neither wanted nor expected, but now saw as possibly the only potentially pleasurable part of the meal. 'You can bring a big pot of ketchup and while you're at it, a *very* big pot of mayonnaise, because a club sandwich can't be called a club sandwich if it's nothing but bread, meat and a few shreds of lettuce and tomato!'

I had taken out my anger — justifiable, but not her fault — on someone innocent, just because I had the power to do so. Because I didn't know her and she didn't know me, there were no consequences. We had no ongoing relationship. As I say, that's the thing about transactional relationships: you don't have to see the people again; they can be faceless, representatives of whatever the service or organisation might be. Although, of course, how many of us have found that the waitress you've been rude to is the grown daughter of your friend, or have heard stories of someone raging at an attendant and found it was someone they knew from their old neighbourhood?

'Certainly. No problem,' the very young girl immediately responded, politely and graciously. In contrast to me, her response implied she was, indeed, taking me as an individual on board, maybe eyeing my wet belongings, my bedraggled hair, maybe stereotyping me as an old person having trouble with the weather, with the world — any of those things would have meant perhaps she saw me, mentalised about me, as someone who needed kindness. Or maybe she was just angling for a tip and was stereotyping me as someone who, if humoured, was likely to show it that way. Whatever, she would have had to override a perfectly reasonable hostile response to my hostility in order to answer me so cheerfully and charmingly. Her part of the transaction showed that even in transactions that are going badly you can act skilfully and turn things around.

And, indeed, it did turn things around. I'm sure things were helped because her kindness emerged in front of my friend, highlighting my irritability, shaming me, but mostly, I hope, I responded better because she'd made me feel better; plus she'd made me feel grateful, a humane feeling towards her as she'd shown towards me. I'd seen her behaving well on my behalf. With the meal ongoing I had a chance to repair, particularly as she'd agreed to bring me my demanded large pots of sauces. I guiltily turned to my friend. I was ashamed I'd behaved badly I said and announced I was going to commend the waitress on her gracious behaviour and apologise for my own poor show. So that is what I did when she came back offering overly generous pots of condiments. 'You were really gracious in the face of my behaviour. It's not your fault about the sandwich, even though the sandwich was inexcusably bad, and I'm sorry I used that tone.' She reddened a bit and then smiled appreciatively. 'Thank you,' she said, warmly. I hope I remedied things: that is, I hope I made her feel good. I know I certainly felt better for having apologised. I hadn't retracted my – I still feel – reasonable point about the regrettable sandwich, but I had behaved badly. I clearly apologised for that.

There have been thousands of times when I haven't apologised as I did with the waitress and I am sure I am typical in that respect. That's especially so when people who are serving you are, in fact, faceless. Over the phone, behind a booth, driving a bus and looking ahead so you don't see their face at all. It may be why customer relations training tells customer-facing people to give their names. Why, just today I spoke to a Kim and a Jay about an electricity and gas account. You do sort of picture someone when you have a name.

Or equally, you can be the service user who feels maltreated by the service deliverer, as the woman felt in the opening scene of this chapter. I remember once while heavily pregnant and with a three-year-old plus his buggy in tow, I tried to board a bus in New York City in the midst of a heat wave. There were two doors for boarding and, by then used to the then London practice of getting on buses on either of the two entrances, I entered the wrong one. 'Get off!' I was commanded by the bus driver, who was looking straight ahead to communicate that, for him, I didn't have a face or identity.

'You have to go to the other entrance!' he continued, still looking ahead, each second he persisted in looking ahead denying me dignity, cancelling out the fact of my existence. It was only the protests of the people in the queue behind me that shamed him into letting me board. I lumberingly hauled my baggage and child, not to mention my pregnant hulk, up the steps onto the bus, within the shadow of his fury, each necessarily slow and halting step infuriating him further, as he maintained his cold, stare-ahead stance of deliberate humiliation. Which had been successful. I had, at first, felt humiliated, then I had become indignant, and finally, while struggling to prevent a restless three-year-old from mounting the steps the driver was forbidding us to climb, had begun to feel almost murderous. However, the kindness of strangers – to me if not to the bus driver – and their collective repair had left me mildly humoured, and tempered my urge to meet aggression with aggression. By the time I was at the top of the steps and paying my fare, I was trying to feel charitable, feeling the weight of a whole hostile bus behind me against the poor driver. I smiled weakly at him and thanked him. He nodded almost imperceptibly in return, no eye contact made. If not leaving me jubilant, my blood pressure went down a smidgeon as perhaps did his.

Stereotyping

When it comes to using interactional skills, transactional relating depends more on using emotional regulation and collaborative language than on mentalising. You can't and won't know much about the other person. Much of what you'll see and think will necessarily be based on stereotyping. We stereotype because it is a shortcut to making decisions about how to behave. Stereotypes, of course, are dangerous, because they are so often wrong. That's especially so when you hold to them as fact, when indeed they are only guesses. Using them in that way is prejudice or literally, 'pre-judging'. You might, for instance, conclude that a dishevelled-looking person with stringy hair at your door is coming to beg for money, but could he be the new neighbour delivering a letter for you that has gone astray to his house?

What else beyond the stereotype might you be able to note about someone coming to your door to deliver a package that adds to the person's humanness? A beleaguered stoop to their shoulders, a smile twitching as they look thoughtful striding to your door? Might you each benefit from a deep breath, a pause and a friendly approach? Are they representing a service you normally resent but have to use? I won't name any here but do fill in your own blank. Can you try to think of them as not just cogs in the wheels you can't stand? They may need the job. They might even resent the organisation as you do. Or they might deliver a service within it that is uniquely good if they are treated as someone who can do that. If so, thinking that can help you shape a possibly more humane response, still your anxiety, resentment, irritation, then shape what you say politely, collaboratively. After all, you are collaborators: you're receiving or giving a service, the other person is in the reciprocal role.

Turning things around

Let's go back now to the moment-to-moment interactions between the token attendant and the customer that we opened with. We are now going to change the body language, the voice tone, the choice of words and the prejudice that denied their individuality, to make their ideas about the other looser and kinder. We'll watch them use skills better and see it unfold more happily. We're going to make these two better observers of themselves and each other, and more skilful interactors.

Customer (her tone of voice is anxious; her body language is nervous and distracted, with her hands going in and out of her pockets as if trying to locate something as she speaks): 'Hello! I am trying to buy a pass to travel or – to buy – what are they called? Tokens? I am not sure. Please forgive me! But what I want to know is . . . I mean, please can you tell me how many rides I get for £10?'

Attendant (he is now looking at her, noticing her nervousness, smiling at her, his tone of voice is soothing): Must be hard in a different city! You get five tokens for £10. Or a pass for £10 for six. Or, anyway, it's £2.50 a ride otherwise and you get something we call 'tokens'!

Customer (she smiles and looks relaxed, stops fidgeting in her pockets, her tone of voice is calm, bright): Oh! Thank you! I guess I can only get three then!

But as you know either party can change the course of an interaction. Let's see how the customer might have turned things positive.

Customer (her tone of voice is anxious; her body language is nervous and distracted, with her hands going in and out of her pockets as if trying to locate something as she speaks): 'Hello! I am trying to buy a pass to travel or – to buy – what are they called? Tokens? I am not sure. Please forgive me! But what I want to know is . . . I mean, please can you tell me how many rides I get for £10?'

Attendant (he is not looking at her, instead he rolls his eyes at his colleague and then stares down, his tone of voice bored, sharp and clipped): 'You get five tokens for £10. Or a pass for £10 for six.'

Customer (looks at him, smiles with concern on her face that registers she sees he has felt put out, her tone is composed, pleasant, almost soothing): Oh, I'm sorry! You are busy – just give me enough of them for two journeys, I'm sure I have enough for at least that.

Attendant (relaxes, looks up at her, smiles, then gives her the tokens).

Customer (smiling, warm voice tone): Thank you!

Attendant (smiling, warm voice tone): No problem!

In either case the outcomes for both will have been both satisfactory and satisfying: together they achieved the transaction they wanted and each added to the sum of pleasure in their own and each other's days.

10

Virtual relationships:
The move online

About eight months into the pandemic, I got a questionnaire from a university asking, among other things, how I'd fared and what I'd learned during the pandemic. Somewhat facetiously I listed, 'Getting good at Zoom and Teams.' I wasn't the only one who gave that answer. When the UK abruptly went into lockdown in March 2020 my psychotherapy and coaching practice, like so many businesses around the world, suddenly radically transformed. I'd already made virtual adaptations over the years for clients whose jobs, for instance, took them on long stints overseas, or those who'd come to me from distant countries or who'd moved away. In those cases the all-important trust and ease had already formed within the crucible of real life. That had been my rule: no virtual without IRL (in real life) first, until trust and comfort had been indelibly established within our in-the-flesh meetings. But even so, when I told clients that March that for an indeterminate amount of time meeting on Zoom or FaceTime was all I could offer, some of my ongoing therapy and coaching clients no longer wished to be seen.

There was no way they could believe in either the efficacy or facility of doing our work virtually, but necessity is, we know, the mother of invention and, it turns out, in the case of relating virtually for work, it's also the iconoclast of received wisdom. In my case this has meant that, even with most new clients, the medium of virtual relating, as long as the technology remains mostly reliable and stable, seems to work well. Trust and comfort can bed in without the expected ripples.

While we have yet to get much hard research on its relative pluses and minuses, and on exactly why relating virtually face-to-face can work well, we've got anecdotal reports – not just about therapy and coaching but also about meetings between people in general, with work and even with friends and family – about these now ubiquitous face-to-face platforms. During the pandemic, our unavoidable immersion in it meant the word 'Zoom' summoned a groan, but it transpires that face-to-face relating platforms bring some distinct benefits to relating. We lived in an experiment on widespread virtual relating imposed by the virus, and the reports came in proclaiming certain advantages and disadvantages. In general, virtual relationships can present particular downsides and dangers, but they also can expand and simplify people's lives.

Michael is an executive I've been coaching for a number of years. We used to meet in London, but now we meet online. As Covid restrictions eased he asked me if I had plans to return regularly to London. I demurred, at that point not yet sure of my ultimate plan, but I asked him if he'd rather we return to that way of working. He looked sheepish. 'Actually,' he confessed, 'this works out a lot better. I've got more on at home now and want to spend more time with the kids – working from home has taught me that. So even though I'm now doing a blend, the thought of having to get across town to see you and then back . . . That takes up almost half an afternoon all together, you know. If we went back to doing that, it would mean me working later and it would cut into my time with the kids. But I didn't want you to feel that I didn't want to see you. It would be great to see you. There's a gap when you don't have physical reality. I know that and I feel that when I do now go into the office some of the time.

But, pragmatically, as long as you don't think we're missing out in not meeting up in person, this is fine the way it is!'

A lot of virtual relating is very new; all of it, from emails onward, is pretty new. Each type – email, messaging, social media platforms, special interest forums – have their own emerging rules of engagement. You try to avoid immediately firing off an impulsive possibly angry or offhand response in emails if you want to avoid aggression. You follow particular grammatical conventions and phrases if you want to be accepted on particular social media platforms. Other newer platforms, or those more recently widely used, such as Zoom, Teams and the like, are beginning to shape theirs. The etiquette of Zoom or Teams meetings, for instance, seems to demand promptness, perhaps even more than IRL. At least during lockdowns some excuses for tardiness vanished: you couldn't blame late trains or traffic, or the queues at the coffee shop.

'You sort of need someone to compere the meet-ups, like a conductor, keeping everyone on the same subject,' commented an executive of an international company to me about this new way of conducting long-range get-togethers among friends. At the same time, she noted that meetings in her business were now more inclusive, which brought up a thorny new question: whom to invite? Now that you can ask anyone around the world to meetings, isn't there a pressure to be clearer about the agenda and your criteria for inviting someone, and to figure out how to convey that without offence? In lockdown you met people you used to visit once every few years more frequently, so what are the new conventions around that? What's expected? What's an acceptable time-lag between contact now?

Some of how we can safely, wisely and productively relate to others is in our control, even if some remains distinctly out of it. Beyond the fact we're in something of a Wild West, because we're only now establishing rules of engagement

– the conventions and expectations around each type of virtual relating – there is the even more problematic issue for conducting relationships online: the quality and sureness of the information you get. We cannot – yet, anyway – remain entirely safe from misinformation and disinformation, from catfishing or other forms of deception. On visual platforms for one-to-one relating, but also for one-to-one relating via messaging or emails, you can employ the principles and deploy the skills of this book, but with virtual relating there is an additional *step* and an extra *principle* to hold in mind.

What I mean is this: in this book the skills for relating rest on you having information. First, that's about yourself: what are you feeling and why in response to or as you approach the other person when there's something that has gone, or could go, amiss. Emotional management rests on you being able to answer that. You can then take steps to be in control of your feelings. Then, to mentalise, you think about what could be going on for the other person and why, to the extent that you know or can make a good guess about it, so you can try to imagine how to act to gain what you need while trying to get the other person on board. Of course, that's to achieve the best outcome and, when relevant, to do so with the least harm. The information that forms that mentalisation then directs how you act and what you say, so the other person will take it in, again so you can get the best potential outcome for going forward. In those skills you are using information about the other person to the best of your ability.

Virtual relating gives you less information about the other person than you'd get IRL. Online you are relating to the presentation authored and engineered by the writer, or photographer, or filmmaker. On Zoom or its like, information is both limited by the fact that you see a fraction of what you'd see IRL – how the person relates within the wider world, for instance

– and also by the amount of control the person chooses to exercise in their presentation to you – their setting, for instance. More than that, you get just their upper body in motion. Offstage, so you can't see them, people have more control over what they'd like to present and what they'd like to hide about themselves; they can exaggerate – or lie. You see only what's chosen. You're relating, but with whom? Even deciphering tone is limited, especially if the online relationship is conducted without visuals. If you're playing games with someone online, for instance, you only get the 'gamer' and they only get the 'gamer' in you. The other person might well be clued up to the fact that you're only a presentation, as well. You're relating to that part-person and they to you as that. As Michael pointed out, you're missing something of the whole, not just the physical, although that as well.

Be careful and take your time

You can't rush gaining the relevant information; you can't assume things. With the only partial information you will always get from relating online you have to be extra careful. This pertains even to email or messaging contact, even when you know the other person IRL. You can't hear tone and you don't have much context beyond the words in front of you. You can jump to conclusions or what you say, if it's ill-considered, can lead to the other person doing so.

You may have had the same sort of lucky escape I had, after sending an email containing personal information about someone else to the wrong person from my address book. I'd hit the wrong name. Luckily it went to someone who knows me well and whom I could trust. She sent it back with a message that reassured me the information would go no further and that the email had been deleted. I've also done the classic error of hitting 'reply all' when the reply was meant for just 'one'. Those were messages sent in haste. Maybe worse was the email spat I once had with a brother. Fast and furiously our emails flew across the ocean, dividing us emotionally further each time, just as the ocean was already doing physically. All we could see were each other's angry words. There were no physical cues to guide us to 'Stop! That looks like you've really hurt him [or her]!' No nuances in tone of voice, no sad bend of shoulders to lend meaning to the words. We didn't talk for a few months. Later in this chapter, though, you'll see that the same skills we've been practising in the book can still lend themselves to email and messaging behaviour.

Aaron, a student, is a prolific tweeter. In addition to his real-life friends, he also considers his 350 followers to be something like 'friends' – certainly he feels that they form a community that makes him feel validated, praised and accepted – they are something like Robin Dunbar's outermost circle of real-life friends mentioned in chapter 7. Aaron tweets about music, politics and films. His tweets are clever and twisty. He thinks the medium – he says its brevity means you need to be pithy and original – suits the way his brain works: 'It's like it releases me; it's really easy for me!' He once thought of being a stand-up comedian. 'This is better,' he claims. 'You can reach more people faster, more frequently, and there's no stage fright.' In person Aaron is deceptively quiet. He considers carefully before responding – there's no rapid-fire quipping, no firebrand remarks. Clearly only certain arenas facilitate his aptitude for those and Twitter is one of them.

One day one of his followers, another young man at a nearby university, managed to track him down and asked if they could meet for a coffee. Aaron was flattered and expected to meet a like-minded soul. In fact, after a fairly desultory if friendly half an hour, Aaron managed to turn the small talk of initial engagement into what he thought was a congenial exchange of political opinions. Later that day he got an email from his follower saying thank you for meeting up, but that he'd really been disappointed. In person Aaron wasn't at all like his tweets. The gist of the deflating message was that Aaron was ordinary and, when it came down to it, pretty boring.

Months later Aaron can tell the story with a laugh, but at the time he was crushed. He realised only in retrospect that his virtual presence through Twitter captures only a small aspect of himself. He recognises that. It's part of why he's been so delighted that a medium like Twitter now exists, even better than his former idea that he'd be a stand-up. It almost uniquely releases that part of him, like oil paints might release the painter in someone else. Anyone expecting his Twitter presentation to be the whole of him will be disappointed.

However, as we'll see in an example later in this chapter, while still limited, you can get quite a bit of information, particularly when you meet visually online, to help you manage interactions well. It's just less information than IRL and you have to tailor your skills to the sort of information you're going to get. But even in Zooms you don't have verification. Even what you see might not be trustworthy: you must take it on faith that the person in front of you is really where they say they are, who they say they are and in their own surroundings. You don't know the 'truth' of what you see or learn from people's online presentation, especially when you aren't interacting visually. Like the conman in *The Tinder Swindler*, it could be all untrue.

Marianne worked as a school secretary and part-time cleaner. She'd been married and divorced twice, and had two sons. To save money after her last marriage ended, she'd moved in with her widowed mother, who helped with childcare on weekends when Marianne did an admin job for one of my neighbours. We both knew her because she worked at the school which our children attended. Everyone liked Marianne: she was bubbly, chatty and helpful. When she asked one day if we

233

knew anyone who needed an assistant to help with admin, because she could use the extra cash, my friend readily signed her up. When Marianne would finish on a Saturday morning Marianne, my friend and I, if I were around, would have coffee together and gossip about the school. We mostly caught up on Marianne's life – she was always quick to offload whatever was on her mind, positive or negative – and one Saturday she sat down with a grin like a Cheshire cat's: she'd met a man online, from rural Texas. They'd met first through a country music enthusiasts' site and begun, over the past two months or so, to communicate. It had stepped up recently to long phone calls. She'd learned he'd been recently divorced because his ex hadn't wanted children. He was thrilled she had sons for he wanted nothing more than to become part of a ready-made family. Because this preceded visual platforms, they sent each other photos. She showed us the one she'd sent – hers was at least five years out of date and in soft focus. The one he'd sent was of an attractive man in his 30s wearing jeans, a checked shirt, a cowboy hat and winking cheekily. This was the man, she told us, she was going to marry.

These were early days of such things happening and my friend and I were aghast, but Marianne was convinced that everything she knew so far convinced her that they were a perfect match, with a shared passion for country music and line dancing, and a meshed need for a completed family. He was of British heritage, undaunted by the prospect, he claimed, of becoming British himself. Or better yet, his late parents owned a ranch that, once through probate, was soon to come to him: she and the boys could come to live there with him. Some intense online relating, some photos and a handful of long phone conversations, and he'd proposed. It was clear that Marianne was not asking what we thought: this was a done deal and she wanted our enthusiasm.

Marianne disappeared from the school and the community shortly afterwards. We heard through the grapevine that she, but not her sons, had moved to Texas, but within a few months she was back in the UK, without the cowboy, in another job. I saw her in the street in town one day and she was keen to go for a coffee. The story came cascading out from a still traumatised Marianne. Although his photos hadn't lied, almost everything else about him had been untrue. He'd never been married. Soon after she'd landed in Texas, hounded into moving there, with the promise that the boys could follow as soon as the deed to his late parents' house came through, an old girlfriend of his had written to her. The letter had warned: don't trust him and watch your wallet. She discovered he'd been given a dishonourable discharge from the US Army only weeks before they'd begun corresponding. She'd spent her remaining life savings on furtively escaping to catch a plane home.

An extreme example, yes, but it demonstrates that extra *step* you need to take in virtual relating: when and if possible establish veracity. It also illustrates the extra *principle* in virtual relating: use caution and take time. The *step*, establishing veracity, as best you can, is clearly the most protective thing you can do. False information is dangerous information. The extra *principle* of caution and time may go against the grain for you, as it did with Marianne, but it is also deeply protective, making your information more secure. Because you both have only partial information and it may not be reliable, the observations and ideas about the other person that inform mentalising and your consequent attempt at collaborative language need more time and more testing than they would IRL. However, when you do develop a relationship virtually, if you want things to go smoothly, as in any relationship the skills still matter, but those skills need to be embedded into those two extra elements of care.

Virtual relating arouses a host of hot issues and it's not within the scope or purpose of this book or chapter to address them all, but it is salient to bring up a few, perhaps to lay some concerns to rest about virtual relating on the one hand, and to spotlight positives on the other.

The cons of virtual relating

The cons have become part of our everyday lore, the subject of tabloid headlines, of TV dramas. You're probably rattled by the existence of unregulated, widely accessible forums, hotbeds of hate and prejudice, that preach unsubstantiated 'facts'.

You'll already have heard reports of children groomed, seduced, kidnapped, killed by paedophiles, who have contacted them online; of teens learning how to self-harm from the internet; of girls who are dying from anorexia encouraged by websites that promote dangerous practices and dispense misinformation; of terrorists fashioned from similarly perilous sites and the relationships they forge through them. We know, again if only from the news and anecdotes, about the bullying of children, women, celebrities, people with vulnerabilities and differences, and those within minorities. And, anecdotally, reports swell of children and adolescents siloed in their rooms by the internet, roaming sites and exchanging posts and messages, sealed off from relating in real life.

There are real dangers for vulnerable, young and unsophisticated people, not just from catfishing paedophiles or grooming terrorists. If you make a mate on a special interest site, that very same bonding that joins people as friends, the ping and pleasure of similarity, bolstered by an assumption that a friend wants the best for you, means that sort of friend will validate and reinforce the shared interest, even if it's a harmful one. And that will be mostly what, perhaps all, you know about each other:

that you both are engrossed, for each other wholly defined, for example, by weight loss. Telling 'Shari', the girl you became virtual friends with from a site that encouraged you to restrict your diet about your new method of cutting calories, and getting a thumbs up from her, tells you you're on the right track. You aren't freakish or singular and she's even giving you tips. For the naïve and unsophisticated, clearly, for the young, for those not schooled in critical thinking and therefore able to sort out real facts from misinformation, and for those not taught to sift evidence from fakery, internet information sites that lure them in and encourage them to make specious relationships can be extremely risky.

And beyond that, if you're a parent you may well be concerned about the amount of time your child spends on online relationships instead of with IRL friends, or what happens while they're talking onscreen. A recent study discovered that during the pandemic more than three times as many primary school-aged children said they'd rather chat to their friends online than in person. Findings like this do increase worry, but there's a perspective to put on this: the findings could be an artefact of the pandemic when the research was conducted. Online relating, not IRL, is mostly all children were able to do. The same study found abuse had been widespread – trolling, for instance – as well as its reverse side: regret about posting some messages. Again, here's the grain of salt: the more there is of something, the more there is of whatever happens within it: if online is where most interactions occur, that's also where more abusive behaviour will occur.

These 'cons' serve to highlight my point: you need caution around virtual relating. The hot debates over parental protection of their children, putting aside the one about how far any parent goes to restrict their child's world, underscore the primitive state society remains in over how to regulate what's available so it can be safer and more reliable; whether there could be built-in protections for all of us, but particularly the young and vulnerable; and whether there could ever be methods to verify people's presentations of themselves online. If you can do detective work to check things out or avoid a site or contact pathway that could be dodgy, then that's sensible. And if you can hold yourself back to reserve judgement and take time to learn more, no matter how enthusiastically you feel attracted to a new internet friend, try to do so.

The pros of virtual relating

Given all that, you have probably benefitted from the other side of the coin too, chiefly the convenience and speed of linking with people, especially those in far-flung places. If you are one of the geographically or socially isolated, virtual relating might be your lifeline. The pandemic has shown that to all of us: we've all been isolated, our connections to others saved in large part by virtual means. Some people with autism, particularly teenagers, make gaming 'friends' using gaming sites, since games obviate navigating through confusing social cues. They're connected to others, some comfortably for the first time. Ditto for those who feel 'other' in some way – for example, those with special medical conditions or unusual sexual proclivities – who find their counterparts online.

BookTok, an outgrowth of TikTok devoted to reading, has garnered over 9.6 billion views and keeps growing. This site joins young readers extolling books they love. Aidan, a 14-year-old boy I know, had felt 'odd' because he loved to read fiction and had no friends with whom to discuss the books that had excited him. Boys tend to 'fall off' the reading platform in adolescence, compared to girls, and girls, a piece of research by the University of Exeter Professor of English, Helen Taylor, has shown, tend to read fiction more than boys. But Aidan has gratefully found a like-minded community in BookTok, although it is largely populated by girls. At this point the anonymity of being part of a virtual group means he doesn't have to expose what he feels to be his 'oddness' to other boys, but he can still revel in his pleasure in reading. Meanwhile, the shared tastes he finds there validate him: others whom he respects for their voices feel as he does. He's also delighted to find suggestions for books to read. He recognised one of the people who posted as a girl he knows, so knowing that he someday might even be able to meet someone with similar tastes in real life has comforted him.

As a member of the board of an organisation working with domestic abuse I became aware of sites that convene people who have experienced abuse; these link people to others in the same boat, to organisations, to ways to get help, and they dispense validated information. These sites can be literal lifelines. Relationships that result from them can be key to helping people leave risky homes, and both to begin and to sustain new and safer lives.

And then there are the parental concerns about children's mental health and virtual relating. In fact, the evidence is beginning to accumulate to dispel some of them. In general, spending time online (not solely in online relationships) does not, it seems, pose harm to teenagers. A recent study from Oxford University found there is no evidence of a growing link between child mental health problems and the use of technology. As a newspaper editorial put it: 'Social media may be no more harmful to teenagers' mental health than television was in the 1990s.' In regard to parental concern about the harm from online bullying, one pre-pandemic study warned that it's not online relating parents should be worried about but IRL bullying. Online bullying of children was found to be less damaging than bullying IRL, which makes sense: you have a real person doing real not nice things, in a nearer, more palpable way, right in front of you. Moreover, a study of suicidal adolescents found that having more online-only friendships was particularly helpful and suicidal thoughts shrank.

And having both IRL and online friends doesn't seem to get in the way of interacting IRL, as you might fear it could: a different study showed that people can tell the difference between the sort of intimacy and trust you get IRL and those online. For example, people tell and discuss IRL friends about health issues, but not their 'only online' friends. Yet another study showed having both kinds is not in conflict, but instead that each make a contribution to wellbeing. Another study established, unsurprisingly, that particularly the oldest generation in far-flung families, who you might imagine had more difficulty travelling, enthusiastically valued virtual relating.

Or it could be in your work relationships that you've derived benefits from virtual meetings. Jim Citrin and Darleen De Rosa, of the Spencer Stuart business consulting firm, write about one advantage that emerged over the pandemic, in particular – that bosses have more intimate contact with staff. What formerly might have been cursory meetings can be both longer and more concentrated, so both parties can get to know each other much better. If you own a business, or run a team, you have probably been grateful for the convenience of people getting the same information at the same time, and saving time and money if your team is far-flung. A journal editor told me that he can now spend time chatting with authors and is able to get across his comments to them much more expeditiously having made a personal relationship with those he would never have had the chance to meet previously.

Or maybe you've had a friendship grow from an IRL group. A friend who lives in London and tweets has 'twunches' – she meets up with a group who have met on Twitter but live locally for occasional lunches. They share the Twitter-based interests that bonded them in the first place, with lunches around that subject, but meeting up bridges the physical gap Michael, my client who didn't want to go back to in-person sessions, spotted. In person you gain information – people's physical movements, aesthetic choices, behaviour both towards you and within the wider world – and this is information that, unlike the unseen presence online, is unfiltered by the individual's control over it. You see more than what they want to present; your information is more complete.

And how many of us know couples who first met through internet dating? This is perhaps not so different to pre-technology days when romances were kindled through letters, as the AS Byatt novel, *Possession*, so elegantly dramatises. People can, of course, develop relationships in part through exchanging words online – messaging, emailing, for example. But – with a nod to the point about partial information and checking out the truth of things IRL – romances that become robust get tried out over meetings in the flesh, over time, as more rounded information gets gathered and is subject to proof.

Written virtual relating

I saw Anna and her ex-husband when they were separating, and amidst angry emotions we concentrated on their communications around childcare. Later, now a single parent, she contacted me again, this time about a different relationship. An online business relationship she'd developed had hit a rock. On both counts she'd not been cautious. She'd not checked out who her new internet friend was and she'd rushed to judgement that he was more to her than he possibly could be.

Made redundant during the pandemic, Anna had been an executive of a fashion chain. Driven by panic and need, she'd garnered every ounce of energy and her full, worldwide contact list and launched in what seemed short order a cherished dream: an online clothing rental business. Well-connected, with worldwide contacts, one became key. This was a man she 'met' online, through a friend three times removed – which probably meant she had little knowledge of and, in her haste, sparse due diligence on him – in Canada, who'd begun an online rental specialising in vintage designs, more niche than her own project. This apparently warm, dynamic and sympathetic young man became something of a mentor, her cheerleader, her guide. 'I thought he was my angel,' Anna sighed. He'd taken her step-by-step through both pitfalls and pathways to success. Their relationship flourished on WhatsApp and other social messaging apps, with some sparsely sprinkled FaceTimes that, given the time difference, could happen only when her children were asleep. Listening to her account, I heard her mad rush, driven by what must have been panic and loneliness. I had little idea about what lay behind the man's engagement with it, but, not rattled as Anna had been, I could surmise and try to put myself in his shoes. Maybe, I wondered, he simply recognised a kindred soul joined in a fervid mission to expand green fashion. Or just maybe – and both motivations could be true – something more worrying for Anna was at work: the lure of control. What Anna related sounded to me like an onslaught of do's and don'ts, so that might have been the case. If that were so, I was guessing, what would happen when fledgling Anna was ready to fly? His own feathers might well be ruffled.

Anna's enchantment and desperation, her mad dash into intimacy and dependency, had short-circuited her ability both to stay calm in the face of the relationship friction that did eventually arise, or to mentalise what could be going on in him, to then productively manage the issue. In her desperation he had been, rather one-dimensionally, her 'angel' and, joined solely philanthropically by their common aim to make fashion more green, that was all she'd seen of him. But it was all she'd wished to see. When that angel fell from grace, the unprepared Anna was, of course, devastated.

Indeed, his fateful fall came in the wake of Anna's flight from the nest. With his considerable help, her platform design and business plan were now firm and she was on to the next step: finding stock. That was in her considerable domain of expertise. She'd been paid for spotting trends for years. His domain was smaller, his advice no longer germane, but he was, Anna assumed, naively as it happened, her cheerleader. Expecting him to continue in that role, she sent him the details of, to her, a wildly exciting new design collective. She was stunned when he fired back: 'I cannot approve of this step. Step away now. Very bad move.' Baffled, even sickened – this was totally out of character! – she fired back. 'I don't get what you're saying. I mean, first of all, what do you mean "approve"? That just sounds so weird! Explain!' And so he in turn fired back: 'Your order to me to "explain" is deeply offensive, as is the accusation that I'm "weird". How could you even say such a thing? And, girl, I am really disappointed. I taught you to do your research! That website is a shambles. I thought I taught you to be thorough!' Anna, in an instant, became again the former executive of a fashion chain. Angry, she fired back, now to her enemy, her detractor, certainly not her angel: 'You "taught" me??!!' She refrained from typing in capitals. But the double question and exclamation marks conveyed the same.

And then there was silence. Anna sat back in astonishment. It had to be one of two things. Either she'd been duped: he'd presented a false self to her all along. Or she'd been stupid: she hadn't seen who he was. Or both. In the end, she wasn't totally off base on either count. She wanted to reflect on how this had happened and what, if anything, she wanted to do about it. Hence, she contacted me to use a session for just that. In it she quickly allowed that her desperation had made her too hasty: she'd assumed too much about her new friend/mentor. Where had she got her evidence? He'd been responsive, warm, helpful. But she only knew what she 'knew' from what he'd written to her; from the snatches of images she'd got of his well-curated collection on their FaceTime visits; from equally distilled Instagram posts.

In her desperate haste to find a benevolent helper she'd not done the due diligence that might have nuanced her rosy view. Who else knew him? What had been their experiences? What was he like when crossed, when his ideas didn't align with others? In her desperate haste she hadn't questioned his motivation to help, nor the limits of his beneficence. When there was new data that put the angel image into question, Anna became desperate once again, hasty, demanding and accusatory: 'Explain!' and 'weird'. Reflecting not just on what she'd been feeling and why, which she could do now because she was calm, Anna went on to reflect about the man she now knew more about. Maybe he had enjoyed being the tutor, both because he did want to help but also because it gave him control, status, made him feel expert. Maybe rather than being as invested in nurturing Anna as she'd believed, his ego was more important. Then her emerging power would make him competitive, rather than supportive. Maybe he assumed Anna understood more about him than she did, that she'd have been sensitive to his feelings as she was shedding him as her mentor. Maybe then he'd felt angry at what he would have seen as Anna's insensitive way of showing she'd moved on. Those seemed reasonable, even charitable, hypotheses. No 'angel' but human.

What could she do now? What did she want to do now? It's easier to shed online relationships than it is to shed IRL ones, especially if they're geographically remote. They could continue to ghost each other, but that didn't feel right to Anna. She wanted both to acknowledge his contribution to her and the warmth that had indeed grown between them. Someday, anyway, she might want his advice about vintage and there might be some way forward for them.

'I'll apologise,' Anna determined. 'I'll own up to being so needy I saw him only as my "saviour" and I realise I didn't think about how he might have felt when I just changed the terms of things, when we never discussed what was going to happen next when I moved on to creating stock.' That seemed the right first step, a repair that put into practice the mentalising she'd just done. And then what? You'll see in her answers she's using repairs, based on her mentalising, and then inviting him, collaboratively, to think of how to go forward, or not.

'I'll see what he says. I'll try to listen to his words and ask if I'm right: did what I'd done offend or hurt him or what? And I really want to tell him that even though I rushed into the relationship in desperation and might not have thought enough about him, he has really been a key reason I've made it through, so I want to thank him properly.' That, too, seemed the right thing to do, grown from her guess that his ego had been injured. But going forward? 'I'll ask him if he feels he wants to. If so, what does he think I could offer him or he can offer me? Could we discuss ideas? Or maybe we could just be "friends". Then we'd be able to trust that we might see ways to do stuff in the future? I'd try to make offers. I'd try to listen to him.' And by what modality would this conversation or conversations occur I asked, given that their relationship had to remain virtual? Written? Face to face? 'I'd write first,' she was clear. 'This time I'd take my time. I'd craft my words. I'd think carefully about my replies. Then I might feel brave enough to talk face to face.'

The end of this story highlights the single distinct advantage online written conversations offer: you can actually take the time when you interact. You can use the advantage of distance to give you cooling down, then thinking time, just as you would try to gain time IRL. Online gives you the luxury of time. You can fashion, as Anna was preparing to do, a repair and an offer.

When I drafted the UK Parenting Plan for divorced and separated couples, we offered couples a list of choices of communication modes – phone, in person and also email – to establish clarity over how they'd communicate about the thorny issues of childcare. Many chose email because it does give you time to cope with anger and manage it, and was therefore safest. Using electronic relating formats in this careful, thoughtful way can in fact help how you relate, whether you relate entirely electronically or also in real life.

Visual virtual relating

Kathy is a young mother who used to run a restaurant in the city in which I once lived. She came to see me for a few therapy sessions when she and her husband were concerned about their daughter's struggle to fit in at school. But one of our sessions focused, instead, on her now Zoom-based relationship with her one-time best childhood friend, Joan. Kathy entered our own Zoom session still furious, troubled and perplexed from their latest encounter. Her friend's ingrained social gaucheness had been amplified in their Zoom encounters. The many adaptations Kathy had made over the years to ease their real-life encounters no longer easily applied when all they had was these virtual face-to-face interactions. Her instinct had been to avoid Joan throughout the pandemic, dreading Joan's email suggestions that they meet over Zoom. Their sporadic, and very brief, sessions never improved, but, as it happened, dissecting Kathy's dilemma with Joan illuminated the actual advantage in using an online face-to-face platform. It gives you a distinct advantage if you 'zoom' in yourself, on certain cues about people you get uniquely from such a format for relating. When Kathy came into my office all she could see were its drawbacks, but Joan was a difficult case for any interaction and, it seemed, her relational deficits were emphasised by conducting a relationship with her solely online, face to face.

'She actually begins by staring at me in silence, even if she's the one who's set up the Zoom. She waits for me to start talking. The staring can go on for minutes until I finally smile and start. She's unmoved, no matter how long I wait. She doesn't think she shares conversational responsibility – at least that's the way it seems – and that's always been the case. Before, when we'd meet up, I'd expect her silence and we'd start out with something like a ritual cup of tea, a hug. If I was at her house I'd look around, or if she was at mine I'd let her wander about and look for the first five or ten minutes and then I'd start. I'd always start. I mean conversation never exactly trips along, but that's okay. I know to wait. She does it on the phone too, and emails aren't much better. Hers are always about a sentence long and that's it. The point is, up to now I knew what to do. During the pandemic, Zoom or FaceTime was all we had, pretty much, and it's made it much harder.'

After 20 years of a difficult but treasured friendship, Kathy could only imagine a solution which had her continuing to avoid Joan, which would end the friendship, but she didn't want that either. The answer was to concentrate on what you do get in face-to-face virtual interactions, rather than what you don't. If you zero in on what information you do get, versus what's left out, it can help you focus your skills, so you pay attention to what you can observe and then work out what you can guess.

The necessity of working with people only virtually during the pandemic taught me it is possible to make deep and trusting connections, to bond over emotionally fraught and intimate problems, despite the limits of meeting only online. I began to see Candace and Dave during one of the lockdowns. Candace had discovered a brief affair in Dave's past. Dave has a public image in their community and concern over leakage about his affair added to the couple's distress. I worked intensively with them for a few weeks and then, as things settled down and the emotional temperature normalised, less so, always over Zoom. 'Intensively' over Zoom meant longer sessions – from an hour to an hour and a half – and more frequent ones. They were not the first or only couple presenting to me this way during the pandemic and we just had to work with the tools available – virtual ones in every case. I found it was in fact possible to work only virtually, even when an affair has thrown a bomb into the middle of a marriage. While everyone had to be on board with believing it was possible even without meeting up in person, something else was also essential: both sides had to be adept at focusing on what information they could get: zeroing in on facial and verbal gestures, words, expressions.

What you get in face-to-face virtual relating is a tight focus on facial and verbal signals. There were reports of new conventions springing up during lockdowns, with one person describing it as like being back in school, because you tend to put your hand up in meetings so people will know you want to say something. You can't nudge or interrupt easily, because that could create too much disorder, so gestures become that much more important.

Of course, you miss out on what the rest of body language might tell you. You don't get the way the person carries themselves, the clothes they put on, the way they fiddle with things or glance around a room, or leave it or stay too long in it. You can't assess well the texture of their skin or, if you would normally make physical contact, how they touch or what they feel like, or what it would feel like if you could. These add to the sum of your conclusions and feelings about people and they will add nuances to your mentalising when you do that about them. These sources of shaping your relating are lost. I don't know how tall Candace and Dave are, or even how tall they are in relation to each other. They sit side by side, necessarily, and there's little room for me to discern. I don't know if they'd choose separate chairs or to snuggle close to each other on a sofa if they'd come to me in the flesh. I can't tell if Candace has healthy skin or Dave really has reddish hair – the lights in their room are always bright and I can't be sure how true they are.

But other things are gained. I do know how they think, feel and relate to me and to each other, because we are tightly, intently focused on every eye flicker, every mouth turned up or down, every leaning in towards or away from each other, every rise and fall of the voice. We aren't distracted by phones or emails, because the conventions attached to relating the way we are dictate constant attention. They have to think hard, as I do, every minute about what these gestures, signals, words mean. The minute-to-minute interactions are under the microscope of the screen each of us are mutually gazing at. We tune in to the particular frequencies of each of our voices, words and faces that we've learned about over time, so we note minute changes in them in ways we'd likely have missed without the intense focus on the selective data we've grown accustomed to focusing on. 'It's so exhausting!' was a pandemic complaint and it is. All that intense and singular concentration, trapped as you each are in your respective gazes, *is* exhausting. The loop of interactions – your expression and utterance, theirs back to you, and so forth – are undiluted, in pure, inescapable form.

In losing information about people's height, gait, where they choose to place themselves in physical spaces, about movement in general, you take your noticing elsewhere, onto a narrower, but arguably deeper level. It has struck me that the more exquisite attunement to facial and verbal information you get this way seems similar to what is said about people who lose one sense but develop a greater skill with others; for instance, blind people hearing more keenly, listening more finely than sighted people. You might also be let into personal information you'd not get otherwise, if you're each in your own habitats and you haven't blurred or disguised your backgrounds. You share each other's personal artefacts: photos, artwork, books.

So back to Kathy and Joan – Joan who was giving very few facial or verbal cues to Kathy. But what about what Kathy was giving back to Joan? In response to Joan's inertness, Kathy became silent and uneasy. Inescapably, Kathy's tiny expressions were broadcast to Joan, who'd have recognised them as discomfort. And what Kathy knew about Joan was that she wouldn't have known what to do to make her, Kathy, relax. That was what was being conveyed, back and forth onscreen, to each other: Joan's general social gaucheness and Kathy's unease.

Pre-pandemic Kathy used to dispel the initial awkwardness of being with Joan with what seemed to me to be certain rituals that eased the way into their initial conversation. Kathy and Joan had grown up across the street from each other, each in their own way witness to and loyal to the other one's childhood sufferings. Joan had for a time been selectively mute; Kathy had learned to play with her soundlessly. Kathy had lived within a domestic warzone; Joan's calm and quieter house had offered her solace. Without realising it Kathy had developed a method of beginning things with Joan, through acclimating herself silently into Joan's environment. She'd not expected immediate words. Instead, she'd walk around Joan's house to get its feel; she'd notice Joan's objects, touch them and use observations about them as a bridge with which to start a conversation. If Joan came to her, she'd let her do the same, watching how she'd move and what had caught her eye, then initiate a conversation in the same way. In each case Kathy would have been entering Joan's world, the Joan she knew, had sympathy with and for. They'd developed rituals to get started so Joan would feel ready. That was how Kathy described it to me.

But wasn't she, I pointed out, also getting herself prepared to relate to Joan? To feel at ease enough, by reminding herself who Joan was as she roamed around Joan's rooms or watched the stiffening leave Joan's body, the leaning towards her she recognised as Joan being ready to speak? Those tools for getting there were now gone. But wouldn't Joan, in her way, be similarly monitoring Kathy? When Kathy looked at ease, remembering how to be with Joan, she probably communicated it somehow to Joan through the way she looked. Kathy looked thoughtful. She'd been so concerned with her own indignation that she hadn't thought about the fact that she had as much effect on Joan as Joan had about her, that Joan would have been searching for signs about Kathy.

To the point at hand, Kathy should remember that, painful though it had been to get there, she had somehow been able to initiate a conversation on FaceTime with Joan. How had she done it? What had happened to release her and to release Joan? It had to have been something in each other's faces. That's all they had available this time. If Kathy could identify that, as she'd identified the tools IRL that had made things flow for them, she'd be able to do it again.

'There was a flicker in Joan's face,' she remembered. 'It was like it didn't look like she was frowning at me, waiting for me to start. Then I knew it was okay, I could start asking her a question, that that drag of a silence could end.' And what had precipitated that flicker, I wondered? Just as Joan had 'read' that Kathy was feeling ready to relate to her after she'd immersed herself in Joan's world IRL, what on the opposite screen had Joan, intently focused as Kathy had been, seen? 'I guess that I was more relaxed?' hazarded Kathy. That was likely. So, what had helped her get to there, in the same way that gazing around Joan's house had done before? She scrunched her face as I watched her on my screen, thinking hard.

'Well' – she closed her eyes, recalling – 'I remember watching her little tic – she does this thing with her mouth when she's uncomfortable, particularly when she's just waiting for you to start, because I know she's thinking she just can't. But it's almost like she's champing at the bit. She doesn't know she does it, but for just a second there I saw it, I realise, and I thought it was sort of sweet. Something about her being almost excited but ignorant. She doesn't know what to do. I guess I sort of felt sorry for her, not annoyed, not uptight. I think what you mean is that she noticed that in my face, like I noticed that in hers. So I saw that tic go. I saw her face relax, like I used to see her shoulders go down. I always used to look at her shoulders, because it was so marked, almost like she was sinking from the weight of finding how to start such a burden. And then as she saw it was okay, she'd look so different.'

I nodded. 'Anything else?' Kathy's eyes were still shut in concentrated reminiscence. 'I looked around the room behind her. I saw the little glass horses she used to collect that we played with as kids. Maybe I even smiled – who knows? I could have, when I spotted them.' She opened her eyes. 'I see what you mean. I guess there are ways I am already using and maybe I can use them even more, get better at noticing what's there in front of me. I definitely found myself when we did talk feeling we talked more intensely than we had in a long time.' When I asked what she meant she answered, 'Well, I see that I was really looking at her, and she really, really looked at me, deeply. Sometimes, particularly in the beginning of our conversations in the past she'd kind of nervously dart glances for a bit. That would go away. But this time there was none of that. We were much more "in sync" when we finally did start going.' And that was without anything but their faces and their words, in close observation and in intense listening mode.

Had there been any moment of difficulty? I asked, wondering what happens when there's a break in their synchrony and how they restart. She closed her eyes again, putting herself back into that conversation. 'Yes, a tiny one. I mentioned hearing from another girl we'd known as children who'd I guess you'd call it bullied Joan. Anyway, wasn't patient with her like I was. Joan never liked her. But she was still my friend and I still see her now and again. Her name came up. I saw Joan's face go tight. Kind of like she goes blank, like the door's shut: her eyes sort of glaze over. Her shoulders go up again. I hate that. It means we might have to start all over again and that's a pain . . .' She opened her eyes. So? I prompted. 'I took a deep breath. At first, I was irritated, but then I guess I did what I'd done before – saw the things about Joan I love, found her sweet again somehow. And I did feel bad for her. I know that girl wasn't nice to her and I probably should just never mention her name. Every once in a while I drop it into a conversation to see if maybe now she's okay, over it. She's not and she'll never be. So, I sort of give that to her. I understand. Even if I think if it were me, I'd forgive – she was only a kid, herself! So, I said something like, "Yeah, she's sort of a dickhead" – because she is or she can be, I wasn't lying – "Don't worry, I know that, but can we go back to what you were saying? I think I'd just asked you something." She was telling me about a project at work, so then we picked up where we'd left off.'

Kathy smiled. I smiled and told her that she had really managed things well. Without realising it, she had 'read' her friend with, compared to previously, very limited information about her, but she had used what she had really well, even using it to get over a roadblock. She had used tools to help her before, but now she'd used different tools – Joan's face, her voice, her upper body. I explained that some of the exhaustion she felt after such virtual encounters with Joan was normal exhaustion anyone would feel after you're using those tools, that intense focus on face and voice. There's little let-up. Encounters might even not go on that long, but they take so much energy that you feel as if they have.

Kathy sighed with relief. She may never look forward to FaceTime with Joan as much as she would to seeing her in the flesh, but cutting her cloth to suit its limits empowers Kathy so she doesn't have to begin by fearing things and being 'uptight'.

By extolling the virtues of virtual relating in no way do I want to minimise the advantages of relating IRL.

The tools empower you to focus on what you can, but, of course, they don't give you back other things. You cannot touch. You can't express or receive what we know are the health-giving, healing, restorative, singularly reassuring and reaffirming benefits of physical tenderness. No matter how productive or how skilfully you conduct it, this is what will be missing in any online relationship.

11

Future relationships:
Habit-forming

So, where does this leave us? It's harder now than ever to be left alone. Technology means the sheer volume of interactions has increased. We're reachable by others and we can reach others all the time. We're learning the dangers and rewards that come from relating over new platforms and we're establishing the etiquette, but it feels like we're in an onslaught of change. However, the principles that this book is teaching remain the same.

The principles do not change and they tell you to observe how you interact in the loops of behaviour, those moment-to-moment interchanges between you and another person. When there are misunderstandings and frictions, when there are breaks in the easy rhythms between you, be careful how you feel, think and respond.

Stop the action as you proceed to check in and consider whether things have gone smoothly – once the skills become habitual for you it really only takes a few seconds. Perceive what happened, who did what, who felt what and get a sense of why. That will show you how to proceed.

Know that you are each responsible for and have the power at each step, each moment of the interchange between you, to make it positive or negative. That means it can be up to you. You can turn things around to make them feel good and be in sync. Or not.

Look and think about both parts of the interaction, you and the other person. Observe tone, body signals. Hear their words. Make yours as clear as you can in a way that they can hear. Attend to you, what you feel and why. Manage that. Attend to the other person and what they are likely to feel in response to what you say or do. Feel for you both.

Then you're on track for a truly collaborative interchange, phrasing things clearly, concisely, inviting the other to listen. In interactions with someone you will benefit if you can find points of understanding, even if that's about ending a collaboration, but more frequently it will be about making it go forwards more productively for you both. That collaboration could be a friendship, a romantic, family or domestic relationship, a work project or even just collecting a package.

It may sound like it will take a long time to think about yourself, the other person and then what to say or do, but it doesn't. In fact, as anecdotes and now clinical findings about mindfulness techniques used to manage emotional states have shown, the sorts of measures this book is suggesting actually only take a few seconds. These pauses aren't perceptible to others, but they can also offer others useful moments for reflection.

In the initial chapters I talked about how insight into yourself wasn't enough, but you do need that too, because now you'll hopefully be looking at relationships as a set of interactions that build up. In a particular moment, as you interact you will, as a skilful person, think about what goes on inside you and why – your past, your likes, your dislikes and how they were formed – but that will only be your half of the interaction. Just remember not to stop there, because the other half is just as important. Ask what effect your behaviour might have on the other person. Ask yourself who that other person might be and why they might respond to you in that way? That tells you what steps are next and that means you'll be collaborating, shaping the best outcome for you – and possibly for them.

Training yourself to do that, to think interactionally, to use interactional skills, is a pathway towards better relationships, whether virtual or in person, whether fleeting or for the long run, whether with colleagues or friends, or with the people you love. And once you've got the skills defined, seen them in action, and then tried them again and again in your own life, you can make them second nature to you.

This book has tried both to define the skills you need and to give examples of them in action across some of the situations you'll probably encounter in life. Now you're on to the next step – to try the skills out in your own situations – and then to keep trying and to keep using them. You will develop the habit of attending to the interaction; to your own emotional state and the why of it; then calming yourself; of thinking about the other person; and of shaping what you say and how you react most productively within that space in between. You'll have become tuned in to misreadings, to moments of rupture, to times when cycles have turned from virtuous to vicious, and because you'll know about making repairs, you'll make them.

Relating skilfully is a constant. Ring whatever changes new platforms, new technology, might bring. The skills will help you in whatever mode you relate to build good, even great, relationships. Having those relationships is the pathway that leads to good, even great, healthy, happy lives.

Resources

Apter, T and Josselson, R. (1998) *Best friends: The pleasures and perils of girls and women's friendships*. New York: Crown.

Apter, T. (2007) *The sister knot: Why we fight, we we're jealous, why we'll love each other no matter what*. New York and London: W.W. Norton.

Apter, T. (2009) *What do you want from me? Learning to get along with in-laws*. New York and London: W.W. Norton.

Apter, T. (2022) *The teen interpreter: A guide to the challenges and joys of raising adolescents*. New York and London: W.W. Norton.

Black, O. and Bailey, S. (2009) *Relationships: The Mind Gym*. London: Sphere.

Bloom, P. (2016) *Against empathy: The case for rational compassion*. London: The Bodley Head.

Bowlby, J. (1969; 1982) *Attachment and loss*. New York: Basic Books.

Byng-Hall , J. (1985) The family script: A useful bridge between theory and practice. *Journal of Family Therapy, 7*, 3, 301–305.

Csikszentmihalyi, M. and Larson, R. (1984) *Being adolescent: Conflict and growth in the teenage years*. New York: Basic Books.

Csikszentmihalyi, M. (1997) *Living well: The psychology of everyday life*. London: Weidenfeld and Nicholson.

De Rosa, D. and Citrin, J. M. (2021) *Leading at a distance: Practical lessons for virtual success*. Hoboken, New Jersey: Wiley.

Dodd, C. (2022) *All grown up: Nurturing relationships with adult children*. London: Green Tree, Bloomsbury.

Dunbar, R. (2021) *Friends: Understanding the power of our most important relationships*. London: Little , Brown.

Duhigg, C. (2012) *The power of habit: Why we do what we do and how to change*. London: William Heinemann.

Eriksen, E. (1963) *Childhood and society* (second edition). New York: W.W. Norton.

Fowler, J.H., Christakis, N. (2008) 'Dynamic spread of happiness in a large social network: Longitudinal analysis over twenty years in the Framingham Heart Study'. *British Medical Journal*, 377, 2338, 1–9.

Gaby, N. (2015) *Dumped: Stories of women unfriending women*. Berkeley, California: She Writes Press.

Gallagher, A.M., Updegraff, K.A., Padella, J., McHale, S.M. (2018) 'Longitudinal associations between sibling relational aggression and adolescent adjustment'. *J. of Youth and Adolescence*, 47, 10, 2100–2113.

Garnett, J. (2021) 'There I almost am: On envy and twinship'. *Yale Review*, 109, 1, 17–31.

Goleman, D. (1996) *Emotional intelligence: Why it can matter more than IQ*. London: Bloomsbury.

Gottman, J. (1994) *Why marriages succeed or fail: and how you can make yours last*. New York: Simon and Schuster.

Gottman, J , Notarius, C. Gonso, J and Markman, H. *A couple's guide to communication*. London: Routledge.

Greenberger, D., Padesky, C.A., Beck, A.T. (2015) *Mind over Mood: Change how you feel by changing the way you think* (second edition).New York: Guilford Press.

Grosz, S. (2013) *The examined life*. London: Chatto and Windus.

Heller, D. P. (2019) *The power of attachment: How to create deep and lasting intimate relationships*. Louisville, Colorado: Sounds True. Publications.

Holmes, J. (2010) *Exploring in security*. London: Routledge.

Iasenza, S. (2020) *Transforming sexual narratives: A relational approach to sex therapy*. New York: Routledge.

Lerner, H. (1989) *The dance of intimacy*. New York: Harper and Row.

Lerner, H. (1985) *The dance of anger.* New York: Harper and Row.

Mischel, W., Ebbeson, E., Raskoff-Zeiss, A. (1972) 'Cognitive and attentional mechanisms in delay of gratification'. *J. of Personality and Social Psychology*, 21, 2, 204–218.

Murray, L. and Andrews, L. (2000) *The social baby: understanding babies' communication from birth.* Richmond, Surrey: CP Publishing.

Murray, L. (2014) *The psychology of babies: How relationship support develops from birth to two years.* London: Constable and Robinson.

Orbach, S. and Eichenbaum, L. (1987) *Bittersweet: Facing up to feelings of love, envy and competition in women's friendships.* London, Melbourne, Auckland, Johannesburg: Century.

Owen, W. (2021) *The mentalization therapy guidebook: The art of becoming aware of one's body, mind and soul.* London: Independently published.

Pang, C. (2020) *Explaining humans: What science can teach us about life, love and relationships.* London: Viking.

Parkes, C. M., Stevenson-Hinde, J. and Marris, P. (1991) *Attachment across the life cycle.* London: Routledge.

Perel, E. (2017) *Mating in captivity: Unlocking erotic intelligence.* New York: Harper paperbacks.

Perry, P. (2020) *The book you wish Your parents had read (and your children will be glad that you did).* London: Penguin Life.

Reibstein, J. and Richards, M. (1992) *Sexual arrangements: Marriage, monogamy and affairs.* London: Mandarin/William Heinemann.

Reibstein, J. (1997) *Love life: How to make your relationship work.* London: Fourth Estate.

Reibstein, J. (2006) *The best kept secret: Men and women's stories of lasting love.* London and New York: Bloomsbury.

Shragai, N. (2021) *The man who mistook his job for his life.* New York: W. H. Allen.

Taylor, H. (2020) *Why women read fiction.* Oxford: Oxford University Press.

'Teens, tweens and screens'. Editorial, 5 May, 2021, London: *The Times* newspaper.

Twenge, J. M. and Campbell, W. K. (2013) *The Narcissism epidemic: Living in the age of entitlement.* New York and London: Atria.

Vaillant, G. (2012) *Triumphs of experience.* Cambridge, Mass. and London: Belknap/Harvard Press.

ACKNOWLEDGEMENTS

The gestation of a book is usually long, starting a good deal before the moment an author commits first words to paper or word processor. This particular book is a case in point. It is the culmination of decades of my own work and thinking. The ideas within it were shaped over time, with legions of people – other professionals, clients, patients, students, not to mention family and friends – helping me to form both the questions it raises and the answers I've come to. There are too many of those helpers to name. I hope you all know who you are. My gratitude to you for all that I've learned in our work together or discussions over the years is deep.

But there are some who very directly helped in this book's creation and they merit particular mention. Among those are the students, trainees and clinical colleagues at the University of Exeter's AccEPT Clinic, which resulted in the refinement of the Exeter Model and its relative, the Intercultural Exeter Model. Specifically, my colleagues both at the University of Exeter, Prof Hannah Sherbersky, Prof Eugene Mullan, Prof Jeremy Holmes, the Child and Family Practice Group and the London Intercultural Couples Centre, particularly Dr Reenee Singh. Penny Mansfield, CBE, and her extraordinary team with whom I worked over the years at the organisation, One plus One, were key in both helping to develop my ideas and in advancing and evidencing much of them through our work together.

The same can be said for my work with Octavius Black and Sebastian Bailey and the many talented, bright and impressive people at The Mind Gym. Dr Mary-Claire Race, Cathy Walton, Emma Seal, and Daisy Goodwin provided feedback on specific chapters and I thank them for making those better as a result. Craig Myhill was a fantastically reliable and resourceful research assistant. His promptness in getting things done so well really sped things up. Gillian Stern made me explain things to her in a way a non-psychologist could understand. Like magic, her help transformed complex ideas into intelligible ones. She was a wonderful interpreter, translator, and friend.

My agent, Elizabeth Sheinkman, cannot be thanked deeply enough. She has believed in me and in this project from the start. She 'got it' at once, seeing its promise and naming it 'a paradigm shift.' She has guided it, helping me hone it through different guises toward its present, finished state. She's not only been its firm believer and promoter, she's been a cheerleader and wonderful friend. She led me to Charlotte Croft, my brilliant editor, who has been remarkable, gratifyingly enthusiastic about the book's ideas, reporting even on how they have worked in her own life. She worked with me through the grimness of the pandemic, responding readily and sensitively to all I sent to her. She was a source both of encouragement and even joy in producing this book. The team within Bloomsbury, Sarah Skipper, Katharine Macpherson, and the design team, among others, who have shepherded it further have similarly been pleasures to work with: easy, responsive and generous with their time.

And finally, a thanks to my friends and family who have patiently spent what I imagine is too much of their time listening both to my expounding of ideas and my grumbles about how to write them so they are fit for purpose. You will recognise who you are and I cannot say how deeply I have appreciated your loving support and forbearance. But I must name prominently among them my husband, Prof Stephen Monsell. He has been in the front-line of that particular support group for a very long time. He deserves the deepest of my gratitude.